THE PETTY-SOUTHWELL
CORRESPONDENCE
1676–1687

Also published in

Reprints of Economic Classics

by Sir William Petty

The Economic Writings, two vols. [1899]
The History of the Survey of Ireland, Commonly
Called the Down Survey [1851]
The Petty Papers, two vols. [1927]

Also edited by LORD LANSDOWNE

THE PETTY PAPERS

Some unpublished writings of Sir
William Petty edited from the Bowood
Papers.

SIR EDMUND GOSSE in the *Sunday
Times :* "Lord Lansdowne treats the
various accomplishments of his extraordinary ancestor in masterly fashion,
and he cannot be too warmly com-
mended for the tact and skill with
which he has performed his difficult
task as editor."

Spectator : "These two volumes will
be found of very special interest and
importance as a quarry for the investi-
gator of economic and general history,
while they will also serve for the delight
of those who would browse over a field
of quaint miscellaneous information. . .

"There are in the *Papers* many
scattered jottings which will serve to
correct or shed some small new light on
history particularly with regard to the
story of Ireland, which was a country
Petty knew intimately."

SIR WILLIAM PETTY

FROM A PORTRAIT BY CLOSTERMAN AT BOWOOD

THE
PETTY-SOUTHWELL
CORRESPONDENCE

1676–1687

Edited from the Bowood Papers

by the

MARQUIS OF LANSDOWNE

REPRINTS OF ECONOMIC CLASSICS

AUGUSTUS M. KELLEY · PUBLISHERS
NEW YORK · 1967

First Edition 1928

(London: Constable & Co., 1928)

Reprinted 1967 by

AUGUSTUS M. KELLEY · PUBLISHERS

by arrangement with CONSTABLE & Co.

LIBRARY OF CONGRESS CATALOGUE CARD NUMBER

67 - 27557

PRINTED IN THE UNITED STATES OF AMERICA

by SENTRY PRESS, NEW YORK, N. Y. 10019

CONTENTS

PART I

UNDER KING CHARLES II

1676–1684

PART II

UNDER KING JAMES II

1685–1687

LIST OF PLATES

INTRODUCTION

THE Correspondence of Sir William Petty and Sir Robert Southwell forms part of the Petty MSS. at Bowood. The origin of that collection has been explained in the recently published *Petty Papers*,[1] where I had occasion to refer to and to quote from many of the letters contained in the present volume. Portions of them have also been used by Lord Fitzmaurice in his *Life of Sir William Petty*,[2] where three (Nos. 44, 46, 184) were printed in full. One letter (No. 48) has been given by Professor Hull in his reprint of Petty's *Economic Writings*,[3] and two more (Nos. 25 and 185), which are in the nature of essays, were included in the *Petty Papers*. The great majority of the letters have not yet seen the light in whole or in part.

The Correspondence, whether viewed merely as an interchange of thought between two men of mark during the Restoration period, or regarded as a ' footnote ' to Petty's Economic and other Writings, seemed worthy of rescue from the oblivion of a muniment room. With the few exceptions to which I shall presently refer, it is now printed *in extenso*.

The documents of which it consists were preserved at the time by their respective recipients, and the two collections were, as will be explained, subsequently merged into one. The Correspondence is thus un-

[1] *The Petty Papers*. Edited by the Marquis of Lansdowne. Constable & Co., 1927. (Introduction.)
[2] *Life of Sir William Petty*, by Lord Edmond Fitzmaurice. John Murray, 1895.
[3] *The Economic Writings of Sir William Petty*, by C. H. Hull. Cambridge University Press, 1899.

usually complete for one of so remote a date. Of
the later letters scarcely any appear to be missing on
either side.

Both contributors were in their time Members of
Parliament and had been employed on Government
service of importance. If they were not amongst
those who have actually controlled their country's
destinies, they were in close touch with the 'Great
Men' of their day, from the Sovereign downwards.
Both were original Members of the Royal Society,
which was instituted in 1662 'for the improvement
of Natural Knowledge'. Each had thus his share—
and Petty a not inconsiderable share—in carrying
into practice the principles which Bacon had formulated half a century earlier, and in giving to philosophic thought the lead which it has ever since
followed. The letters, though they touch little on
the major events of the time, are thus not devoid of
historical interest.

In a secondary aspect the Correspondence is of
value from the side-lights which it throws upon
Petty's printed Writings. Southwell was at once his
most intimate friend and his literary censor. It was
Petty's habit to send to him in the first instance almost
everything which fell from his pen, and Southwell
was not slow to express his opinions thereon, whether
favourable or otherwise. If he sometimes—as the
letters will show—dissuaded Petty from publicity, we
owe to him at all events the preservation of the greater
part of the papers which he thus received, while an
interesting commentary upon them is supplied by his
criticisms and Petty's replies thereto. Incidentally
also the letters give the dates when many of these
papers were written and furnish biographical material
concerning Petty which is otherwise lacking.

The story of Petty's Life has been told in the
volume by Lord Fitzmaurice to which I have already
referred, and some of its more salient facts were
repeated in the Introduction to the *Petty Papers*. It
does not therefore require recapitulation.

Of Southwell less is generally known. Though he is frequently mentioned in contemporary documents, the only account of his Life is to be found in the *Dictionary of National Biography*. His claims on public recollection, if not on a par with those of Petty, are, however, by no means negligible.

Sir Robert belonged to a family of English 'Undertakers', as those were called who, migrating to Ireland during the reign of Queen Elizabeth, 'undertook' the administration of the newly forfeited land in that country. His father, Robert Southwell, was sometime Collector of Customs at Kinsale in Ireland, and afterwards 'Sovereign' or Mayor of that town. Born in 1635, Sir Robert went to Oxford and read for a time at Lincoln's Inn, after which he travelled for two years (1659–1661) on the Continent. In 1664 he was appointed Clerk to the Privy Council, an office which he held till 1679. But meanwhile he was several times employed on confidential diplomatic missions. He went twice (in 1665 and 1668) as special envoy to Portugal, where he was instrumental in negotiating the Peace of Lisbon. This treaty, though ostensibly concluded between Spain and Portugal, was of the first importance to England as preserving the integrity of the smaller power and checking the aggrandisement of her more powerful rival. His services on this occasion were rewarded by a knighthood. In 1671 he was sent to Brussels, and in 1680 to Berlin, where for six months he acted as Envoy Extraordinary to the Elector of Brandenburg in furtherance of the Government's plan for the formation of a defensive alliance against France. Amongst other activities he was Commissioner of Excise from 1671 to 1679, Member of Parliament for Penrhyn from 1673 to 1678, and deputy Vice-Admiral for Munster, becoming Vice-Admiral on his father's death in 1677. In 1679 he bought Kingsweston, near Bristol, where (as his letters to Petty show) he kept as much as possible to himself during the troubled period which immediately ensued.

In 1685 he was once more elected to the House of
Commons (for Lostwithiel), but since James II preferred to rule without the assistance of Parliament,
Southwell's legislative duties interfered but little with
his life in the country. He emerged, however, from
his voluntary retirement after the Revolution, was
President of the Royal Society from 1690 to 1695,
and for several years Secretary of State for Ireland.
He died at Kingsweston in 1702. His great-grandson
succeeded to the De Clifford barony. Southwell's
papers thus found their way into the possession of that
family, where they remained for upwards of a century.

While still a young man Southwell had come into
contact with James, Duke of Ormond, thrice Viceroy
of Ireland. Their acquaintance eventually ripened
into a close friendship which found its expression in
an important and intimate correspondence preserved
among the Carte MSS., as also in an account of
Ormond by Southwell which has been printed in
Mountmorres's *Life of the Irish Parliament*.[1]

Southwell married Elizabeth, daughter of Sir
Edward Dering, of Surrenden in Kent, and by her
had two sons and three daughters. His elder son,
Rupert, died at the age of eight in 1678 (p. 56
infra). The younger, Edward — the " Neddy " of
these letters—after succeeding his father as Irish
Secretary, was knighted for his services, and died in
1730. The daughters are generally referred to in the
Correspondence as ' the spinsters '. It should perhaps be explained that the appellation was jocularly
employed, for they none of them attained to marriage-
able age until some time after its termination.

Southwell and Petty had from the first several
points of contact. As members of the Royal Society,
both took a keen interest in the philosophical dis-
cussions in which the ' Virtuosi ' of the day were fond
of indulging at Gresham College and elsewhere.
They were both deeply concerned in Irish affairs.
Following on his Down Survey of Ireland and the

---

[1] Cf. *The Life of James, Duke of Ormonde*, by Lady Burghclere.

Cromwellian Settlement of that country, Petty had become possessed of large Irish properties, notably in Kerry, where he established ironworks, fisheries and a considerable trade in timber. Southwell owned part of the port of Kinsale, as well as land in its immediate vicinity. Both he and Petty depended for their tenure on the maintenance of the Act of Settlement which had been passed by Charles II soon after his Restoration ; they suffered from a common anxiety when under the rule of James II it became apparent that this Settlement was in danger. Through Petty's marriage to Elizabeth Waller, who was a cousin of Southwell's, the two men became related. They were thenceforward on terms of the closest intimacy. Petty, who was often in Ireland, kept an eye on Southwell's interests in that country, and poured forth by turns his schemes and his grievances into Southwell's receptive ear. Southwell appears to have been *persona grata* with Charles II, and as Clerk of the Council had easy access to those in authority. He was thus in a position to assist his friend when, as not infrequently happened—whether in the pursuit of some new phase of 'Political Arithmetic', or in some quarrel with the Chancery or the Treasury —Petty's zeal outstripped his political discretion.

The Correspondence contains a number of allusions to Samuel Pepys. They are for the most part very brief, but they indicate the relations which existed between Pepys and Petty, and are deserving of some notice.

Pepys' position when alive was of course by no means commensurate with that which he has posthumously achieved through the publication of his famous *Diary*. But if not one of those 'Great Men', to whom both Petty and Southwell agreed in showing all due civility, he held an official position which brought him into close contact with our correspondents and made his good offices often desirable. As Secretary of the Navy he was professionally interested in the building of ships, which

Petty, who started life before the mast, considered one of his own specialities, while in virtue of his membership of the Royal Society, he could claim to be one of the ' Virtuosi '. Thus when Petty was first engaged in his plans for a Double-Bottom ship, Pepys' approval of the invention became indispensable, for without it there was little hope of obtaining that of his Royal Master. It is clear that Pepys at this time entertained a very high opinion of Petty. He speaks of him as " One of the most rational men I ever heard speak with a tongue, having all his notions the most distinct and clear ", and on the occasion of a symposium at which Lord Brouncker and some of the leading lights of the Royal Society were present, he remarks that in this excellent company and good discussion "above all I do value Sir William Petty ". This was in 1665, shortly before the third of Petty's Double-Bottoms had come to grief; possibly when the boat foundered with all hands Pepys' enthusiasm may have been somewhat modified. Friendly relations were nevertheless maintained, and Pepys seems to have been one of the chosen few to whom Petty's miscellaneous papers were exhibited from time to time, for, as Southwell informs his friend, he " takes a mighty share in all you say and do " (*infra*, p. 54). In the present volume Pepys is most often mentioned after he had been reinstated in his post of Secretary to the Admiralty. Petty (assailed once more by his " fits of the Double Bottom ") was then engaged in his fourth and last attempt to make good his invention. Of the letters, however, which passed between the two men at the time none from Pepys and very few from Petty have survived.

It may perhaps be inferred that the relations between them were founded on community of interest rather than of sentiment. Pepys was essentially of a practical nature. So indeed was Petty, up to a point, for few can have been more proficient in the art of obtaining what they wanted. But Petty, as will

appear in this Correspondence, had another side to
his character, and this was reserved for more intimate
friends than Pepys. The workaday Secretary of the
Navy would surely have been a little impatient if he
had been treated to all the processes of ' ratiocination ' which were inflicted on the more long-suffering
Southwell. It is noteworthy, however, that two of
Petty's latest papers come from the Pepys MSS.
One of these, entitled " The Spiritual Estate of W.P.",
is or was in private hands (Historical MSS. Com.,
XV Report, App., p. 180); the other, a " Dialogue on
Liberty of Conscience " (Rawlinson MS., A 171, ff.
274-275), is endorsed in Pepys' hand, "Sir Wm. Petty's
Paper written at my desire and given me by himself
a little before his Death. S.P." The religious views
of the Secretary, not perhaps quite strongly enough
defined to please either party in the State, had brought
him into disgrace eight years before. Petty, though
he managed to steer clear of trouble in these matters,
was also broadly inclined in religious belief. He
probably started life as a Roman Catholic; he later
professed the Protestant faith, and he would seem, from
a passage in his will, to have died an Agnostic. The
two men had thus no doubt more in common than
would appear from the scanty communications between
them which are still extant.

As already mentioned, the letters in this volume
are derived from two sources :

(1) The Petty Papers (properly so called) which,
through the marriage of Sir William Petty's daughter
to Thomas, twenty-first Lord of Kerry (the grandfather
of the first Marquis of Lansdowne), have come down
to their present owner.

(2) The Southwell Papers, part of which were
bought by the third Lord Lansdowne at the sale of
the De Clifford papers in 1834.

Petty's letters are of course in the second, and
Southwell's in the first of these collections—though
in each there are some drafts and copies of letters
sent, which have often helped to elucidate the script

in the corresponding letters as received. The originals, however, were never collated, but were bound up intermixed with much other material and with an almost complete disregard of date and sequence.

The Correspondence in its initial stages is of a fragmentary character—only fourteen letters are extant from its inception in the year 1668 up to the summer of 1676. Though these have been omitted in the following pages, they should perhaps be briefly referred to, since they indicate the genesis of the more regular epistolary exchange which subsequently supervened.

The earliest letter—surviving only in the form of a draft — was addressed by Southwell to Petty in March 1668. It was in the previous year that the two men had become related by Petty's marriage, while Southwell was then just back from Portugal, after the conclusion of the Peace of Lisbon mentioned above. He addresses Petty (for the first time) as " Cousin ", a title which he says " I have celebrated more than the late peace, as being the best alliance I have to mankind ". He goes on to assure his friend that during his absence he has constantly " fed upon the memory of our oracle ", whom " in my small geography I have ever reckoned among the kingdoms of the world ", adding that he is prouder of what Petty has done at home than all that he had himself compassed abroad.

The response to this letter is no longer extant, but Southwell's tributes show that he had already conceived for his friend that peculiar admiration which subsequently led him to play the rôle of ' Boswell ' to Petty's ' Johnson '. He seems indeed to have made it his peculiar business to elicit and to collect Petty's views on all subjects. " Nobody regards the wise man," he afterwards wrote, " I will believe that your papers had more effect than you are told of, and seeing they turn you no better to account, let me at least have the transcript of what you gave in. For I shrine all up and fancy that in after times I shall be resorted to for your works as Mr. Hedges is for the true Opobalsamum " (*infra*, p. 102).

Southwell was, however, almost immediately to go back to Portugal for a further period of twelve months, and when he returned in the summer of 1669, the necessity for letter-writing did not often arise, for Petty was in London. The infrequency of their communications is the subject of one of Petty's characteristic comments. " Tis a strange thing," he wrote in December 1672, " that we who are no onely cousens and gossips but friends also, should never write to each other ; upon the opinion that friendship is not onely immortall, but also so spirituall that it needs no food at all—not so much as a drop or 2 of ink once a year. The Tryall wee have made of this truth is fitt to be registered at the Societie." We must conclude that the friendship continued to subsist without epistolary nourishment, or that the correspondents at this time did not think each other's communications worthy of preservation. There is at all events a complete absence of letters on either side for the eighteen months which succeeded Petty's complaint.

It was not till 1676 that the exchanges began to assume a regular form. In that year Petty went to Ireland in order to take up his duties as Judge or Registrar of the Admiralty Court in Dublin. He remained there, except for an occasional visit to England, for the best part of nine years. Southwell was meanwhile at home, but when Petty returned to London for good in 1685 his friend had migrated to Gloucestershire. Thus from the autumn of 1676 onwards nearly all their communications had to be committed to paper, and so frequent did these become that both writers often left their letters unsigned. It is at this point that I have commenced my selection. Of the subsequent letters extant I have printed all but ten, omitting in the rest only a few passages—relating to business and money affairs — which are of no present interest.

From 1676 onwards Southwell appears to have

kept almost every letter he received, though those
which he sent were not at first so scrupulously preserved by Petty. He becomes, however, increasingly
represented in the exchange as the Correspondence
goes on, but it is not till after the accession of James
II that this becomes practically complete on both
sides.

A distinguished critic (Mr. Keith Feiling), when
reviewing the recently published *Petty Papers*, pre-
dicted that Petty, if better known to votaries of the
seventeenth century, would take his place among such
figures as Evelyn, Pepys and the rest, "whose
readers are their friends". It is in the hope that
the prediction may be fulfilled that I am publishing
these letters. I must leave them to tell their own—
quite simple—story. It is a tale in the main of business and family affairs, intermixed with such excursions into philosophical thought as became two 'Virtuosi' of the Royal Society. It may seem astonishing
that in letters of so intimate a character there is
scarcely any mention of the great political events of the
day. There is not even an allusion to incidents such
as the Popish Plot, the Exclusion Bill or Monmouth's
rebellion, though these occurrences can scarcely have
left our correspondents unmoved. Southwell, moreover, never breathes a word of his own political or
diplomatic activities. He was, as we have seen, sent
on an important mission to Berlin in 1680, but his
departure is scarcely mentioned, and apparently he
told Petty nothing at all of what he did there. It
may be remembered, however, that the letter post did
not then enjoy that immunity from prying eyes which
it has since acquired. Communications were constantly tampered with, and Petty himself has occasion
more than once to complain on this account of the
agents of his arch-enemies, the Farmers of the
Revenue. Moreover, both he and Southwell were
servants of the Government, with whom they could
not afford to quarrel, and in the uncertain state of
feeling which prevailed under the later Stuarts, any

comment on political or religious affairs could not fail
to be dangerous.

The letters bring out the marked contrast in
character between the two writers. Pepys tells us that
Lord Sandwich, the British Ambassador to Madrid
at the time of Southwell's diplomatic activity in
Portugal, had complained of his coadjutor as an
"unmannerly" and "a forward young man" (Pepys,
vii. 32), but Southwell must at the time of this
Correspondence have lost the self-confidence which
he had formerly possessed. He appears indeed as
something of a pessimist, ready to expect the worst,
and when difficulties arose always anxious to take
the line of least resistance. He would pass days (or
sometimes weeks) in meditation before venturing to
reply to Petty on some new line of philosophic enquiry.
When, towards the end of Charles II's reign, religious questions began to become once more acute,
he immediately gave up his public position (which,
as we have seen, was a good one) and buried himself
for ten years at Kingsweston. He was cautious by
temperament, as also no doubt by his diplomatic
training, guarded in speech and action, careful not
to offend those in authority, and constantly urging
similar caution on his more impetuous friend.

Petty, on the other hand, was a fighter, always
ready to attack his opponents with word and with
pen, and even on occasions—though he was both
lame and short-sighted — with cudgel and sword.
His mind was for ever effervescing with new ideas,
'expedients' and grievances, and he seems to have
taken as much pleasure in demolishing a rival philosopher's theories as to the size of London as in
scoring a more material point over his lifelong enemies,
the Farmers. His optimism was invincible. He
could never bring himself to believe, even after the
accession to the throne of a Roman Catholic sovereign,
that all would not be well for the Protestant interest
in Ireland ; nor would he accept defeat in the matter
of the 'Double Bottomed ship', though the last of

his four attempts in this direction ended more disastrously than any of its predecessors. Southwell soon became the recipient of all his thoughts, and evidently had the greatest difficulty in dissuading his friend from ventilating some of his more extravagant notions, and from prosecuting attacks on such as were in a position to make their resentment felt. Nevertheless, Petty for years carried on his fight with the Farmers and his dispute with the Treasury about the Quit-rents on his Kerry property, while most of his Irish Lawsuits seem to have been still running at the time of his death. In his last letter, written *in articulo mortis*, we find him still fulminating against the Duke of Ormond on account of wrongs suffered more than twenty years before.

The printing of the Correspondence has necessitated numerous allusions to the *Petty Papers*, which are referred to under the short title of *Papers* throughout. The other works mentioned at the beginning of this Introduction (Fitzmaurice's *Life* and Hull's *Economic Writings*) are cited for brevity's sake under the name of their respective authors.

I have prefixed a few words to such of the letters as seemed to call for explanation, but they are printed as in the MS., with the original spelling, the only changes made being in the contractions and punctuation.

The likeness of Petty which figures as a frontispiece is taken from a portrait by John Closterman at Bowood ; that of Southwell from an engraving by John Smith after the portrait by Kneller at the Royal Society. Petty's coat of arms is from his original " Grant of Arms " at Bowood.

I have again to thank Mr. A. Bence Jones for reading through my proofs, as well as for his assistance in placing some of the quotations with which Petty and Southwell were so fond of adorning their epistolary communications.

LANSDOWNE.

BOWOOD, 1928.

THE DISPUTED AUTHORSHIP

As an addendum to the foregoing Introduction, it may not be out of place to recur once more to the disputed authorship of the *Observations on the London Bills of Mortality*, a subject on which I offered some remarks in the recently published *Petty Papers* (ch. xxvii.). The book in question, it will be remembered, was published in 1662 over the name of John Grant, or Graunt, but it was freely stated at the time that Petty was its author, and this view seems to have remained unchallenged for nearly two centuries. More recently, however, the question has been reopened, and modern criticism has on the whole inclined to the side of Graunt.

In the *Papers* I was able to bring forward a number of fresh factors in Petty's favour, and I ventured to express the opinion that, by the addition of this new evidence to that which had been previously adduced, Petty's authorship of the *Observations* was established beyond all reasonable doubt. My remarks have since been called in question in an interesting article [1] from the pen of Professor Major Greenwood, who is unable to agree with me, or with the reviewers in the " lay press " who accepted my conclusion, that Petty was the author of " one of the Classics of Statistical Science ". Though a layman may well hesitate to dispute the verdict of so eminent a statistician, I am impelled to urge some further arguments in defence of the view that I have previously expressed.

I would, in the first place, suggest that my critic dismisses somewhat lightly the evidence of Petty's and Graunt's contemporaries, six of whom (Evelyn, Aubrey, Halley, Burnet, Houghton and Southwell) have definitely pronounced in Petty's favour. It is, at least, curious that their statements provoked no

---

[1] " Graunt and Petty ", *Journal of the Royal Statistical Society*, vol. xci. Part I., 1928.

retort from Graunt's many friends when they were made, and that no one until comparatively recent times has felt tempted to take up the cudgels in his defence.

Professor Greenwood, moreover, does not attempt to explain the fact that Petty himself included the book in a private note of his own works—which is demonstrably accurate in other respects, and was written only nine years after the publication of the *Observations*. This circumstance gains special significance from the fact that he never claimed the work publicly. It is true that he came near to giving away the secret by implication in the original title-page of the Dublin *Observations* (*Papers*, ii. 274), as well as in a passage in his paper on a *New Instrument of Government* (*Papers*, i. 105), but with these exceptions he almost invariably speaks of the book in conjunction with Graunt's name. It was his friends, and not he, who insisted that his was the authorship.

In my former article I had occasion to remark that I could not discover any difference in style between the *Observations* and Petty's known writings. Professor Greenwood characterises this statement as "ingenuous", but his arguments in a contrary sense are all addressed to a comparison of *method* and not of *style*. For literary style, neither the *Observations* nor Petty's Writings are conspicuous, but I have yet to learn what differences can be detected between them in this respect. The question of their method is a separate matter.

In the *Petty Papers* I gave a number of parallels or similarities (additional to those which had previously been noticed by others) between passages in the *Observations* and in Petty's works. Professor Greenwood dismisses them all, both old and new, on the ground that either they are not, strictly speaking, 'parallels', or that they are such as might occur between any two writers on similar subjects. The last argument would be more convincing if it could be shown that Graunt had in fact ever dealt with any of these subjects elsewhere. It is, however, well known that he did not. Though elected to the Royal Society, he did not contribute to the *Philosophical Transactions* of that body. Nothing, indeed, appears to have been elicited from him except a paper on the growth of Carp and Salmon—of which merely a brief note is preserved.

Consideration of space makes it impossible to go into a detailed examination of all the parallels I had suggested, but I will take that which Professor Greenwood specially singles out as unworthy of being " taken seriously ".

The writer of the *Observations*, in his chapter dealing with " Particular Casualties ", devotes something more than a page to a classification of deaths arising from the " French Pox ", and is at pains to show that from the medical point of view many of those which probably arose from this cause had been wrongly attributed to other forms of disease. Petty, when practising at Oxford in 1646, had written an elaborate Latin treatise, *De Lue Venerea*, still extant in MS., on this subject. Parallels apart, may it not be seriously contended that the passage in question was more probably written by a Doctor of Physic of sixteen years' standing, who had made a special study of this disease, than by a London tradesman who was, so far as we know, totally unversed in medical matters ?

For the rest, I would still maintain that every one of my parallels show a definite similarity either in thought or expression between the *Observations* and Petty's other Writings, and that they constitute a chain of evidence which cannot be dismissed as mere coincidence. The instances remain on record, and may be studied by those who care to investigate them.

But I must pass from Professor Greenwood's negative criticisms to the more positive part of his argument in favour of Graunt.

He gives three principal reasons for attributing to him the authorship of the London *Observations* :

(1) That the book opened up a "field previously uncultivated", from which important results were obtained.

(2) That the writer applied to this field a new "critical method".

(3) That it contains the first "London Life Table".

As to the first point, the greater part of my Introduction to the *Petty Papers* was taken up by an exposition of Petty's remarkable originality in thought and writing. There is surely no necessity for looking beyond him for a possible or probable "cultivator of new fields".

As regards the second, the example cited, viz. Graunt's critical disquisition on the subject of Rickets, Spleen and Liver-grown, is one which in itself goes far to support my contention. The paragraph in question, with its nice distinctions between these allied diseases could, like that mentioned above, scarcely have been written by a man unacquainted with medicine, but would have come easily to one like Petty who had been practising physic for nearly twenty years.

On the subject of the Life Table Professor Greenwood remarks: "It is strange, if Petty had made or even realised the importance of this discovery, that neither in his published nor unpublished writings should one find any reference to it. It is particularly strange since what one might call the financial side of the matter, the utility of the instrument in computing the values of annuities and life rents, speedily appealed to men whose financial instincts were certainly not acuter than those of Petty." It is difficult, for a layman at all events, to understand this statement, for the writer had in an earlier passage himself quoted portions of Petty's *Essay on Duplicate Proportion* dealing with this very matter ; moreover, in the *Papers* there may be found several references to "Scales of Longevity" and "Scales of Salubrity", which Petty hoped to construct when he had obtained the data necessary (*Papers*, i. 188, 193 ; ii. 263). There is even evidence that he was prepared to make such a ' Scale ' for the natives of Pennsylvania! (*Papers*, ii. 115). These Scales evidently connote some form of Life Table, if not exactly that which might commend itself to a modern statistician. The passages in question might indeed have been included in my list of "parallels". In one of the papers above mentioned Petty goes so far as to detail some of the statistics which would be required for the making of such a ' Scale ' (*Papers*, i. 187). There can be no question then that, even if he was not himself responsible for the Table in the *Observations*, he fully realised the importance of this discovery. It is equally clear that the "financial side of the matter" appealed to him. He takes care to point out that the Scales which he was contemplating would in fact give "the value of any person's life at any age", and would "make a par between the value of estates for life and for years" (*i.e.* between life rents and annuities) (*Papers*, i. 193). Can it be that these passages had altogether escaped Professor Greenwood's notice?

If Petty can be shown to have practised statistical analysis, there is also ample evidence that his efforts in this direction were not the result of mere chance, but were the outcome of a clearly preconceived theory. Why did he desire to collect all the statistical information demanded in the *Papers* (Nos. 49 to 59)? It was precisely in order that he might apply to it the same critical analysis which had already been applied to the London Bills. When writing of an Irish Land Registry (*Papers*, i. 105), he advocates it on the plea that "a thousand inferences might be made from it by a prolific genius", and in "Lands and Hands" (No. 58) he explains at some length the nature of the deductions which he hoped to extract from a general census of the people. The statistics he hoped for were never obtained, and the Mortality Bills remained for the time being the only complete set of figures on which it was possible to practise critical analysis; but there are few of Petty's papers which do not show, in one form or another, the striving after this ' new method '.

The same may be said of his letters in the present volume. We shall find again frequent references to the value of " Ratiocination " and " Argument by Number, Weight and Measure ", as well as recommendations to practise ' the matching and comparing of *sensata* ', a word which in Petty's vocabulary seems to have indicated things which can be appreciated by measurement rather than feelings or thought. But one might well despair of convincing one who has not already been convinced by the publication of his *Papers* of Petty's zeal for statistical analysis.

I have elsewhere (*Papers*, ii. 279) referred to the very few surviving letters from Graunt to Petty. There are, however, in one of Petty's letter-books copies of several addressed by him to Graunt in 1672–73. Though these contain no mention of the London *Observations*, they are not without an indirect bearing on the question of the ' Disputed Authorship '.

The letters show how closely connected the two men had been, and remained till the end, in spite of certain differences which arose between them. Graunt acted as Petty's representative during his absence in Ireland, and as such he was responsible for the collection of rents from the London property which his friend had acquired with the proceeds of his Survey of Ireland. Graunt was in financial difficulties at the time, and it seems that he withheld some of these rents which Petty had destined for the payment of his own creditors. Writing to a relative, Petty explains that " not knowing how to understand the Major ", he was forced to place his interests in other hands, and he goes on to say : " Whether Major Graunt be more decayed in his fortunes than I imagined, or expects more from me than I think reasonable to comply with, or accounts upon me new principles and interests, I know not. But upon the whole matter, I think it fit and high time to pay my debts, and also to dispose of my rents as I think fit. . . ." After some further directions he adds: "Do this in case he be contumacious, for I still love him better than he hath of late loved himself" (Petty to Brookes, December 7, 1672). To Graunt he wrote about the same time : "I have been many years tender to your credit, but you too hastily abandon mine. However nothing shall be wanting in me to serve and support you, but you must not weary or discourage me too much." The subsequent letters show that Petty was as good as his word. He made constant efforts to procure for Graunt employment (suitable for one of the Roman Catholic persuasion) in Ireland, whether by way of an official post under the Lord-Lieutenant, or as Seneschal or steward of his own Irish property. Graunt, however, seems to have been unwilling to leave London, and nothing came of these proposals.

There are some significant references also to Graunt's change of religion, of which Petty seems to have disapproved on temporal rather than on spiritual grounds. "You have done amiss", he tells him, "in sundry particulars, which I need not mention because you yourself may easily conjecture my meanings. However we leave these things to God and be mindful of what is the sum of all religion, and of what is and ever was true religion all the world over" (January 18, 1673). And a little later he writes again: "I think I understand what puts you out of humour, and how it is your own fault several ways. If you are willing to throw me off, you therein do me an unkindness. I shall never do the like towards you. My wife is landed in England. I hope through her there may be yet a right understanding. Adieu" (February 22, 1673).

This was apparently the last written communication which passed between them. Petty was about to return to London, and a few months later he wrote to his friend and correspondent, Dr. Woods: "Captain Graunt is now an open and zealous champion for Popery, wherefore I have not so much intimacy with him as formerly". Graunt died in 1674. It is to be feared, therefore, that the 'right understanding' was never reached.

But the outstanding feature in these letters lies rather in what they do not, than in what they do contain. Except for a single enquiry as to the *Political Arithmetic* (the MS. of which appears to have been left with Graunt in order that he might submit it to some of Petty's friends), they do not contain a word beyond business matters. There is no attempt at 'ratiocination' upon any of the problems political, medical, religious or statistical, which were continually occupying Petty's mind and pen. If Graunt, as we are asked to believe, had really been the inventor of statistical science, if his was the mind which evolved an entirely new method of statistical analysis, if Petty owed to him in the first instance most of the ideas which he afterwards developed, it is surely inconceivable that there should have been no mention of such things in their Correspondence.

In the present volume Southwell explains that calculation was never 'a herb of his garden' (p. 146), yet Petty's 'notions' were continuously ventilated for his benefit, and there are few of his extant letters to his fellow 'Virtuosi' which do not contain some allusion to them. If Graunt had been responsible for the *Observations*, his views would have been infinitely more valuable to Petty than those of Southwell or anyone else. The conclusion seems to be irresistible that Graunt was not consulted because his opinions on these matters were not considered of value.

In the concluding paragraph of Professor Greenwood's article a somewhat different line of argument is pursued. The writer is at pains to show that Petty owes much of the support which he has received as author of the London *Observations* to the fact that he was a graduate of Oxford, one " who knew all the best people " (though perhaps like Bacon, " not quite one of the best people " himself), and " the founder of one of our great families ". He appears to suggest that it is unfair and somewhat unkind to urge the claims

of such a man against those of a " poor London shop-
keeper who died bankrupt ".

It may be observed incidentally that the distinctions drawn are a little lacking in historical reality.
Petty was the son of a poor Hampshire clothier. He
started life with sixpence in his pocket, and all that
he did was achieved without any outside influence or
assistance. Graunt came of a family which carried
on a well-established drapery trade in the City of
London. He was launched in business about the time
when Petty was still hawking sham jewellery for a
living, and he had sufficient influential friends to enable
him to obtain for himself a succession of civic offices,
and for his friend the professorship of Music at Gresham College. It might be added that he was intimate
with some of the leading artists of his day, and a collector of rare prints. The initial advantages would not,
therefore, seem to have all lain with Petty. Again,
Petty did not, in the usual sense of the expression,
" found a family ". Both his sons died without
surviving issue, and his only daughter married into
a family actually " founded " some three centuries
before.

" Arguments of this class " may perhaps, as Professor Greenwood suggests, " influence all of us one
way or the other ", but in the present instance they
should not be allowed to do so. We are not discussing
a question of right or wrong, but attempting to unravel
an historical sequence which cannot be affected by the
antecedents or the posterity of the two men concerned. Nor should the matter be made (as some
have seemed inclined to make it) a question of faith.
Earlier conclusions may always be reviewed in the
light of fresh facts, and those which I have been
able to adduce on Petty's side have yet to be
answered.

It is from Anthony à Wood, the compiler of the
Athenæ Oxonienses, that we derive most of our
knowledge of Graunt and of his many virtues. Yet
Wood was compelled to admit that Petty had " put

Graunt in the way to write " the London *Observations.*
Graunt's hand may perhaps have held the pen, but it
was surely Petty who supplied the ideas which have
caused this book to be regarded as " One of the
Classics of Statistical Science ".

L.

PART I

UNDER KING CHARLES II

1676–1684

THE PETTY-SOUTHWELL
CORRESPONDENCE

AT the opening of the Correspondence Petty, as already explained, had just assumed office as Judge and Registrar of the Admiralty Court in Dublin. Southwell was at the moment also in Ireland, having come over to visit his father who was lying ill at Kinsale. He was soon, however, to return to his duties as Clerk of the Privy Council in London.

The first letter begins with a lengthy dissertation upon the elder Southwell's symptoms, and contains a brief allusion to a speech, apparently of a controversial character, which Petty had recently made on Admiralty affairs. Petty also refers to a 'discourse' or essay upon the *Scale of Creatures* and to his 'Battle with the Farmers'—the most persistent of his many quarrels. The juxtaposition of these last is typical, for with Petty 'ratiocination' and litigation seem to have gone hand in hand. Indeed, his literary output was always greatest when he was involved in legal controversies. Both the *Scale of Creatures* and the Farmers will frequently recur and require a few words of explanation.

Petty, as we have seen, had become, partly by grant and partly by purchase, the proprietor of large tracts of land in different parts of Ireland. Acceptance of the Cromwellian Settlement had been a condition precedent to the Restoration of King Charles II., and this Instrument was ostensibly taken over *en bloc* by the new monarch. The far-reaching transfers of property which it involved had not, however, had time to become operative, and difficulties in regard to their completion soon became apparent. Some of the Cromwellian soldiers and Adventurers were still unsatisfied of their expected share in the booty. New claimants had arisen: 'Innocents' who demanded restoration to their lands on the plea that they had not actually taken part in the rebellion;

' Constant good affection men ' who asserted that, even if they had drawn the sword against the Parliament, they had always remained loyal to the person of the Sovereign ; ' The Forty-nine Officers ' who had first served the King before the peace of 1649 and had afterwards transferred their allegiance to the Parliament—besides a host of others. Many of these claims were allowed, and in order to obtain the land to meet them, the Parliamentary grantees were ' retrenched ' of a portion of their original shares. There was still, however, not enough forfeited land to go round, and Cromwell's settlers had to fight hard to maintain their possessions.

In addition to the inherent difficulties of their position the new grantees had to contend with the ' Farmers ' of the Taxes. The practice was for the Farmers to contract by the payment of a lump sum down for the collection of the Irish Revenue. They seem to have been allowed to recoup themselves as best they might, being permitted to assess and collect Quit-rents from all landowners on the King's behalf— though the proceeds went into their own pockets. Petty had had occasion to advance them a large sum of money, but when he claimed repayment, he was at once met by a demand for Quit-rents increased by a sum equivalent to his debt. The quarrels which ensued, complicated by a separate though parallel dispute with the Government as to the amount of Quit-rent due from his Kerry lands, persisted till his death. It was not indeed finally settled by his successors till the year 1696.

Petty's case as an Irish landowner was, no doubt, typical of the confusion which existed in these matters at the time. Most of the property he had purchased lay in the mountainous part of County Kerry, which until the final subjugation of the last Earl of Desmond in the reign of Queen Elizabeth had formed part of the territory known by that chieftain's name. Not long after King Charles's restoration it was discovered that the Duke of Ormond, by virtue of his marriage, had succeeded to the Desmond ' Chieferies '. The Duke had been expressly restored by the Sovereign to all his former possessions, and Petty's purchase thus came to be included amongst them. After a few years, however, Ormond, who owned plenty of broad acres elsewhere, surrendered his claims in Kerry, and Petty tried to get his original title confirmed. Here again he was met by a demand from the Farmers for all the arrears of Quit-rent, which, in spite of the fact that he had not been in enjoyment of the land in question and that it was at best of a highly unproductive character, were assessed at an exorbitant figure per acre.

There was a further complication. Part of Petty's Kerry property was ' soldiers' land '—bought no doubt on very easy terms, since Cromwell's Ironsides showed no desire to settle down amidst the Kerry mountains. It had formerly been the heritage of the McGillycuddy of the Reeks, a chieftain of ancient lineage whose family had long controlled large tracts of land around the mountains from which they took their name. The McGillycuddy was believed to have taken part in the Rebellion, and was consequently included amongst those whose land had been declared forfeited, but he was subsequently in King Charles's service during the time of his exile, and one of the King's first acts was to restore him to his former possessions. No countervailing provision seems to have been made for Petty, who thus became involved in contest for the ownership of the land in question. The Correspondence shows that this dispute was likewise running when Petty died, and we have no precise information as to the time or manner of its settlement. At the moment of Petty's death, the McGillycuddy was clearly in the ascendant (*infra*, p. 291), but some sort of compromise must eventually have been effected. Successive McGillycuddys have remained to this day in control of much (though not of all) the land which their family had enjoyed prior to the Rebellion, but there is evidence that a considerable portion of their former territory passed for the time being into the hands of Petty's descendants.

The discourse on the *Scale of Creatures*, or so much as remains of this work, including a letter which gives a sort of synopsis of its contents (pp. 44-48, *infra*), has been printed in the *Petty Papers* (Nos. 87A and 87B). It was an essay designed to prove a scale of affinities downwards, from Man to the lower animals, and upwards, from Man to God. It may be noted that the affinities which Petty sought were rather those of the mind than of the body ; he cannot, therefore, be claimed as a Darwinian.

From the letter which follows it seems that Petty had recently delivered a discourse on this subject which had provoked some comment. In the *Papers* (No. 129) will be found a portion of a Lecture which was addressed to the Dublin College of Physicians about this time. So far as it goes this Lecture is concerned only with Anatomy, but the concluding paragraph points to a sequel dealing with the differences between man and other animals. There seems reason to believe that this was the discourse alluded to below, and that Petty's conception of his *Scale of Creatures* was first ventilated in Dublin in the later part of the year

1676. Southwell's curiosity was, as we shall see, roused to the highest pitch by the promise of this novel idea. Pepys (with perhaps other friends) was kept informed through extracts from Petty's letters of its progress (Hist. MSS. 15th Report, p. 175), but their expectations were destined to be disappointed, for the essay was apparently never finished.

1. *Petty to Southwell.*

Dublin, ye 30⁰ Octob[r], 1676

Deare Cosen

This Munday morning I recevied your Letters and doe hereby answer them Imediately, for feare the stress of Buisness which I expect between this and the next going away of the Post should disable mee to do it then ; and I wish I could answer your Letters as successfully as I do it readily.

Your Good Father's Case hath nothing of strange or monstrous in it. It is any ordinary Dropsy, as yet under Mediocrity. The Nature of the Disease, the approaching winter, and his age, is the worst that can bee said ; and his Temperance, Prudence and good Naturall Constitution, is the most I can say to ballance the other. The discourse of Serouse humours, ' Genus Nervosum ' and ' Genus Vivosum ', may be spared. . . .[1]

As for the Admiralty Eloquence, it was onely such as I have not heard Reprocht, even by my many enemyes that were present, and but moderately applauded by others. I will trade no more in glittering performances and hereafter will *praestare officium* but *taliter qualiter*.

The discourse upon the *Skale of Creatures* was not Vulgar, nor easy to be answered by the Libertine Scepticks, of whom the prowdest cannot be certain but that there are powers above him which can destroy him as they do Nitts or Vilar Animalls. Tis hard to say where the Skale ends, either upwards or Down-

---

[1] A number of medical directions for Robert Southwell (senior) here follow.

wards ; but it is certain that the proud Coxcomb Man is not the Top of it. Wherfore Let us bee sober and modest, and conforme to the generall practise of good Men and the Laws of our Age and Country, and carefully study the Laws of Nature, which are the Laws of God.

And now Cozen, I am prepareing for Battle with the Farmers this afternoone and for an other to morrow. I perceive no publicq nor great designe in them, nor doe I heare any Thing of a free-port at Kinsale, but from Mr. Hodges. When I took leave of my Lord Chancellor of England,[1] hee treated mee very civily, and as if I needed not to feare oppression from his hands ; but I spoak nothing of any buisness but what he himself proposd. I am now in Mourning for my Brother Napper[2] who was buryed the 10th Inst. For want of buisnes I have the care of a woman and 5 children added to my Imployment.

Salute all with your affection as from

Yours &c

WM PETTY

2. *Petty to Southwell.*

Dublin, Novr 7 1676, in ye morning

Deare Cosen

This day I am to have a double Battle and yet I wright — but not elaboratly as I promisd, because I thought the paper of Medicaments prescribd and directed to Dr Cox[3] had been sent to mee ; but, as I was going to bed, one raps at my dore to deliver them, which I did before I could take any Coppy of them. Wherefore I cannot as I intended run Division upon every point, but in lieu thereof they are gon into abler hands. . . .

[1] Sir Heneage Finch, who had succeeded Lord Shaftesbury as Lord Chancellor in 1675.

[2] James Napper, son of Sir Nathaniel Napper, Bart., of Loughcrew, who had married Sir William Petty's only surviving sister, Dorothy.

[3] This was probably Thomas Coxe (1615–1685), sometime physician to the Parliamentary Army. He was one of the original members of the Royal Society.

As soon as my present trouble of Quit rents is over, I will do something in this matter[1] which shall shew that the Admirall's foot hath been [in] Ireland, and will begin from the foundementalls ; that is to say, from the accounts of the shipping and seamen of all sorts, belonging to or ordinarily trading with Ireland. I have already begun it.

I myselfe who am 13 yeare older than my wife, my widdow sister who has 3 sons and 2 daughters, present our service in a parallel Line to you and your sister, wishing earnestly the health and long Life of your father and mother. Wherein there is also something more of paralelizme—but how can I bee witty who am intended this day to bee worried !

I will observe your com̃ands to Mr Hodges who tels mee that Sheridan[2] is the great obstructer of the free port, but saith that his reasons for it are no better than blackberryes, much lesse reasons of [? like] the sun for their cleerenesse. Nay hee saith that all his whole cluster of reasons are not worth a ffig, nor what the Spaniards left of their ffigs at the seege of Kinsaile.[3]

Adieu.

3. *Petty to Southwell.*

Dublin, 14⁰ Novbʳ 1676

Deare Cosen

What you writt in yours of the 10ᵗʰ Novbʳ concerning your Father's thirst, swellings, effect of fomenta͠cons and Asthma, affords no matter at all of further discourse ; nor no other Theorem or practic than what is conteined in my former Letters. God Almighty direct his takeing or forebeareing what shall bee

---

[1] The business of the Admiralty Court in Ireland.

[2] ? Thomas Sheridan, the elder (*fl.* 1661–1688), a leading 'Farmer' and prominent Jacobite. Fellow of the Royal Society, 1679. He was imprisoned in connection with the Popish Plot. Later became Chief Secretary for Ireland (1687) and went into exile with James II.

[3] In 1601 the Spaniards under del Aguila had landed at Kinsale and held the town for some months against Mountjoy and Carew. Their surrender marked the end of the rebellion in Munster under Queen Elizabeth.

appointed unto him. I say again, do not torture him, nor let him part with certain ease for uncertain and conjecturall advantages, purchasd at the Rate of payn and Anguish, and let him think the least hee can of his Distempers. I can but repeat what I have said before.

I take notice of all you have said of Admiralty and Chancery matters. Wee must let things take their Course. The two Chanceryes, one of England, and the other of Ireland, are two soare Blisters upon my affairs. My throat is also Soare with crying for Releife, nor hath purging or bleeding don mee any good.

I cannot continue the parallel between your fortune and mine in the point of recovering Losses. Those who wrong you are in Irons and Chayns, and those who abuse mee have Rods of Iron in their hands. However I am glad that I have any fortunate friend, how much soever otherwise I am myself.

I am glad my Ld Chief Justice Hayle hath undertaken the work you mencõn,[1] but Galen[2] *De usu partium* will not do it. 1°. The point is to prove that the most admired peece in the world, which Galen takes to be Man, was made by designe and preconceivd Idea, which his maker had of him before his production. 2°. What shall wee say to the flaws and many Infirmityes in the said peece Man, and of the Dificulty of helping either your soare throat or of your father's Dropsy ? 3°. The question is whither man was designed to performe the things which hee performeth, or whither he performeth by the same necessity of his fabrick and constitucõn wherewith ffyer burneth ?

My Medium or Organ of the *Scale of Creatures* doth not wholy remove these Dificultyes, but it doth sufficiently humble man and check the Insolent Sceptisismes which do now pester the World, and is

---

[1] *The Primitive Origination of Mankind*, by Sir Matthew Hale (1609–1676), published in 1677 (*vide infra*, p. 12).
[2] Abraham Hann de Galen, a 17th-century Dutch doctor; he founded the sect of ' Galenists ' whose views coincided generally with those of the Socinians.

a good Cautien against the slighting of Religion and practise of good Men. And as for the other grand point, men take too much pains to prove it, for it is necessary that there should be a first and universall cause of all things, by whose designe and according to whose Idea all other things must bee made. And wee may feele the blessings of this incomprehensible being, altho wee do not see it ; as blind men may bee comforted with the warmth of the fier.

Abysus abysum invocat. Wherefore let us returne to wish well unto and to do well for one another. I hope when our Case of Clay is broaken by Naturall Death, Wee shall no longer peep through its Craks and Cranyes, but then look round about us freely, and see cleerely the things which wee now do but grope after.

I perceive you are returning for England. God conduct you and make you what hee would have you to bee.

W. P.

4. *Petty to Southwell.*

[Dublin, December 1676]

Deare Cousin

I hope you are safely arrived from a Winter's Journey to London. I doe not heare any thing touching your Father's Condition wherein I can rejoyce, yet I shall continue my best Offices, God willing, to the last.

I have writ to my Ld Conwey [1] to procure for me some reasonable favour with my Lord Chancellor in the dispatch of my businesse. For these farmours study nothing more than to perplex me in my interrest and defame me in my Credit, As I have formerly intimated unto you. And by reason also of my absence, matters goe very ill with me In the Chancery there. . . .

And thus you see how I am willing to purchase my

---

[1] Edward Conway (1623–1683), third Viscount and first Earl Conway. He was influential in Northern Ireland and sometime a Commissioner of Customs.

quiet and putt matters to an end with these angry Men, and returne to talke of a little Philosophy among our Brethren at Gresham.[1] Therefore see what you can effect herein by the opportunity of your relation and accesse to his Lordship, and I will be as carefull of what concernes your good Father, As Lyes within the skill and power of,

S^r, Your affectionate Cousin and servant

W. P.

[Endorsed by Southwell "L^r supposed from Sr Wm Petty; shewed my Lrd Chanc^h., 6 Jan. 1677".]

5. *Southwell to Petty.*

Spring Gardens, 2^d Jan^{ry} 1676 [1677]

Deare Cosen

I got hither in safety on the 23rd past, and can tell you that my Lady and all your Brood are in as healthfull and chearfull a condition as your heart could wish. I have testifyed to my Lady your great tenderness, and your excellent Counsells to my poor Father in the midst of all your troubles.

And I have had since my coming, the further proofe of your concerne by receiving here what you writ, and should have gone to my father at Kinsale, witnessing your desire to know the progress of his condition. I left him under the effects of great cold newly taken, which as it put him to fitts of violent coughing, soe it helped to discharge a great quantity of compacted plegme. His feet were soe very cold that hee was fain to keep warm bricks to the soles of them. And this together with what I have told you before was his case when he pressed me to come away, and hoped that he should not dye whilst I was there, least it should delay mee. It were strange if I could relate at full unto you with what Tranquility of mind hee discoursed of Death, and how gratefully hee took from the hand of God all the Memorials of it. Socrates

---

[1] *I.e.* with the members of the Royal Society.

and Seneca did by the help of Words and Witt, leave greater Monuments of their Firmity when they came to this great experiment ; but I believe hee will expire as little concerned as either of them.   I here enclose you the copy of his last, to which hee only set his hand ; and of many thousand letters is the first from him by another hand.

I called on my Ld Chiefe Justice Hales five days before his death and I found him then expiring.   His Book is now in the Press, (whereof I gave you some hint) entitled *The Origination of Mankind*, where shewing the necessity of his being made (he) confirms the Creation layd down by Moses, and soe Impugns the business of the Atheist.[1]

I met at his house, Mr Stevens, an ingenious person that puts forth his books, and shewing him what you had written touching the *Scale of Creatures* hee was extremely inamourd with it, and with your expression that it was hard to say where this Scale did either begin or end.   Pray as you have leasure, compleat some essay upon that subject, for the Notion is excellent, and will I am sure prove very fruitfull in your hands.

I wish I could hear any (of) the rubbs or difficulties you meet withall were within my strength and good offices to remove.   When you think they are, let mee have your particular Instructions, and I will endeavor to acquit myselfe as becomes

S[r], Your most affec[t] Kinsman and humble servant
ROBERT SOUTHWELL

6. *Petty to Southwell.*

[In the midst of his ' rubbs and difficulties ' Petty characteristically sought an anodyne in the invention of the

---

[1] *The Primitive Origination of Mankind Considered and Examined according to the Light of Nature* was published soon after Hale's death.   It is a formal treatise in defence of Christianity, but forms only part of Hale's work on that subject.   MS. copies of other parts (some of them made for Southwell) are amongst the Add. MS. at British Museum.

'pacing saddle' or single-wheeled chariot which is described below. He continued to play with this invention in after years. It is mentioned in 1677 (*infra*, p. 41), and again in 1678 (p. 51), when he informs Southwell that he is about to set out in it for 'a three weeks' progress'. In 1684 the scheme was once more taken up during a moment of depression 'to stupifie a little the sence of my sufferings', and the chariot was sent to England so perfected that its author 'verily believed it can never be much improved' (p. 125).

Nevertheless, yet another chariot was made in August 1686 (*Papers*, Nos. 124 and 125). The new one was apparently built on a somewhat larger scale than its predecessors. It could be drawn alternatively by one horse or by three men, upon two wheels or four, carrying as many as four persons, while it could be used as a 'sedan' without either wheels or horses. It was only to cost one-third the price of an ordinary chariot, and was guaranteed to "passe rocks, precipices, and crooked ways". It was a truly amazing invention—in its author's estimation at all events. We can only regret that it is impossible to test the attributes which he assigned to it, for unfortunately neither model nor drawing of the 'Pacing Saddle' has survived.]

Dublin, 13th Jan.ʸ 1676/7

As for an Essay, which you desire I should write concerning The *Scale of Creatures*, I shall, God willing, compleat it the next fair Weather that shines upon my mind; for that matter must not bee treated in the Clouds. Yet let mee tell you that even in this last Storme which has blown upon my concerns both in England and Ireland, I have (to shew mine Enemies that they cannot give mee business enough) actualy made and finished the Chariot which I was modelling in England, in which I maintain these following points :

(1) That the Rider is at extreme ease, and may, for ought I know bee able to travel in it 3 days together, night and day.

(2) The Horse hath noe weight upon him, carries nothing but draws only, and the Rider can help him going up or down a hill by the Inclination or Reclination of his Body.

(3) Overthrowing may bee most easily prevented, but if it bee overthrown (even upon a heap of Flints), the Rider can have noe harme.

(4) It turneth as short as a horse, and can goe wherever a horse can (for it was designed for Kerry). Notwithstanding all which you may, if you please, call it ' The Pacing Saddle ', as a name that will best please those that smile at Inventions.   I wish I might have speedy Justice in my Concernments, upon the condition I were bound to come in it from Holyhead to London in 3 days without alighting one foot of the way.   It will cost about 15£.   One stout horse will draw as much as is designed to bee carried in it ;   And for want of such a great horse, I suppose that two small ones (taken by chance) will suffice—that is any two common post horses.

And thus with a story of my Christmas Gambal I conclude, and am Yoᵣₛ &c

Wᴹ Petty

7. Petty to Southwell.

[We now find Petty a prisoner in Dublin Castle for contempt of court.   It was alleged that he had cast animadversions on the English Lord Chancellor, Sir Heneage Finch, though it was the Irish Lord Chancellor, Michael Boyle, who was the immediate cause of his incarceration.

This misadventure drove Petty into fresh literary activities which took the form of a translation into Latin verse of the 104th Psalm.   George Buchanan, the well-known Scotch scholar and historian (1506–1582), had done it before in his *Psalmorum Davidis Paraphrasis Poetica*, but Petty was in no wise deterred.   After much sending backwards and forwards the translation into both English and Latin verse was completed.   The Latin version was finally published by William Jane in 1679 under the title *Colloquium Davidis cum anima sua (Accinente Paraphrasim in 104 Psalmum) De Magnalibus Dei. Fecit Cassid aureus minutius* (cf. Hull, *Bibliography*, p. 638, No. 9).   It appears to have been greatly admired by Southwell, as well as by the ' Virtuosi ' of the day.]

Dublin, ye 10 Febr 1676/7

Deare Cousin

This day about 11 o clock I and my councill (one Mr Whitchett) were comitted prissoners to a Sergeant at Armes by My Ld Chancellor,[1] upon a very great mistake as I think. The matter was thus, vizt : I drew up materialls for a Bill to be preferred in Chancery against the Farmers, and as I use alwaies to doe, I gathered up all Matters and moĉons which I thought might have any affinity or Relaĉon to my intentions, expecting that my Councill would have made such alteraĉons in Matter and forme as might answere the practice of the Court. Whereupon hee made a few notes up and downe upon my papers, as if hee had thoroughly perused it ; but when I myselfe came to review it, I found that hee had not corrected some nonsense and other defects which I myselfe had left in it. In soe much as I went to him my selfe, showd him his oversights and desired him that hee would take a speciall care of it. For that although my Matter was sharpe, yett I would have it soe temperd by him as to give noe offence, nor spoile my business ; telling him that I had severall times sufferd (as you know I have done) by oblique advantages which my Adversaries have taken upon some faults in forme and circumstances, when they would not doe it directly upon the matter itselfe.

But hee having much business lett pass these 2 following points, vizt : I complained among other abuses the Farmers had done mee, that they (as I believed) had instigated my Ld Chancellor of England to speake sharply to mee, and That *they stood laughing whilst the dreadfull grinding of your oratour to the nether Milstone was denounced.* And the other point was thus : That the farmers had given out in speeches, *That they would force your Oratour's plainest pretences at Coĩon law into Chancery, and that they had secured the Chancellors of both Kingdomes against him.* Upon

---

[1] Michael Boyle, Archbishop of Dublin.

this reading of these paragraphs, and haveing heard both Mr Whitchett and myselfe speake somewhat in explicačon and excuse of the matter, hee gave sentence as aforesaid ; saying that hee could easily pass over the reflečon which was in those words upon himselfe, but not what concerned a principall minister in England, meaning (as wee all think) My Ld Chancellor.

Now see my misfortune—that I who had lately received an account out of England how my Ld Chancellor there publiqly expressed himselfe to this purpose, vizt : that although hee had granted an Injunčon against mee with some favour to the Farmers, yet that hee did not intend that by delayes or other devices the Justice of the Court should be discredited, and therefore bidd them to dispatch theire cause by Easter—upon which news I was very much pleased and my thoughts of My Ld Chancellor's former severity were quite vanisht away. I say my misfortune was that when I was well reconciled to my Ld Chancellor's proceedings, I should be thought to throw dirt in his face, whilst I was endeavouring to wipe off what I conceived had been throwne upon him by others !

Now the mistake (I think my Ld Chancellor was in) is That hee punishes mee for telling him that some others had abused him, without Ever questioning them whom I accused for soe doeing. There bee 2 or 3 points more which I lett pass, for I doe not love to believe that persons in great place doe mistake soe much as it seemes to mee they doe. In briefe I am now a prisoner for haveing scandalizd my Ld Chancellor of England, whereas I verily believed I was doeing the quite contrary, and at a time when his Lordship was as kind to me as I desired. All that I can accuse myselfe of is That I tooke such a method as was not absolutely necessary ; but which way soever I had proceeded, it is an easy matter to say ' An asses eares are hornes ', as mine are now esteemd. I presume you will here this story with much flourish amongst my enemies, but in those 2 above menčoned points doth lye the *Ratio formalis* of my suffering.

Yesterday I had 2 large Letters from your father's own hand, of his own hand writing, wherein he talks very cheerfully of his gathering of strength and that as hee thinks hee is able to Travell; but Mr Baker (his Chirugeon) tells me that his Scrotum and Belly doe swell, which I take to bee a badd matter. But I believe hee is a great way from death, and will see some vicissitudes of good and badd dayes before that time. I tell him that, if we can putt off his Tryall till May, that wee may then send an Injunčon to stopp the proceedings of his disease.

Deare cousin, I know you will have some sympathy with me in these troubles, and I am sorry for it. I am in the Right and my Adversaries are in the wrong, at least I am soe happy as to think soe; and my mind is soe quiet that when I have done my Letters, I intend to make an end of translateing the 104th Psalm into Latine verse, for which amongst all others Buchanan himselfe was most famous. I doe not hope to reach the Admirable purity of his Latine, but in some other points to come neere him. I pray God bless you.

Your obligd servant &c.

W. P.

. . . Since I finsht this Letter I received the inclosed order which will give you a little more light in the matter, but must tell you that in the said order there are 3 mistakes in matters of fact. (1) That I never acknowledged to have drawn the Bill, for I onely offered materialls to my Councill out of which he should have drawne a Bill, and twas properly his fault that the Bill was not as it should have beene. (2) There was no Menčon in the Bill that my Ld Chancellor of England was concerned in the passage of 'grinding to the nether milstone', although the Court did upon comon fame conceive that the said expression related to his Lordship. (3) I did not bragg in the Bill of any thing done to Vernon,[1] but

---

[1] For Vernon, *vide infra*, pp. 68-72.

complained that the farmers abetted the evill that hee
did to me.   Soe that there remaines nothing, but that
I informed the Court by my Bill that the Farmers had
abused both my Ld Chancellor of England and his
Grace, by boasting and frightning me with the interest
which they had in them both.

8. *Petty to Southwell.*

Dublin 13 Feb. 1676/7

Deare Cousin
        I writt unto you the last Post.   I now give
you notice that a Gentleman will wait upon you with
a Coppy of the Farmers Bill against my Sallary, with
a Coppy of my Answer thereunto, which answer is the
history of the farme and is worth the keeping by you.
You will also have a true coppy of my Bill concerning
the Kerry Quitrents, which is called ' Scandalous ',
and containeth in some smale Measure the History of
the Farmers, as the last mentiond answer was of the
farme.   It is endeavoured here to incense My Ld
Chancellor of England against me, but whatever
Sinister Construcõn may be made of it, I doe assert
these following posicõns, vizt :
        1°. That I do detest and abjure all intencõn or
design to scandalize or offend either of the Chancellors.
        2°. I gave the rough draught to Councill, giveing
him Speciall direcõns out of my Materialls to cutt out
such a Bill as might be fitting ; and hee, after 3 days
haveing it in his hands, at length signed it.
        3°. When I first heard that my Adversaries in-
tended to make [complaint of] it, whether the Bill
be right or wrong I endeavourd to withdraw it.
        4°. It is plain, that in the same Bill whereby
I craved reliefe of my greivances, I would not incert
anything to offend them from whence I hoped for
reliefe.   And this besides my own Abjuracõn will
(I hope) excuse me from all Shaddow of Malice,
and will prove that I did not beleive that either

of the Chancellors could be secured against my Right.

5°. If there be any words which may give just offence, I do heartily ask pardon for the same, although my Councill, whose buisness it was to guide mee better, ought to take me off.

And this, Deare Cousin, I begg you to say for me where and when you see occasion. I received an Order from the Chancery dated the first of February Instant, the makers whereof I have no reason to revile. I will trouble you with nothing more at present.

I am, Yo˜ affˡ servˡ & kinsman

W^M PETTY

[Petty's imprisonment was not of long duration. The Duke of Ormond, at Southwell's solicitation no doubt, intervened with the Lord Chancellor, who thus wrote in reply:

Lord Chancellor Finch to the Duke of Ormond.

London 20 Feb. 1676/7

My Lord

I have had the signification of your Lordship's respects touching the matter of Sir William Petty, and at the same time receiving a petition from him full of sorrow for what had hapned. I desire by your Grace's example not to take any notice thereof, and therefore request that on my consideration he may not be any longer in custody.

This is all that the busy time of the Parlyament gives me leave to say, but the greatest respects wherewith.

I am, my Lord, your Grace's most obliged and very humble servant

FINCH C.]

9. *Petty to Southwell.*

Dublin, ye 3° March, 1676/7

Dear Cousen

I did hope by this Post to have sent you a piece of our *Scale of Creatures*, but the Devill hath interposed this week and retarded it. But I verily beleive That the next shall bring you the same, with something else, and the return of my thanks to my Lord Chancellor ; for I see no reason why the next week of my life may not be fairer and calmer weather.

I receive your Letter of Mr Brown of our post office and do presume to send the inclosed under your Cover, for that the Rats of the Farme have been knawing my secrets of late.

I have this day written a long letter to Kinsale, where as I said there is much ebbing and flowing. The last newes I had from him was very good, and I hope this warmer weather will mend it.   Noe more at present, but that

I am Y^{rs}

W. P.

10. *Petty to Southwell.*

Dublin, ye 10th of March, 1676/7

Dear Cousin
        I have inclosed the return of my humble thanks to my Ld Chancellor and desire you to present them.   I have been very brief, partly for the reasons mencõoned in my Letter, but chiefly out of diffidence in my own discretion, and, least meaning well, I should let fall some words which might be otherwise interpretted.   Wherefore I rely upon your discretion, of whose felicity and dexterity I have had good Experience.

Of the great sum I owe you, I can pay but part at present, but Ile assure you the rest is in the Collector's hands—I mean the *Scale of Creatures*, and the application thereof to Religion.   As to this first payment—the Poem [1]—you will see what it is ; and I have sent the touch - stone with it, which is the substance and sence of the thing in English prose, the which I am content should be compared with Buchanan's.   As for the purity of his Latin, I did never hope to reach it, nor do I think any man can

---

[1] *I.e.* the 104th Psalm in Latin verse (*supra*).

surpass it. The Censure which some have given here of the exercise is, vizt :

1°. The Sence is (as you see) in the English Translation, which (as I said before) you may compare with Buchanan's and the Psalm it selfe.

2°. The Lattin words are generally Strong and Significant, but the Legaments by particles, the Phrase and Lattinity, is but mean.

3°. As there are some things very sharp and well said, soe there are other things flat and vulgar, especially at the latter end.

4°. The Chancellor of both kingdomes was the cause why it was done at all, and the farmers why twas done noe better.

I have sent it you because I said I have done it, but desire you not to shew it—at least not as myne. For I do not value my self by my Poetry no more than by my discretion, but the pride I take is in the love of truth and of a very few friends.

But you will ask why I meddled with this Poem at all ? To which I answer you, that my mind was sick, and that I tost and tumbled from place to place to find these, which when I had in vain sought from truth and reason I fell to this Poetry. And when I was vexed in considering the wicked works of man, I refreshed myself in considering the wonderfull works of God, and writt about fifty of these verses the same night I was comitted, after I had writt my post Letters.

I shall now thank you for your Theory of the Deluge,[1] but do candidly say that I know not what to say in that point ; but take it to be a Scripture Mistery, which to explain is to destroy. For of the waters above the firmament, I mean the Orbe of the fixed Starrs, we have noe experiment. The distance of that Orbe from us is vast and Immense, and [I] think that as much of those waters (if the backside of the firmament be covered with them) as answers in

[1] Was this Edmund Halley's theory, referred to by Southwell *infra* p. 235 ?

proporčon to a Spoonful of our Sea, is more in quantity then all our whole sea.   Now how the winds which sweep the surface of our Earth (and which perhaps are not a perpendicular myle) should operate upon those super-Ethereall waters, is a mistery fitter to be humbly admired then Critically preyed into.

Well Cousin, pardon this Poetry, and we will try to repair your patience by the *Scale of Creatures*, which shall be the next act on the Theatre of my gratitude.   Farewell, Dear Cousen

W. P.

Pray direct the Inclosed to my Lord Chancellor.

11. *Petty to Southwell.*

Dublin, ye 3^d of Aprill 77

Dear Couson

My brother Tom Waller [1] is very thankfull for your effectuall answers to his desires, and I thank you for enduring the trouble of my well meaning fooleries.   Lord ! that a man of 54 years old should, after 36 yeares discontinuance, return to the makeing of verses, which boyes of 15 years old can correct ; and then trouble Clerks of the Councill and Secretaries of the Admiralty to read them !   In your last you seemed gently to reproach mee that I had not (like my master Buchanan) kept close to the text, which I took so ill at your hands that I took pen presently and translated the Psalme again verse for verse without any Paraphrase at all.   I have in 3 or 4 places borrowed from Buchanan, where I could not come nearer the text than he had, and I broke of at the 27 verse upon the same reason.   Thus you see what trouble you brought upon yourself by finding fault with me.   I have also sent you the additionall verses which are the conclusion of the first Essay, whereby I hope I have tag'd the Ribon I first sent you.   I would have sent

---

[1] Thomas Waller, the eldest son of Sir Hardress Waller and brother-in-law to Petty.

you the whole corrected and amended coppy,—for so
it now is in severall false quantityes,—but I protest
that the school boyes to whom I delegated that power
have not yet done with it, but are still tumbling over
their Smetius and Prosodia for a further detection of
the false quantityes in the Poem ; which when they
have done you shall be sure to have it, for I will see
what admirable delight (as you call it) you can take in
my dottage.

Present my hearty service to Sir John Lowther [1]
and tell him that the quantity of Coles spent in Dublin
is between 25 and 30,000 Tun per annum, and this
I have from account taken about 12 yeares since and
since corrected by some aditionall computation. Tell
him likewise that the number of chimnyes in Dublin
is about 18,000. Tell him also that the Coles imported
into London in one year is 288,000 Chadern ; whereof
I suppose as many Tun was spent in London, the rest
in the county about London ; and Dublin (as I have
often told you) is about the tenth part of London.
Tell Sir John I will inquire of the Modern Authors
further into this matter, though I dare say this estimat
will serve his purpose near enough.

As for the *Scale of Creatures*, I thank you for the
paragraph you have sent me out of Doctor Bates.[2]
You know I am no good book man, and therefore do
not know what authors have written of this subject ;
but should wonder that any thinking man should overlook it. I desire you to enquire further what hath been
written already ; But whatever it be, you shall shortly
see mine, which will be an originall, altho you
should find the like hath been done a thousand times
already.

I am heartily sorry for what you write of my
Ladye's miscarriage. My wife has not recovered the

---

[1] Sir John Lowther (1655–1700), Member of Parliament. He was later
a supporter of William III., by whom he was created Viscount Lonsdale.
On the matter of the coal consumption of Dublin, compare *Treatise of Ireland*
(Hull, p. 589).

[2] ? William Bates, D.D. (1625–1699). The Nonconformist (known as
' the silver tongued ') Divine, author of several works, including *Considerations
on the Existence of God and Immortality of the Soul*.

ill consequences of hers to this day, but I hope it will be better with you.

The farmers or their tools do plague me much by intercepting my Letters. I must therefore beg you again to let the enclosed be sent and delivered in my wife's owne hand, and so God reward you for all your kindnes.

W. P.

I do not find that the people here concernes themselves a jot in the Cattle Bill,[1] nor do I, otherwise then to have the naturall Liberty of subjects and the rights of English men, tho liveing in Ireland. I hope if it succeed it will make exchange full.

12. *Petty to Southwell.*

[Robert Southwell senior had at length succumbed to his long illness. Petty ingeniously makes one letter of condolence do for two, by enclosing to Southwell that which he had written on this melancholy occasion to his sister, Catherine Lady Perceval. From exigencies of space I have forborne to print this enclosure.]

Dublin, ye 7⁰ Aprill 77

Dear Couson

Letters of Condoleance are decent and customary, and therefore I write this; but I doe in my conscience beleive that in truth and reallity there is no cause of great lamentation, otherwise then that you have lost an able and a faithfull Steward, who had onely the latter quallity when you lost him, and by the course of nature, which was God's Law, could have noe more. The whole country and the comon wealth have the same reason to mourn as you have.

I enclosed sent you what I wrote to Lady Percivale; not to spare my own [pen] of writeing as much more

---

[1] There had been an Act passed in 1663 prohibiting the importation of fat cattle from Ireland into England. Cf. also Petty's "Observations upon the Trade of Irish Cattle" (*Papers*, No. 63).

to you, but to shew you what Arguments I have given her, in which I think there is not a word of fancy or Poesy.   In briefe, I desire you on my behalfe to pray God that I may dye with the same circumstances that your father did, and that my wife and children may have noe more Cause of excessive sorrow then your father's now have.

Lastly I desire you to look into Sir Tho Moore[1] how good people did lament their deceased friends; and do accordingly pray [that] God Sanctify the severall sorts of visitation wherewith he is pleased to try us in this World.

13. *Southwell to Petty.*

[April 21, 1677]

Deare Cousin

To give wisdome to the Ignorant, Entertainment to the Knowing, Physick to the sick and Consolation to the afflicted, is what falls within the Portion of very few mortalls in this Life.   But such has beene your felicity, that in most of these Relations I stand Indebted to you.

My poore Father is gone, but yett after soe many experiments of your love, that seeing it was not in humane power to prevent it, I doe humbly bend to the determination of God therein.   And tis my comfort that I [need] not goe farr [for] the Rules of a good life or of a Christian death.   Now *Pater Eneas exitet.*

In yours of the 30th [2] I had the variety of (as well the addition unto) your divine Poem.   The first part has here gone into [other] hands, soe that I must depend on one entire copie (as it escapes all eyes there) for the Satisfaction of Severall here; and pray lett a distinct paper beare the English translation of all that is altered or added to the first I had.   And as for the *Scale*, tis with Impatience that we looke for it.   I never

---

[1] Sir Thomas More (1480–1535). The reference is apparently to his *Utopia* (cf. *infra*, p. 201).
[2] *Sic*, but 3rd (*vide supra*) seems to be intended.

heard tydings of it till from your mouth, nor that any but Plato went before you in that reflex[ion] ; and all that I heare noted of him is what I sent you in my last.   I have Inclosed to Sir J Lowther your friendly Report in the matter of his enquiry.

By the Inclosed warrant you will see how I still relate to that Element you dipt me in at Gresham Colledge, and how still I must be linkt unto you on further Accounts.   There is a young agent of mine, Mr Robert Holmes, that will attend and take your order for the necessary steps towards a Patent for Vice-Admiral of Munster.[1]   He will find a patterne of my Father's there enrolled.

We are in this family in a State of health, and I must ever continue under the many tyes of
Deare S^r
Yr most affect Cousin.

14. *Petty to Southwell.*

Dr Coz^n Dublin, 28 Aprill 1677

To yours of the 21 instant.   I am glad you submitt so well to what could not bee refused.[2]   I have also his Royall Highnes' Warrant, but Mr Holmes hath not been with mee with your father's Old Patent, but so soone as he comes all shall be dispatcht.   Tis an affaire as much out of order as can bee and without some extraordinary help not worth the mending. Nevertheless I am glad you have it, that it may be soe mended, and it was in my thoughts to have minded you of it in the very next letter to that of Condolence.

I wrote Sir John Lowther (since what I sent you) a more perfect accompt of the Coales brought into Dublin, and guesse that not above 26 thousand tons of all sorts are brought thither, of which above halfe come from his towne of Whitehaven ; from whence some ships have made 16 returns in a yeare, many

[1] Southwell, who had been Deputy Vice-Admiral for Munster since 1665, now succeeded his father as Vice-Admiral.
[2] *I.e.* the Vice-Admiralship of Munster.

12, all 10 one with another—which is more than hath
hapned in any other sort of Trade.

The last post but one brought suspicions of My
Lord Duke of Ormond's return hither,[1] but the last
of all brings such a certainty as that all speake
of it openly.   I have but a word to say upon that
occasion and you know from our former discourses
what that Word is.   Have also an eye to mee this
Easter Terme.

Col Vernon [2] arrived here on Thursday.   The
same night I meeting with him reasoned with him
concerning some injuries hee had done since the first,
and since the fines &c.   But hee behaved himself as
usually hee doth.   But yesterday with 2 men assaulted
mee in the street and run the picque at the ferrull of
his Cane full into my left eye, and then drew his
sword.   Whereupon I cudgelled him well before the
many spectators would suffer mee to draw mine, and
so wee parted for the present and are at this time
under a sort of confinement.   Where this will end at
last I know not.   Many here have a great mind that
one may kill tother, that something considerable may
bee forfeited ; but let God's will be done !

. . . The Poem is now finished and mended so much
that I am weary of it.   Such as it is you shall have it
with the English, which yet wants the addition of the
Epilogue in English.   Tis much that after 35 [years]
discontinuance a man should doe so well, but otherwise tis a Thing not to value oneselfe upon, excepting
the designe.

The *Scale of Creatures* had also been done (and
shall be very shortly unless I bee suddenly killd or
hangd) if this news of change [of] the Terme,[3] and the
return of our Kerry commission, and this new tangle
with Vernon had not hapned all together at this very
time.

[1] As Lord-Lieutenant in place of Lord Essex, who was actually recalled
a few months later.   [2] See *infra*, p. 68.
[3] *I.e.* of the term of the Farm of the Irish Revenue.   This had been extended for a year, thus putting off the settlement of Petty's dispute with
the Farmers which he hoped to effect at the close of the Term.

I hope my eye will recover.   If I sue Vernon here, the fine shall go to the farmers, and They who have employd him herein will remitt [it] to him as his wages in their service, and consequently may give License to any Scelerat act punishable by fine.   This also must be endurd, that wee may bee lesse in love with the world and lesse afrayd of death.   But tell my Wife (to whom pray show this Letter) that I am now Settling the rest of my Estate,[1] seeing the necessity of it, and desire your leave to make you a Trustee for my children ; and shall take care in the doing of it that it shall bee very Little Trouble and I hope no other danger or other Inconvenience.   It seemes to me that there are snares of many sorts layd for it and my life both, and such as no innocence can prevent.   Surely I am either not Good enough or not Bad enough to live in this World !
However I am Yr^s entirely

W. P.

15. *Petty to Southwell.*

Dublin, 6 May 1677

I send you 3 Papers—I feare not free from *vitia scriptoris*.   I have none about mee that understand calme or sense, and my owne troubles are many and my eyes exceeding bad, and by the wonderfull machinations of my enemyes I am returning apace to bee nothing.   All the good I can doe doth but encrease them, but *invidiam augendo ulciscar*,[2] and whilst I live I will do the things that I think best, not fearing what man can do.   We are all in expectation of his Grace. Col Vernon is hasting back for England, intimating that My Lord Duke cannot budge without him.   I am in a pretty condicion here—if I stir, I am fined to the farmers who have the casuall revenue ; but if any body wrong mee, even to willful murder, the

---

[1] He appears, from a paper among the MS., to have settled part of his estate in the previous year.

[2] Petty printed this motto at the beginning of the *Five Essays in Political Arithmetic* (1687).

farmers can remitt. I do not wish it at present, but could bee very well sent to bee with your father. Adieu, deare Cousen. You shall have the *Scale of Creatures* for all this, and somewhat more

W. P.

16. *Petty to Southwell.*

Dublin 26 [May] 1677

Dr Co˙

I received yours of the 19, but not my wife's which is ment̃oned.

I say nothing now of poems or *Scales of Creatures*, but that on the 23ʳᵈ instant the enclosd petition and opinion [was] moved.[1] I send you them and my Notes upon the text. You see now what these farmers are; how they abused the Chancellors of both King-domes; how they plead disability and extremity before the time (but that time will come); how they fly to prerogative for protection. In their first bill in Chancery They allegd That I had promised them 6 monthes forebearance; in their bill here That I was not to bee payed till the King payd them, and now That I am not to bee payed till they pay the King. By their first bill they would destroy my bond, by the second my articles, and so leave me nothing for my wrong. They have done all that knaves and fooles, and that sharks and beggars could desire to doe. I hoped yesterday to have had judgement against them, but tis put of till the 2ᵈ day of next terme, or the 17 June. They now labor to get pretended arreares of Kerry quitrents to be satisfyed out of what they owe mee. All is naught. The delay of indulgence which I have sufferd will endanger my whole.

Adieu, dear Cozen. You shall have the *Scale* for all this.

Yʳˢ &c

W. P.

[1] The Petition in question was one from ' Sir James Shaen and partners, farmers of His Majesty's Revenue of Ireland ', to the Lord-Lieutenant demanding the King's ' protection ' from the debt which they owed to Petty (Petty MSS.).

17. *Petty to Southwell.*

Dublin 9 Junii. 1677

Dr Cos^n

We have finisht your patent for Vice-Admirall. I will shortly write you a Letter entirely upon this matter.

By Letters of the 2 instant I heare of a decree that the farmers shall give me judgement next terme and pay mee within 6 months after &c. I might now say (as before you instructed mee better) That the Justice of my cause was such as it was impossible to have judged otherwise, and that I have great wrong that the same was not done the first terme &c. ; but now I say tis well That it was not judged I shoᴜld never have my money at all. But leaving these extremes I attribute the judgement that is to your care at the fountayne, without any deeper speculation into the right and wrong of the matter. In brief I thanke you and thank my Lord Chancellor, which pray tell his Lordship as you find occasion, and that I, am sorry I mistooke him. But God grant this judgement bee not too late ; and if it bee, God's will bee done in all things. I am now in my bearing throwes about the quitrent, and then for the *Scale of Creatures* agayne. Pardon this abruptnes in

Yr^s

W. P.

18. *Petty to Southwell.*

Dublin, 4° Aug. 1677

D^{re} Coz^n

I was surprized at the reappearance of your Letter, but you did not say how the Bath had done with yourselfe and Lady &c.

I send you some part of the fabrick described in my former letter to you.[1] But have been anticipated

---

[1] *I.e.* the first four chapters of the *Scale of Creatures* which are referred to in the next letter. This fragment of the finished Essay is no longer extant.

so much (out of him whose shoes I am not worthy to untye), that the remainder goes heavily on ; though as good as what I now send you, and I think as different from any thing I ever saw or heard of, as my translaçon of Buchanan was from what preceded. But remember There is one glory of the Sun, another of the Moone and another of the Stars &c. Besides I have of late learned some discretion of persons, times, and places, and that truth and sincerity signify little. Wherefore if I write *in Re Ardua* anything heterodox, what shall I get if I do well ?—R̶[1] oooo. What shall I suffer If it please not the censorious and Envious, the Sciolous &c?—R̶ 99999999 &c.[2] Wherefore shew not these things but where you are sure of Candor and Safety.

Now a Word to the Maine. I have no reliefe either by the King's letter of 28 April 1676,[3] nor by the generall reducements of quitrents, but am most absurdly dealt with by mistakes as well as prejudice. I doubt things are not well for mee with the ——[4] ; because since you first mençoned him I have heard nothing, but neverthelesse give mee rules how to make my unlucky condiçon tollerable if you can.

19. *Petty to Southwell.*

[The fight with the Farmers still continued, but, with the arrival of the Duke of Ormond (here recorded), Petty no doubt felt more hopeful of a successful issue. James Butler, first Duke of Ormond (1610–1688), had already been twice Lord-Lieutenant of Ireland. As such he had been instrumental in suppressing the original rebellion under Charles I. in 1644–1645. Re-appointed to the post in 1661, he held it till 1669, and now replaced Arthur Capel, Earl of Essex

---

[1] *Recipe, i.e.* ' take thou '.
[2] Petty means, of course, that should his writings please the powers that be, he will get no reward ; but should they displease, he will be blamed *ad infinitum.*
[3] This was a letter in which the King, in lieu of an abatement of Quitrents, granted part of them to Petty (Petty MSS.).
[4] Blank in original. The Lord-Lieutenant is probably intended.

(1631–1683), whose anti-papist proclivities had been the cause of his recall and ultimately led to his confinement and suicide in the Tower. Ormond had long been on friendly terms with both Petty and Southwell, and perhaps with a sense of favours to come, the former thought fit on this occasion to welcome him with a somewhat fulsome poem. It is headed " A Navall Allegory—by the Register of the Admiralty of Ireland. To his Grace James Duke of Ormond, as Grand Pilot of the good ship Ireland, upon his fourth expedition on that Bottome." The poem was not apparently published at the time, but I have printed it amongst the *Petty Papers* (No. 151). I have also identified (though I have not printed) the other verses alluded to by Petty in this letter. They are entitled respectively " On making a Nayle " and " Upon the 4 o'clock Bell and my neighbour Kit the Cooper ".]

Dublin Aug. 22° 1677

Deare Cousin

To yours of the 11th instant. I hope you have received the 4 first Chapters of the *Scale*. Honest Hales saith that the six points which hee taketh out of the Bills of Mortality are cleerer than a hundred notionall arguments can refute;[1] And I say that what I pretend to concerning the Farmers and concerning the Kerry Quitrents, is as Cleere and Justifiable as any of the said six points, and all the Tricks which have been used against mee are as cleerly false ; which makes mee admire and lament either the obliquity of other men or my owne Madnesse. I am terribly affraid of my money, besides which and the interest, it hath cost mee and lost mee above 900£. Besides which I sufferr concerning Kerry, insteade of the reliefe I expected. Soe that at this day I may say I am 5000£ the worse for having medled with them, and notwithstanding theire many Lyes, if I would have taken 2000£ for the whole, I did never cleerely see that I might have had it otherwayes then in promises and vapours.

---

[1] In *The Primitive Origination of Mankind.*

Deare Cousin, if I might purchase a lasting peace and Settlement by the way you propound, I believe I shoulde have an end. But since that may not bee, I must gett my right to greater matters adjudged, and I wish they[1] may be able to pay what I hope to obtaine. And I wish it may not bee to late for the King and his Ministers to understand both them and mee ; nor doe I beleive My Lord of Essex dooth vallue himselfe for the Letter which hee wrote concerning this matter. In brief they are a Crazy body and are at this day fallen into two bitter factions of 5 against 3 ; viz. Rider, Gourney and Piggott against the rest.[2] They had yesterday a greate contest before the Council, where they outed Piggott. My opinion is that if the Farme houlde, it must come into a very few hands.

This day my Lord of Ormond landed at Skerries and preparation is making to meete him tomorrow about Finglas. Severall verses have been made and printed to Entertaine him, and among the rest the Officers of the Admiralty have don what is heere inclosed, but are affraid to show them, much lesse to print them. Lett Mr Pepys[3] see them, if you thinke fitt, and thanke him hartily for lending a hand to rowe mee ahed in this foule weather.

I alsoe send you the late Report which my Lord of Essex hath made uppon the letter I obtained from the King when I was last in England,[4] togeather with my new Peticõn to his Majestie grounded uppon the same. You see that my opinion is that *Right is Immortall* and much more the Soules, and that I have the Courage to sufferr in hopes of the Resurrection of Slaine truth, like the seaven Sonnes in the Maccabees;[5]

---

[1] *I.e.* the 'Farmers'.

[2] The 'Farmers', as evinced by their signatures to a petition dated June 1677, were James Shaen, William Rider, Edward Richbell, William Muschamp, Stanhope Mill, Lawrence Stanyon, John Gurny and Robert Pigot.

[3] Samuel Pepys (1632–1703), the author of the famous *Diary*. He was Secretary to the Admiralty and in high favour with King Charles II. (see Introduction).

[4] Cf. *supra*, p. 31 *n*. These documents are among the MSS.

[5] The seven sons in the Maccabees were slaughtered by order of Antiochus Epiphanes, the persecutor of the Jewish nation, in 168 B.C. Their martyrdom is celebrated by the Church of Rome on August 1 (cf. II. Maccabees).

And you alsoe see that my wealth lyes in greate rights with little hopes &c.

I have of late made or trimmed upp two Latin Coppeys of verses, The one about making of Hobb nailes and the other about hoopeing of Tubbs, and some other conceipts; all which shall not hinder the remainder of the *Scale*.

I thinke, Deare Couzin, you must gett a presse a-purpose to lay by the many Papers I send you. Perhapps an ould tubb or bagg may serve well enough !

Sunday 26. ditto.

The rest of what is mentioned here you shall have from my Wife. All is glorious here. Lord Essex went off hence last night with generall regret.

Adieu

W. P.

20. *Southwell to Petty.*

Spring Garden, 15th Sept. 1677

Deare Cosen

I have already acknowledged in part yours of the 22nd past, and your kind entertainment in verse relating to my Lord Lieutenant's Reception. But those other parts of Poetry relating to Hobnails, Hooping of Tubbs, and other conceits which you have lately trimd up, I must needs have them alsoe, or I shall not fill that Ebony Cabinet wherein I keep, as in an Archive, all the effects of your Pen. For I look on them as materialls fitt for those that I would take most care of, and hope they also will hand them over with like estimation.

Soe that while I am thus posest, you may imagin whether it be not a grief to me to see you involvd in the Anguish and depredations of the Law, begining the sute with one Complaint and ending it with Twenty ; running in consequence the Hazard of your Life, or the ruin of your Wife and Chilldren by the

life of others. Nor can I foresee a period of such like
Calamities till you resolve absolutely upon other
measures than what you have taken. For if ' Right
be Immortal ', and can never die, yet you have not
a Corporation of lives to assert it in all that variety of
Channells and Courses wherein it runs ; And there
are some wrongs whose revenge must be remitted unto
God Almighty alone. And therefore if even so dear
a thing as the right eye be offensive, pull it out, and
enter maimed into the smoothing and Peace of this
Life, which is next Doore to the Joys of another.

And suffer from me this expostulation, who wish
your prosperity as much as any man living; and having
opportunities to see and heare what the temper of the
world is towards you, I cannot but wish you well in
Port, or rather upon the firm Land, and to have very
little or nothing at all left to the mercy and good will
of others. For there is generally imbibd such an
opinion and dread of your superiority and reach over
other men in the wayes of dealing, that they hate what
they feare, and find wayes to make him feare that is
feard. I doe the more freely open my soul to you in
this matter, because I see tis not for the vitells that
you contend, but for outward Limbs and accessions,
without which you can subsist with Plenty and
Honour. And therefore to throw what you have quite
away, or at least to put it in dayly hazard onely to make
it a little more than it is, Is what you would condemne
a thousand times over in another. And you would not
think the Reply sufficient that there was plain Right
in the Cause and Justice of their side, for iniquities
will abound and the world will never be reformed.

After all this is said, I mean not that you should
relinquish the pursute of your 2500£,[1] which is money
out of your Pockett and for which you are a Debtor
unto your Family. But for other pretensions, lett
them goe for Heaven's Sake, as you would a hott
coale out of your hand ; and strive to retire to your

---

[1] This was the sum which Petty had actually advanced to the Farmers,
though he now claimed £5000.

home in this Place, where you had the respect of all,
and as much quiet as could be in this life, before your
medling with that pernicious buisness of the Farme.
But you may reckon it as a storm wherein you were
seized, and if it has obligd you to throw over board
some rich Bales, tis but the Common Case, and what
others doe for the safety of the rest.

I will not burthen you with more of this nature ;
but be assured, that it comes from the bottom of my
heart ; and that, wherever it may lye in my Power, I
am, with all truth and affection, Deare Sr Your most
affectionate friend & servant

ROBERT SOUTHWELL

21. *Petty to Southwell.*

Dublin, ye 29 of Sepb^r 1677

Deare Cosen
I see nothing to the contrary, but that I may
comply with Mr Mead's desires. Wee are at present
setting our Judges and officers in many places, but
have finished nothing as yet. I wish you were here
to help us. On Munday next wee make more speeches
to the Gabbard[1] men and ffishermen at Ringsend.

The last had little in it, but this will have nothing,
for I am not well, yet better in my mind than in my
body ; my Leggs swelling, my belly is not onely big
but hard, and my breath short, and mee thinks I see
the same horse bridled and sadled for mee, that caryed
away your ffather.

You shall have the verses about the Hob-nailes
and Tubs you mençon ; but why will you trouble
your self with them ? I had indeed some pleasure in
makeing them, but doe not see why you should have
any in reading them. They (as my other things) are
cramd with a sort of dry matter, and describe the truth
of things, but they all want the fflame and very spirit

---

[1] A *gabbard* was a sailing barge or lighter.

of Poetry. So also do my other preceedings want the
Poetry of Craft, the Lying fflatery, dissimulation, base
complacency & c, and therefore are unsuccessfull.

I heartily thank you for your advice concerning
the Farmers. You may remember how much I have
already declared myself willing to comply with it, but
I do not find that even what you advise will doe
mee any good as to the maine ; and therefore I must
follow Providence, and the working of nature from day
to day.

The *Scale of Creatures* goes on, but will produce
onely more mischiefe against mee. There will bee
many things in it which the World cannot beare, and
for which I shall suffer. But suppose all were tran-
cendently well—what shall I get by it but more envy ?

Do what you will about my petition upon the Ld
Essex his report.[1] Really I think my selfe wholly
uncapable to advise or act [any] thing in these matters.
I despaire of help from right, reason, and truth, but
cast myselfe upon Time, Chance, Constellations of
lucky humors in the heavens, if pos[sible].

Wherfore, Dear Cousen, Throw the dice for mee.

22. *Petty to Southwell.*

[The letters which follow are largely concerned with
Admiralty business, in which Petty, as Judge of the Irish
Admiralty Court, represented the Admiral of Ireland.
James, Duke of York, who had been Lord High Admiral of
England, had been forced to give up that post after the
passing of the Test Act in 1673, in favour of Prince Rupert
and a body of twelve commissioners. He appears, however,
to have retained his position as High Admiral for Ireland.
Southwell, as Vice-Admiral of Munster, was also interested
in these matters, though he seems to have delegated his
duties to the Mr. Mead who is mentioned below.

The Irish Admiralty was, in Petty's words, " a very raw
thing ", and his efforts to maintain its prestige seem to have
met with scant success. His work must, however, have

---

[1] *Vide supra*, p. 33.

brought him into close touch with the Lord High Admiral, and the good relations which afterwards existed between King James II. and Petty were no doubt largely due to the latter's activities as Admiralty Judge at this time.]

Dublin, ye 10° Novb^r 1677

Deare Cosen
                    I directed my wife to shew you my last Letter, concerning the *Scale*, the *Post Chariot* &c. I might write a Treatis and call it *The Scale of Devills*, of whom I find many sorts and degrees, and am now studying whereabout to place the Farmers in that Scale ; and yet I am not provoaked by them to decline the Peace and moderation you have advised mee unto.

I am not well, yet do not appeare to everybody to bee otherwise : in two words my Belly seems to my self to bee a wodden Belly &c.

What followes is concerning the Admiralty ; wherefore I say : That Mr Meade is now come to Towne, so as wee shall finish with him this Terme. Birne and Tam are contesting in our Court. I heare Tam hath caused Monsr Leyinburg [1] to write something to my Lord Lieutenant reflecting upon my Justice, which is totally untrue in matter of fact ; Wherefore let it passe, along with the Farmers.

There came in to Youghall a French man in a Dutch ffliut,[2] without comission, and without bringing with him any of the taken Ship's Company. Hereupon wee accuse him of a Piraticall Act. Hee (as the readiest way to cleare himself) clayms from us the Adjudication of his Prize. Wee, upon discussion of the matter, cleere him of Piracy and adjudge the said ffliut unto him as lawfull Prize, and demand of him the tenths, in right of the Admirall of Ireland. Hee denyes these tenths to bee due. The expedient wee have used is That he pay or secure the said tenths, and have given him 6 weeks time to sollicite a remitall of the same from his Royall Highnesse. Now you

---

[1] ? James Barkman Leyenburg, sometime Swedish representative in England.
[2] The word is probably Petty's rendering of the Dutch word *Vloot*.

being Vice Admirall of Munster (unto which Province this matter relates) must acquaint his Royall Highnesse, or Sir John Worden[1] herewith. Wee here are the Blind, leading the Blind. Wee have neither Doctor nor Proctor, nor any other ancient experienct officer, nor have Wee the late treatis between his Majesty, and other Princes for our direction.

You may have heard that there is a new Bridge lately built at Dublin,[2] below the old one, without leave of the Admirall. This Bridge I allow to bee A good worke, but have questioned the Builders for passing by the Admirall. I have also upon the presentacõn of the Grand Jury, proceeded upon severall Trespasers upon the Harbour of this place, but do find that the Citty are instigated to dispute the Admirall's Jurisdiction ; which if they do (as in many other places they are also doing) I know not from whom to ask mony or other assistance and countenance wherewith to ascert the same.

In my opinion, this Court increases apace, I meane the trouble and businesse of it, which chiefly concerns poore men ; so as the Fees I get do not defray the Postage of the many Letters I receive concerning this matter. Wherefore, and since my Predicessors had their letters free, pray [inquire] whither the same may bee granted mee. Tis a happinesse to the Poore Judge that wee have a Vice-Admirall at Court.

I say nothing about the Kerry buisnesse, for feare it should looke like interposeing any of my unluky advice into your proceedings. God blesse you therein and reward your good indeavours. No more at present from

Your most obligd servant & kinsman

W^M Petty

---

[1] Sir John Werden, or Worden (1640–1710). He was a Member of Parliament and secretary to the Duke of York. Petty, as will be seen later, was always at pains to maintain friendly relations with him.

[2] This was Essex Bridge, built in 1676. Two others were then in existence above it—' Bloody ', afterwards called ' Barrack ' Bridge, built six years before, and the great bridge ' going to Ostmantown ' at the end of Bridge Street, which up to 1670 had been the only communication across the Liffey.

23. *Petty to Southwell.*

Dublin, ye 18⁰ Novbʳ 1677

Deare Cosen

I thanke you heartily for yours of the 10 Instant.

Concerning Kerry I say nothing. What you say of D. O.[1] I will indeavour to deserve. As for printing the 104ᵗʰ psalme, what I count good will bee diserned by few, but what is harsh and stiff by very many.[2] As for the *Scale*, it will conteyne somewhat of extraordinary, but whether extraordinary good or extraordinary bad, I know not.

As for Admiralty matters I troubled you pritty well in my last. Admiralty buisnesse growes upon Us. Wee can brag of Justice and dispatch, and forgiveing of ffees. I am trying severall wayes how to divide the Judicatures, and am loath to fix any thing without some experience. I doubt T. Meade grumbles inwardly That he is not Judge of all Munster, whereas I designe him but for Kinsaile and all the coast of Corke Westward thereof. Pray tell mee freely what you would have done therein. The Admiralty of Ireland is a very raw thing, and must bee brought to Maturity by many and mature thoughts. When I have done with the Farmers I will make some signall progresse in it. Present my service to Sir John Worden, and the Registers also.

I cannot send the draught of the Chariot [3] this day; nor am I willing to do it, till I have rumbled up and downe the Country, through thick and thin, and over Ruffe and smooth, and till I have compared it with the many other wayes now in practise. But for the present pray him to bee contented with the discription following, vizt:

The Intencõn and end of this engine is to carry

---

[1] ? Duke of Ormond.
[2] This poem was printed, probably through Southwell's instrumentality, during the year following.
[3] *Supra*, p. 13.

an unweildy, inferme, and blindish carcas over the
Rocks and Bogs of Kerry ; and to carry him by night
or day, in all weathers and wayes, through faire and
Christian Countryes, not excluding Penman-more [1]
in Wales ; and That by the help of any 2 Jeade
draught horses and Driver, such (as I thinke) are
everywhere to bee had.

This Chariot and its wheeles doe weigh 3 hundred
and $\frac{3}{4}$, the Rider and his servant and the Driver will
weigh 4 hundred and $\frac{1}{2}$; and the necessaryes of them
all, I estimate at $\frac{3}{4}$ of a hundred more. Makeing in
all 9 hundred weight. Now, forasmuch as wee find
by daily experience, That garrons [2] here in Ireland
of 20 or 30£ price, will draw a car or carriage weighin
neere 5 hundred and $\frac{1}{2}$, 20 miles per diem upon truck
wheeles of 30 Inches Diameter ; I conclude that 2
better horses upon wheeles of 5 foot diameter, will
draw $4\frac{1}{2}$ cwt. a peece 30 mile per diem, or 12 stage
miles in 3 howers.

In this cariage there is all the ease that springs,
braces, cushions and change of all posture can give,
and consequently I hope that a man can as well
continue to ride in it as to bee in his Inne.

This Toole is not exempt from being overthrowne,
but if it should bee overthrowne (even upon a heape
of flints) I cannot see how the Rider can have any
harme.

Memorandum : That the Horse beareth no more
burthen then you please, besides his draught. As
for easy turning, and its going in narrow and crooked
wayes, it is no better nor worse than other Callashes
with 2 wheeles.

Upon the whole matter, I hope that a gentleman
and his servant may travell 60 miles a day upon
Post Roade at 6^d per mile expence, and may have 8
or 9 howers per diem for such Refreshments, as they
shall not please to take in the Chariot it self. And

[1] Penmaenmawr, Carnarvon, between Bangor and Conway. Petty, no
doubt, had often had occasion to pass this way in his journeys to Ireland.
[2] Small country horses.

it seemes to mee that this cariage can afford to carry fine goods betweene Chester and London for lesse than 3ᵈ in the pound.

So much for the present from

Yours most entirely

W. P.

I am not worse in my health.

24. *Petty to Southwell.*

Dublin, 22 December 1677

Deare Cousin

Yours of the 11ᵗʰ instant did not come to my hand till 5 days after my wive's of the same date, which menc̃oned your sending mee the King's Letter,[1] just as you have done. After two dayes were spent in inquiring after it without effect, I concluded twas either stopt in England or intercepted by the Foe, or that the Devill was still pursueing his old trick as to this Matter of Kerry. And my heart being hardened against all that even the Devill can doe in that matter, I tooke a slight occasion of buisnes to goe about a 20 miles Journey to try the Charriot to the quick and to review my matterials for the *Scale of Creatures*; for both which, also some Admiralty matter, I referr you to the 3 distinct inclosd papers here withall sent you.

As for your Letter of the 11ᵗʰ instant, it is the Card by which I will Sett my dayly course; for you have therein well diserned and described my miscarriages and misfortunes. In short I will tye my hands behind mee, and put a gagg in my mouth, and try whether this contrary course, which you have advised and I approve of, may not prove a contrary effect. As for what you intend further to doe, I say 'doe it or do it not', or what ever else you think fitt; for I will interpose no more, but pray God to

---

[1] This was a letter, dated December 8, 1677, from King Charles II. to the Lord-Lieutenant ordering that a reducement should be made on the Quit-rents chargeable on Petty's property in County Kerry (Petty MSS.).

reward your kindness in the sympathy and concernment you have had with mee, not onely in this buisnes,
but in that of the Farmers and many others.

And soe wishing you and your Lady and the whole
fire-side, including Sir Francis Edward Dearing [1] and
his a Merry Christmas. Thus my charriot, my court
and all the Creatures of my *Scale*, with myselfe, thank
you and are, dear cousin,

Yours entirely &c

W^M PETTY

I am pitching upon such a soft Sollicitor as you
advised. Sir J Shaen [2] talks of coming for England.
Many Parliament men are also hastning hence. I
am drawing the scheme of *A New Wooden or Woollen
wall* [3] against all the Enemyes of England &c.

Adieu.

25. *Petty to Southwell.*

[The letter which follows, though forming part of the
present Correspondence, has already been printed (as an
example of Petty's efforts in philosophic thought) in the
Petty Papers (No. 87A). Though without date, it can be
approximately placed, for its allusions to 'the Platonist'
and to 'the excellent Hale' must refer to Southwell's communications of January and April 1677 (*supra*, pp. 12 and
26), while the Psalm mentioned in the concluding paragraph is that with which Petty had been so much occupied
ever since his temporary incarceration at Dublin (p. 15).
It might well indeed be the paper which Petty calls his
" review of materials " in his letter of December 22, and I
have accordingly inserted it at this point.]

[1] Sir Edward Dering (1625–1684) of Surrenden-Dering in Kent, first Bart.
His daughter had married Southwell, and another daughter had married John
Perceval. He was a commissioner for customs from 1675 to 1679 and afterwards
a commissioner for the Treasury.

[2] James Shaen had been a commissioner for the ' Civil ' Survey of Ireland
which preceded Petty's Down Survey of 1654. He subsequently (1667) became
Surveyor-General of that country, and as such he appears to have consistently
endeavoured to thwart Petty's plans and undertakings.

[3] Cf. " Of Coarse Irish Wooll ", " The Uses of Wool in War ", " Of Wooll
Walls " (*Papers*, Nos. 101, 102, 103).

[December 1677]

Dear Cousin,

I have sped soe well by pretending to say something of the *Scale of Creatures*, that I have got more from you, then you might reasonably think I could have imparted to you ; for I have gotten what the Platonist, and what the more excellent Hales, have said of that matter.

I told you (and truly) that I had never read any thing about it ; but I also told you that noe considering man (who syncerly minded the great point) could well overlook it, and consequently I believed that many had already handled the matter better then I could doe. And I now doe with joy see that honest Hales hath said much of my scheme, vizt :

(1) That, between God and man, there are holy Angells, Created Intelligences, and subtile materiall beings ; as there are between man and the lowest animall a multitude of intermediate natures.

(2) That good man inferreth from thence, that man hath noe reason to put soe high a value upon himselfe as if he were chiefe or next to God. Which very notion (as I expressed in my first Letter to you) tended only to humble the proud coxcombd man.

(3) Hales makes an Affinity between mettalls and vegetables, and another between vegetables and animalls, and a third affinity between animals and man, a fourth between man and his subtile materiall being, a fifth between those beings and created Intelligences, a sixth between those Intelligences and the holy Angells, and another between the Angells and the Creator himselfe.

(4) He saith that the nature of man is very much worth enquiry, because the brightnes of God appeared in the Man Christ Jesus ; and because man was made after God's image, and doth faintly resemble God, as the sun in a Bason of water doth the sun in the heavens. Moreover the Platonist saith (i) that between Superior and Inferior species there are midle natures (ii) that man is a meane between Angells and

Beastes or between Intelligent and sencible beings
(iii) and that there is also a meane between inanimate
and living natures.

And thus (Deare Cousin) haveing given you to
understand that I apprehend the Drift of your two
excellent papers, I say that to write of this subject
after these great personages, is the same kind of
Insolence and Temerity as to paraphrase the 104th
Psalme after Buchanan. Neverthelesse, as I have
done the one, so I shall doe the other ; without any
designe of disturbing anything that those worthies
have said, but rather with hopes to cleare and exemplify
the meaning of such words used by them as are not
of a single signification : for the heads of my intended
Discourse are these, vizt :

1. I beg leave of the world to decline the words,
Infinite, Eternall, Incomprehensible, when I speake
of Almighty God ; being words not soe fitt for Ratiocination, but rather for Adoration, and such as beget
an honorifick amazment, so as to worke upon our
affections, but not to cleare or brighten our understanding. And therefore I mention Almighty God
but in part, and only as the maker of the firmament
or orbe of the fixed Starrs, and of all things within
that Orbe, which is indeed the visible world and the
greatest things our senses can reach.

2. I make two Scales of animate beings, that is
to say, of beings which act by souls. The one whose
top is Man, and whose bottom is the smallest and
the simplest animall that man can discern ; and of
the other scale, the make of the aforemenĉond visible
world is the top and Man the bottome. Nor do I
presume to offer at a third scale, but stop here and
say " Abyssus abyssum invocat ", or quit it to the
sublimer thoughts of others.

3. I demonstrate the vast and immense difference
between the said two scales, and doe shew the great
multitudes of gradations which are upon the small
scale, from thence inferring that there bee many more
upon the greater scale.

4. Before I determine that Man is the chiefe and noblest Creature, and worthily the top of the small scale, I doe in termes and words of sence expound what I meane by the words Noble, Chief &c, and do then by many comparisons show wherein some particular creatures doe excell man ; but do withall shew that man doth exceed every creature in soe many other particulars as that he deserveth the pre-eminence. And in this Chapter I describe both the Powers and Infirmities of man in some variety.

5. Placeing Man on the top of the lower scale, I make many sorts or species of Comparisons between him and his Inferior animalls, downe to the lowest, and presume to infer the like gradations to be in the upper scale.

6. Having proved many gradations to be also in the upper scale, and haveing scripture grounds that Man (part of that scale) beareth the Image of God ; I inferr that man is nearer in likeness to the top of the upper scale (which I suppose to be the maker of the firmament, if that maker be anything lesse than the Infinite God himselfe) then to God, concerning whom I doe not presume to ratiocinate at all, but (as I said before) to admire and adore only ; fearing to grow stark blind by gazing upon him, rather than to discerne him more distinctly by soe doing.

7. I doe not only compare man with the Inferior Creatures of the small scale, but I doe also compare the highest emprovements of mankind in his masse, with the rudest condition that man was ever in ; thereby inferring that if man hath improved soe much in the severall past Centuries and ages of the world, how far he might proceed in six thousand yeares more, or in any other number of ages, that is to say how farr he might advance from the bottome (where he now is) towards the top of the great scale.

It may now be expected all this should be applyed to Religion :—as first

1. To prove that there is a God. But this In-quisicõn I show to be needles, and alsoe dangerous ;

though not in itselfe, yet in respect of the offense
that many may take at speaking of mysterious things
in clear words. But I doe much labour to state
that question truly and intelligibly, and I hope to
doe it soe as may amount to a sattisfactory Determination thereof. So as the principall use of considering
these *Scales of Creatures*, is to lett man see that
beneath God there may be millions of beings superior
unto man. Wheras Hee generally taketh himselfe to
be the chiefe and next to God : (1) because it hath
been said of him more than of others that he beareth
the Image of God ; (2) That God appeared in the
shape of man.

Now these two arguments are safely answered
thus : first, for that God appeared alsoe in the shape
of a Dove, and the spirit of God hath spoken through
a more contemned animall. And as to the Image of
God, Tis certaine that these creatures must in some
sence or sort beare the Image of God which beare
the Image of man. Soe that, although the Image of
God be more plane upon Man than upon the Inferior
animalls of the lesser scale, nothing hinders why the
same Image may not be yet more plane upon the
superior beings of the greater scale then upon Man
himselfe—onely wee must by Image meane figure
only.

2. As to Religion, I do in the next place pitch
upon two points, which I call the poles, upon which
all Religion turneth, and I sett downe alsoe severall
powers which make Religion to move upon those
two poles. Of which powers some move it steadily,
as weights doe a clock ; some lesse uniformly, and
but as springs doe a watch ; others yet more unequally,
as streames of water influenced by droughts and land
floods doe a mill ; and some as irregularly and unequally as vapors and exhalations drive a wind mill.
As for other opinions which do not turn upon those
two poles of religion ; they move but like chaffe and
feathers driven to and fro, upwards and downwards
by every puffe of wind, and by the vapors of dis-

tempered blood, humors, and spiritts. And thus I have epitomized what you have sent me, and what I intend to send to you, as soon as I can calmely review it—all of which you see to bee the same that others have and must think of.

I heer again send you the Psalme, as it hath been inspected and corrected by many. The sence and designe hath pretty well past muster with them, as you will find by comparing it with the first coppy. I have also sent you the English which keeps very neare the sence of the lattin, at least neare enough. What I have done of this kind must be looked upon with kindnesse and candor, otherwise you spoyle me for a Poet, so as to meddle no more, till 35 years hence ; making my next pawse as long as my last.

[Endorsed " Sir Wm Petty's Scale of Creatures " : no date.]

26. *Petty to Southwell.*

Dublin, 19th March 1677/8

Deare Cousin

Yours of the 9th of March — As it made mencõn of some storme wherein your self had been tost, so it delivered mee from another and easd me from Busking upp and down the sea of all that had ever past between us, to find the cause of your long silence. Many times when I had wearied my self with seeking you to Noe purpose, I did applaud my own doggett Temper (as I had before bewailed it) for not haveing courted the friendshipp of many. For, thought I, if what I thought so sure bee soe easily and wonderfully lost without my being able to find any kind of reason for it, I have done well in having Traded soe little in that perishing Commoditie of friendshipp. I have ever thought that no Man ought (nor indeed can) love many entirely well, so I now incline to think twas to little purpose to love

any att all ; but your Letter, after I had long laid
waveing in the Bedlam of these ugly Speculacõns,
like a good Opiat brought mee to sleep ; and my
Sences are now so well recovered, that I can give
you hearty thanks for the cure you have wrought upon
mee, but am grievously sorry for the occasion.

As for my own health, I was never heart-sick, and
my head (at least that I flatterd myself) more serene
than at other times ; but all my Limbs from the
Hipps downwards and one of my Arms were as Lame
as Loggs of Wood.   I have now in a great measure
recovered that Lameness, but am still heavy and stiff,
and kept backward from a totall restitucõn by the
harsh weather that hath been and still is.   My Leggs
and feet swell near an Inch every night, but are
aswagd in the morning.   This is my present Case,
and *God's will bee done.*

Since I gave Mr Mead his Commission[1] I have
beene peppard with Letters accusing him to bee a
Puritan Papist, devoted to the French, and that his
name is Myagh and not Mead ; with such other
Circumstances as envy and prejudice uses to accumu-
late.   The poor gent hath of himselfe (hearing these
things) offerred to surrender his Commission, but I
have as yet given no Answer thereunto.   Pray advise
herein ; I seem to bee between Scylla and Charybdis
in this Matter.

I never received any Letter from Sir John Worden,
nor more than the Coppy thereof which you sent mee,
and shall do what I can to comply with your desires.
But Cousin since I have been a Judge I am grown
pestilent cautious, finding that every little tittle is
snapt at, and made matter of accusation and pretended
offence—which is a scurvy Case for a Man who may
suffer much and hopes to get nothing.   As to the
Merrit of this buisness, this french-man[2] had upon
him severall Marks of Piracy, which being cleerd,

---

[1] As Registrar for the Court of Admiralty in Munster.
[2] *Supra*, p. 38. Some letters among the MSS. show that Petty's conduct
of this case had been animadverted upon by the Admiralty authorities in
London.

the shipp was condemnd as Prize to the French ; no Creature (not soe much as Mr Galwey) having to this day appeared to the Contrary, which is by good luck expressd in our Sentence.   Much less could wee divine what was transacted at Nimingen [1]—Nor indeed have wee any helps of that kind.   But the blind lead the blind, so as had wee not some glemerings of naturall Justice, wee had long since dous't into some ditch of Iniquity.   The very thing you move was long since granted, nor was ever any security tendered, nor do I here a word concerning it to this very day ; and my Opinion is, That if the Dutch would have their right, they must reverse our sentence in the ordinary Course—which whither they doe or not, I think the Admiralls 10th will bee due, and that the damage thereof must bee repaird by the first wrong Doer.

Tis expected that I should some time or other build Hospitalls [2] &c, but I assure you that the Paines, the attendance and expence I am at, and the fear of treading awry in order to doe poor men Justice, may well commute *pro tanto* for the Charitys I ow the world.   I am not weary of what I do, because I beleive I do well, but have often wisht I never had ingaged in it ; and truely, without the appeals into England be taken away or Limitted, I will throw up, for I cannot do the good which is necessary to bee done.   E.G : The last week I adjudged three considerable men of Dublin to pay wages unto 5 Seamen, in the plainest Case imaginable.   Now, although no case requires a sumary and speedy Decision more then this, yett those men appeal to the Admiralty of England, knowing the poor seamen have not a penny amongst them, and must be forc't to go to sea and disperse themselves before any thing

---

[1] The treaty of Nimeguen (August 1678) was not yet signed, but the French, having been successful in the war against the Allies, were no doubt already in a position to secure a favourable decision in cases such as this one.

[2] Possibly an allusion to the idea of a Hospital "for the Relief and Maintenance of Antient and Infirm Officers and Soldiers serving in the Army of Ireland " which was mooted about this time.   It took shape in 1680 in the founding of the present Royal Hospital at Dublin (Hull, 166 *n*.).

can bee done therein. Besides, why should one kingdome appeal to another ? Can matters of fact bee better examined in Remote parts, than in the very place where they happen ? Should appeals bee from his Royall Highnes to inferior persons ? Should such appeals bee allowd as would absolutely destroy Trade and Justice, by leaveing poor seamen to the meer Mercy of their Imployers ? Pray mind this in due time and place, and move also that the first money wee get for the Duke may be bestowd to defend his Right. For Cuning fellows seeing our Lame and blind side, do use the Admiralty most villainously ; for I myself and the rest of my officers do now stand Indicted for holding an Unlawfull Assembly, which indeed was in impannelling a Jury to inquire how a dead Corps came by his death and for (Like honest Tobit) burying the dead !

As for the Charriott, there hath been nothing but sleep and silence dureing my Illness, but even to Morrow, I begin a 3 weekes progress with it. Wherefore Sir John Worden (to whom present my humble service) will have good interrest for his forbearance.

As to the King's Letter you sent Mee,[1] something is a doeing, but little done, and my feares concerning it do increase for these reasons, vizt :

You know my virtue and vanity lyes in prateing of Numbers, Weight, and Measure ; not sticking to talk even of the proporcõns of Kingdomes and States. Now upon this Head I have sometimes said That England is tenn Times richer, and Scotland a third poorer than Ireland ;[2] That Ireland doth now pay 240^m£ per annum ; That the charge of Collecting the same is *viis et modis* per annum 60^m£ more, so as the poor people of Ireland do pay 300^m£ per annum to some body. Now if England paid tenn Times as much, and Scotland $\frac{2}{3}$ds of the same, the whole would bee 3 millions and a half ; which sum (said I) would sett forth and maintaine the ablest fleet that ever was

---

[1] *Supra*, p. 42.
[2] Cf. *Petty Papers*, i. 264 and ii. 55—but the estimate therein is different.

known, and about 80ᵐ Horse and foot besides ; over and above the Charges necessary and ornamentall of the Civill Government in the 3 kingdomes. So as wee need not (said I) bee so much afraid even of the mighty powers of France, being able (as aforesaid) to maintain a mighty power at home, a mightier in our Enemies Country, and the Mightyest of all at Sea.[1]

This discourse did not tend toward the intended raising and increaseing of the Revenue here, and was said to have been more properly held forth in the Parliament of England, which therefore I now tell you ; and this is the reason why I fear ill success in my busness. But I assure you Cousin, that I had rather live upon Herb Pottage all the daies of my Life (as I did with advantage all the time of my sickness) than not to studdy truth and those Symiteries wherby the world stands and which are the causes why *Res nolunt mali administrari.* But oh that I had the discretion not to value truth nor scorn Lying !

But you will say what is all this to the *Scale,* or to that *Wall of Wood and Wooll* which I hinted to you in one of my latest letters. Thus haveing tired you, and necessity bauling at Mee to instruct my agents for the buisness of severall Assizes, I break off without subscribing the name of the Character or Relaçon I bear to you ; but onely leave this Blank for your self to fill upp (without the descripçon of what you would have mee to bee) whilst I am

W. P.

27. *Southwell to Petty.*

Spring Garden, 30 March 1678

Deare Cosen

Yours of the 19ᵗʰ instant falls fowle of my Hawzer and such reproach of my silence drives me quite upon a Lee shore.[2] But all this I cherish and

---

[1] Cf. the argument of the *Political Arithmetic,* ch. viii.

[2] As Vice-Admiral of Munster, Southwell seems to have considered it fitting that he should make use of nautical phrases. It will be noticed, however, that he officiated as such almost entirely from Spring Gardens.

esteem as the highest testimony I ever had of your friendship, because it appeares nothing else but sollicitude concerning mine. It seems my letter of the 9th instant had yet testified some sparks of life, and had you received my other (about the like date in February) which inclosed Sir John Werden's original, it would have hinderd the wideness of the Casme, and shewd that I was mindfull how in the old play of Hyde and Seek, it was the rule sometimes to Hoop out. For I neither intended to loose, or to be lost. My Heart was still with my Treasure, though my Eye were sometimes off; and that for a time I was born away in the crowd of other matters.

After this preamble give me leave to bemoan with hearty trouble the crazy state of your health. This, Deare Cosen, and the care of it, must now be the Great Thought and business of your Life. Tis truly that which Ben Johnson called it, 'the Riches of the Poore and the Blessing of the Rich'. For my own part I live only upon Good behavior and having the Rod at my girdle, doe account for every little trespass as it happens. Soe that I neither can brag of health, or complain of heavy sickness. But the rule of strength being (as a friend of yours usd to say) when all the parts are equally strong, it may bee that a Pocket Watch may last as long as a Town Clock.

As for our friend Mr Mead, I ever thought him only a papist and free of any imprudent byasses. Born in the towne of Kinsale among the English, restord by the Court of Claimes, with all other circumstances that might concurr in one that was not a Protestant, and being otherwise not obnoxious either in behaviour or ill life, I believe, as you doe, that 'tis either personal malice, or indignation of the Common Law that any Justice but their own should be upheld. But when all this is said, you our Grand Pilot must neither bee left to Scilla or Charybdis; and if Cander and good words will not appease the Adversaries, they must prevail, and the business of the Admiralty must sink down flat to the ground.

However I would in this matter advise thus : That you would desire the persons complaining to nominate unto you a fitter man than Mr Mead, and particularly whether any such have arisen thereabouts since my father's death ; who did for many years lament the want of any kind of help in this matter, or any thereabouts fit to bee imployed, and was therefore fain to do the whole drudgery himselfe. You may desire to know if hee have made any trip in his Office. For, as they chuse to take phisic and counsel from the ablest in these professions, without considering their Catechisme, so have you had noe other bent herein than the care of preventing a failure in Justice. And you may finaly tell some of the superiors at Dublin how the case stands, and steer therein according to the sence they express. For my own part I shall think all at a loss when Mead breaks off, not being able yet to advise who should supply the roome.

As to your next point touching the Greenland Prize,[1] I writ you my thoughts about a week since in that matter, and therewith sent you what is the sence of the Admiralty here touching their pretence to the right of appeals from and concurrent Jurisdiction in that Kingdome. But your doliance herein I will impart to Mr Pepys, who takes a mighty share in all you say or doe ; and being on Monday to make an excursion together, wee will endeavor to hammer out something tending to your redress. In the meantime the enclosed List will acquaint you with what Weapons I furnish your Magazine, being a collection of all the Treaties I can get, and some other peeces, which I send to your Lady for conveyance.

I rejoice to hear that you are to begin a 3 weeks progress. I hope your health and chariot too will be settled in that due proportion and improvement as either you or Sir John Werden can covet.

As to the progress of His Majesty's Letter, I am glad you say somewhat is a doing, and sorry to hear

---

[1] *Sic*, but evidently the French Prize mentioned above (pp. 38 and 49) is intended.

you foretell that all may not bee done, especially
when the Impediments arise, not *ex re nata* or from
others, but as it seems from yourselfe.   Now when
danger ensues from dangerous premises, To blame
others for your not being silent, and to call this
Liberty the ' Valuing of Truth ', and ' scorn of Lying ',
and that 'Discretion' indeed would otherwise advise—
I can by noe means subscribe to your sence herein.
For it is Discretion and everything else that is good,
when a man being called forth and Interrogated for
the service of his Country does assert the Truth and
even seal it if the case required with his bloud.   But
for a private gentleman to throw forth his thoughts
as rubbs in the Bowls way, and so to speak in a
fresh man's cast who by authority is commanded
into the Green—this is I think to be Righteous over-
much, and why shouldest thou destroy thyselfe ?   I
am not against your studying of the Symmetry of
the World, or calculating the Mistakes of the Time,
but I am against your publishing them unseasonably
to your owne disadvantage, and the hurt of your
Family and concernes.   And now having said thus
much, let me see by your patient sufferance of this
liberty and what I imagine to bee alsoe Truth, whether
others might have more patiently borne with you.

Lastly as to The *Scale*, The *Wall of Wood* and
The *Wooll*, you know I must bee charmed with
everything you name ; and though nothing can come
amiss or shall want the attention of your Admirers
when they come, yet I am afraid to press for the two
latter least I weaken my Title, and indulge your delay
to the first, which I can by noe means endure, having
had my expectation bent upon it soe long.   And
since your head was clear during your late sickness,
I beleeve your sickness did rather promote than
hinder a subject matter that lay in the way of your
thoughts to Heaven.   And since you leave me a
blank to subscribe the character I would give you,
I have filld it up with your being the Finisher of the
The *Scale of Creatures*—And soe I am ever

28. *Petty to Southwell.*

[Petty had come over on a flying visit to Chester in order to see his wife and family. He was met there by the news of the death of Southwell's eldest son, Rupert, aged eight. Petty had himself lost three children in infancy, but three more survived, and figure in the pages which follow: (1) Charles, born 1672 ; died 1696. (2) Henry, born 1675, and succeeded his elder brother in the title which the latter had been granted after their father's death. He died, without living issue, in 1750. (3) Anne, born 1673. She married, in 1692, Thomas Fitzmaurice, who afterwards succeeded his father as twenty-first Lord of Kerry and Lixnaw, and was subsequently created Earl of Kerry. The first Marquis of Lansdowne, better known as Lord Shelburne, was their grandson. Southwell had, however, another son, Edward —the " Neddy " of this Correspondence—who survived and succeeded him, besides five daughters. These last are generally alluded to in the letters as " the spinsters ", but they were all as yet of tender age.

Petty was still busy with his Latin poems. The Latin verses to which he alludes below are among his MSS. under the title *Ad Gulielmum Pettaeum oculis et artibus morbosi captum et decumbentem.* There is another set in English, *Upon Sir William Petty's Bad Eyes*, written in a jocular vein as a reply to the first. They purport to be by one " Dorothy Arswacker ", but their manner, as also the *nom de plume* employed, are, I think, unmistakably Petty's (*Papers*, No. 149).]

Chester, ye 29 May 1678

D^{re} Cos^n

When your father dyed, I sayd what I thought reasonable to comfort you, for I thought that a feasible designe. But I have not been so venturous in the Case of deare Rupey. I now deale like cunning Physicians who administer *in deliniatione Morbi.* I heard of your anxiety till hee dyed and of your happy patience immediately after ; for both these I admire and praise you.

I came to this place but to see My Wife and children, for I was promisd to have all 3 brought hither, tho I had onely Charles. But I find such pleasure in him as makes mee unfitt to persuade you

that the losse of Rupey is a tollerable Thing, Insomuch
as I take him with mee into Ireland and will shew
him the sea more early then it was shewne to his father
—but upon other Circumstances.

The 17 of next month the terme ends, and in the
long Vacation *The Scale* shall be finisht.   In the
meane time Compare what hath been already done
with all you have seen before.   The Conclusion can
never bee more, nor shall it bee lesse ;   but that
there are powers as far exceeding Man's, as the King
of France doth a Magot's.   But Vernon I heare hath
started such new aĉions (though I have scornd to
bring any against him for his severall base doings) as
will put mee to new labors here and in England.

I have another latine Poem being a lamentation
upon blindness and late lamenes.

I will not turne over, nor repeate That I am

Y^{rs}

W. P.

29. *Petty to Southwell.*

Dublin, 20 July 1678

Dear Couzⁿ

With your last I received a Coppie of yours
to your Mother concerning Rupy which was much
to my satisfaĉon.

I promised in my last to finish the *Scale* this
Vacation and to send you the Poem I then Menĉoned.
But, as to the latter, I am grown so timorous That
I dare not—though I know not why.   And as to the
former This long Vacation is no Vacaĉon at all to
Mee.   So that to tell you I will do a Thing in the
Vacation, is another way of declaring I will never
doe it.

If I could gett a Vacation from heart breaking
anxieties, not from 10 hours labor per diem, I would
take that for a Vacaĉon and think myself bound to
performe with you.   But Couzen so it is That in

this month of July, when I thought to reap the fair fruits which seemd to grow in his Majesty's late Letters, There hath happened a flood of two *Custodiums* which has swept all away. That is to say: when I hopd to have the arrears of Marshall's Lands [1] reduced, It was sett to the farmers (my enemyes) *in Custodium*, and when I thought to have had Letters pattents for the other Lands, They were also lett *in Custodium* to the same Persons; nor could anything I could say to the Lord Lieutenant or the Court of Exchequer stopp the Torrent. And Notwithstanding all this I can never believe but that my Case at some Time, or in some place or other, will find Consideracon; and our case is briefly thus; viz, The Estate wee contend for hath been rated by My Lord of Essex &c att 2405£ per annum. Wee never received out of it but 3900£, have paid out of it in Quit rents, *Custodium* rents &c 4200£, and have expended 9100£ in Emprovements.[2] And now when wee thought to bee repaired and settled, all is taken away for an Intollerable quittrent, grown due whilst the King himself enjoyed the Lands. I write this to Vent my grief, not to trouble you, and am sorry I canot pursue some more pleasant subject.

I sincerly am Yo^{rs}

W. P.

30. *Petty to Southwell.*

Dublin, ye 10th of Sepr 78.

Dear Cousin

Last night I returned hither, and read yours with Sir Peter's [3] and Mr Mead's inclosed.

Kerry interest sprouts upp a little againe, although

---

[1] Marshall was a partner or nominee of Petty's, and had extensive grants of lands in Kerry. Lands of which the ownership was in dispute were at this time frequently granted to one or other of the claimants *in Custodium* for a limited period.

[2] *I.e.* the ironworks which he had established in County Kerry.

[3] Sir Peter Pett.

the Divell bee still hard at work. Such is the vicis-
situde of all humane affaires !

Did I never shew you my Colleċons of the State
of New England,[1] wherein is more Materiall truth
than ever I heard from others ?

I think Sir Peter is in the right concerning the
flanin (?) Act, at least hee hath gotten the true touch-
stone whereby to try it and many others. I have
lately perused all the Acts relating to Trade and
Manufacture which are of force in Ireland, and could
without Tears see them all repeald as Incroachments
upon the Laws of Nature. For Trade will endure no
other Laws, *nec volunt res mali administrari.* But
Lord, Cousin, to what Magnitude will the Statutes
both of England and Ireland swell if they grow at
this rate. How hard will it bee for our Lives, Liberties,
Limbs and Estates to bee taken away, upon Statutes
which wee can never remember nor understand. Oh
that our book of Statutes were no bigger than the
Church Catechisme !

In my Country progress I sped a Commission for
3 *Perambulaċons,* whereof one was very Illustrious.
I will not describe it, because the case was the very
selfe same with what Mr Mead hath writen you, and
the effect the very same.

" *Te columus jus ceu rem sed tu nomen inane es.*" [2]

I am loading my gunns and primeing them against
the Terme, and tis very late. I onely condole with
you for my Lady's too early delivery. Pray take
notice whether what bee written of the 8th month bee
true. I was once present at a Laborious Disquisiċon
of the Causes, but was never well satisfied of the Thing
itself.

I bidd you good night, and am Yo^rs Every Inch

W. P.

My wife's humble service to you and My Lady.

---

[1] " Notes about New England. Taken 4° February 1674/5 by Sir Wm.
Petty and Dr Taylor from Mr Frost and Mr Bartholemew " (*Papers*, No. 107).
[2] I cannot identify the source of this doggerel.

31. *Petty to Southwell.*

[Sir Peter Pett (1630–1699), of the length of whose letter Petty here complains, came of a family notable for having produced several distinguished shipwrights. He was himself by profession a lawyer, with a turn for literature, and an original member of the Royal Society. Pett was evidently a great admirer of Petty's writings, and appears to have acted as a go-between in the matter of their publication. Petty repaid his care by translating his " Catterwauling song " into Latin verse—a somewhat ribald affair to which he gave the title *In laudem vini Clareti et Peti* (Petty MSS.). It seems that we owe to Pett rather than to their author, who was always diffident in such matters, the publication of some of Petty's works. The *Treatise of Taxes* (first published in 1662) was reprinted in the year following that in which this letter was written. The Paraphrase on the 104th Psalm, *Colloquium Davidis cum anima sua* (*supra*, p. 17), had in point of fact been printed in August, though Petty had evidently not yet seen it.

The allusion to the *Political Arithmetic* is the first which appears in this volume, though not the first in the Correspondence. In an unprinted letter of March 10, 1672, Petty, who was just leaving for Ireland, had written to Southwell as follows : " I have left the *Political Arithmetic*. I hope you will be so wise as not to trouble your head with these things, seeing of how little advantage these fames have been to your humble servant "; while later on in the same year (December 7) he tells Southwell that he has " a worid more of Political Arithmetic " though he " cannot calculate the dimensions of the King's Reformations any more than those of his last year's victories ". The moot question of the date of composition of the *Political Arithmetic* is thus settled, and that given (1671) in Petty's " List of Writings " (*Papers*, ii. 262) and also in the Rawlinson MS. is confirmed, since it is clear that it was in existence in MS. at the beginning of 1672. The possibility suggested by Hull that the text as published in 1690 had been altered in the interval is not, however, precluded (Hull, p. 235). This letter also explains the reason for the non-publication of the work during Petty's lifetime.]

Dublin, ye 5th Octb^r 1678

Dear Cousin

I have lately received a Letter from Sir Peter Pett of a full houres reading. My wife and Tom Waller are both down with Soar Throats with the length of the Lecture, though they both tooke their turnes. Hee mençons you with great respects in severall parts of it, so as you can do no less than give him the frank postage of the enclosed answers, especially since his ' Catterwauling song ' in English deserves your sight. As for my Translation of it into ' latine Leonine ', I send it you as an Act of my Courage, and to lett you see what I dare undertake for my friend ! I esteem that this my rapping upp of Sir Peter's Catterwauling in latine, Is the burying of it in flannell ; this I say in case his Poetry were mortall, or that there is not enough in it to tempt all Nations to learne the English Tongue.

Hee talks of reprinting the *Booke of Taxes*, and of printing *Politicall Arithmetick* and that the Paraphrase upon the 104th Psalm is already printed. But, Cousin, absence being the Image of death, I hope you will doe in this my absence as you must doe when I am dead, and take a care of these matters. You know I have no Luck with my politicks. Slight Court tricks have advanced many men, but the solid study of other men's peace and plenty ruines mee. Wherefore lett the Stationer doe what hee pleases with the *Taxes*. I am against printing the *Arithmetick* and wish the *Paraphrase* undone. I have latine enough to serve my owne Turne, but not enough to spare the wide world. That Poem has sence and words good enough, and is a good body or Carcass of a Poem, but wants much of the true life, Soule and Spiritt both of Latine and Poetry. Sir Peter is an able Cajolist, but the fox must not perswade the Crow that such a Bird can sing. I will trouble you noe more.

W. P.

32. *Petty to Southwell.*

Dublin, y[e] 4th Jan[y] 1678/9

Dear Cousin

I am indeed sorry for your long silence, but am neither amazed nor picqued at it, for wee hear aloud upon what important matters you have been lately buisy.[1] Good men are bound to return good for evill, and I by the Parralel thereof (instead of being sullen at your silence) do revenge myself upon you with the Tedious inclosed Letter—not of a Cock and a Bull, but of a Whale of the Admiralty Court.[2]

Pray direct this Letter either to your self, and (by virtue thereof) represent as much of its contents as you please to his Royall Highness. Perhaps Sir John Worden may expect such an Accompt, if so bee pleased to direct it to him. Perhaps Sir Allen Apsley,[3] who hath sometimes written to me about these matters (and who lookes out sharp after the Duke's profitt) may expect an account of this *Mighty Thing.* If so, then direct it to him.

You know, Cousin, that I cannot dance upon the Roapes of criticall honor and Courtshipp, But in this Letter have trodden true figures and measures upon the plain ground of Truth. If any body wonder why you meddle with the *Little Thing* of Irish Admiralty, you may tell them you did not doe it till you had a Whale to couple it with.

I lately transmitted 1100£ into England by Bills of Exchequer upon one Matthew Elliston, a merchant in London, who is failed since his acceptance of them. I hoped to have spent this money with my friends in London this Sumer, but now——?

I have formed all my Kerry complaints into Pleas and Bills in the Exchequer, as if I might have relief

---

[1] I cannot explain this allusion. It may refer to Southwell's Parliamentary duties or to those connected with his Clerkship of the Council.

[2] See in letter following.

[3] Sir Allen Apsley (1616–1683), another prominent Royalist, who held several minor offices of State during the reign of Charles II.

that way rather than by the Kings Letter. The issue of which I know not, but doe sorely feel the trouble and expence of this wild-goose chase. God will at some time or other find eyes which will bee able to read my Text Letter Oppressions.

I find Vernon is bringing actions for words I said at the affray.[1] My witnesses are dispersed, But he hath so tuned his in the long intervall, That I find they intend to swear what I know to be false; and consequently I presume hee will pack a Jury to inflame damages for his being called Knave and Coward. Now I, to ballance his Moçons, must comence to revive four more suits against him, which I scorned otherwise to have done. The tryall will bee before My Lord Chief Justice North.[2]

By this concurrence of accidence, I am like to bee brought upon the high way to say *Date obolum pauperi Bellezario.*

It is a sadd Thing that I (almost in all things) do endure both the wrong and the punishment. These effects of Law and power do make me an ugly Cordiall against the comon evills I fore see.

Well Cousin, God send you a Merry New Year.

I am really Yours &c

W. P.

33. *Petty to Southwell.*

[*Enclosure to previous letter*]

Dublin, ye 4th January 1678/9

Dear Cousin

I have not troubled you with many Letters, since my first coming to serve his Royal Highness in the Admiralty, nor need I begin now for the importance of the matter I write of; but I do it to prevent the mistakes unto which the undermentioned matter is very obnoxious.

---

[1] *Supra,* p. 27.
[2] Francis North (1637–1685), Chief Justice of the Common Pleas, 1675–1682, and afterwards Lord Chancellor as first Baron Guildford.

Upon Tuesday last there came a rumor to this Town that a Whale of great bigness (and consequently worth) was cast up in Wicklow about 17 miles from this place. Soon after Coll Dillon (the Vice Admiral) sent his servant to look after it. Upon Wednesday I also sent a precept by the Marshall, who impanneld a Jury upon the Place in order to enquire not onely into the value of this Fish, but into the Propriety also ; for that several Lords of Mannors (especially Sir Richard Parsons[1]) pretended to this Fish. But before I could hear either from the Vice-Admiral's Agent or the Marshall of the Court, another rumor came to this Town (together with some small parts of the Fish itself) that the Whale was all cutt in pieces and carried away by the Country people, but more especially by a principal Tenant of the said Sir Richard Parsons.

Hereupon the Vice Admiral and myself went down in person on Thursday, and the next morning (being Friday the 3rd Instant) wee held a Court of Enquiry, whereupon wee found as followeth, vizt :

(1) That this Whale, having offered at 2 other places, did upon Sunday the 29th past at 3 in the afternoon (and at one hours flood) come aground on the place where shee last rested and where the people began to break her up and divide her ; together with the names of the persons with whose hands, Ropes Boats, and Anchors shee was stayed in that place.

(2) Wee found that upon Monday the 30th several persons, by the direction of Sir R. Parsons's said Tenant, opened her belly to ridd it of the intrals, and then cutt off as many big pieces as they could carry and with Horses and Oxen, drew them to Sir R. Parsons' Land ; housing some part of it within the said Tenants out-houses.

(3) Wee found her dimentions to bee 16 yards and a half [long] and, by the best estimation wee could make, about 7 yards [in] Compass, and the fat under

---

[1] Sir Richard Parsons of Bellamont, County Dublin, afterwards created Viscount Rosse.

the Skin to bee no where above [blank] inches thick, and the Gills placed about the mouth to consist [of] about 200 small flakes of that substance or matter which wee commonly call Whale Bone, one side whereof was fringed with a stuff like small pack thrid. Of which flakes many persons took one or two a peece out of curiosity, being of noe real value or use wee know of.

(4) Wee found that about 3 quarters of the whole Whale did lye collected in the places before mentioned, and the rest carried away by Hundreds of Country people as a novelty.

Besides the Enquiries, which are upon oath and publicly taken (as well as before many considerable Gentlemen as the Jury), our conjectures upon other particulars were as followeth, vizt : (1) That the fish was very young and a femal, the former appearing by the softness and poroseness of her biggest Bones, and the Latter by the relation of those Men who first vieued her. (2) Altho shee had been Dead several days before shee was fixed at this Place, yet the thinness and redness of her blood and the smell of her flesh, makes us think shee had not been dead above 8 or 10 days. Neither did any such wound or mark appeare upon her, by which wee could learn the cause or time of her Death.

Upon the whole matter wee guess that this Fish in its p[resent] Condition is of very little value, by reason of her smalness, Leaness, and the want of all manner of Utensills to mak Oyle of her. It being neither worth the while to bring necessaries from Dublin to that place, nor to carry the flesh from thence to Dublin.

Wee also think that those who first cut her and broke her up, did act very foolishly and illegally therein ; and that many of them are punishable for the same for the injury they have done the Lord High Admiral so far forth as they could.

And lastly wee guess that about 50£ might have been had for her from some who would have made a shew with her and afterwards extracted some little oyle out of her, For many people went out of curiosity many miles even to see the mangled Carcus of this Animal.

This is all I can say upon this Subject, and have said thus much onely to temper the representation which rumour and vulgar Report may make of this matter. Whether you will trouble His Highness with this account, I leave to your own discretion ; onely advertising you upon this occasion That the Admiral's Authority is in soe tottering a Condition here, that I cannot promise to defend his Highness's Interest even in this Fish had it been considerable. For wee have sufferd as followeth. 1. A Bridge hath been made across a navigable River, without the Admiralty leave ; and a Prohibition brought to the suit comenced thereupon.

2. A Prohibition hath been brought, after an Execution in the Case, of using unlawfull ways of Fishing.

3. The Like prohibition in a suit for stopping and annoying a Navigable River.

4. The like in the case of a Pilot condemnd to pay Damages for casting away a Ship in a gross manner.

5. A Prohibition hath been brought (in the case of Mr Thomas Fleming) for putting a Decree in Execution made by his Majesty's Authority, and by his Majesty himself personally confirmed. Moreover there was formerly an appeale from the Court here to the Admiralty in England in the last mentiond case, altho' it was thought an Appeale could not lye therein.

Lastly an Appeale hath been brought unto the Admiralty of England in Case of poor Seamen's Wages, where so much as a probable Tale could not be told in prejudice of the sentence given here for those poor seamen.

I say nothing of other causes which have been removed out of the Court even without apparent reason, much less necessity.

All which matters if they be not remedyd and regulated, This Court is but a greevance to the Nation ; Whereas wee humbly conceive It may bee made an effectual Instrument to promote the Trade and Navigation of this Country.

I am Your most humble and faithful servant

W^M PETTY

34. *Petty to Southwell.*

[Dublin, February 1679] [1]

Dear Cousin

This is onely to owne the Receipt of your last about the whale. I did by Algebra find out the cause of your silence before you told it mee, and take nothing ill concerning myselfe that you doe or omitt. I thank you for pittying my Losses and troubles, and that you keep blowing upon Pepis that the fire of his kindnes should not go out. I take hold of what you offer mee concerning Vernon. But will not trouble you with it till the Time draws neerer (for who knows what may happen between this and that), and then I will send you a distinct paper which will contain nothing else but that fowle stuff.

I have 2 or 3 things to send you or bring you, one whereof is a *System of Divinitie*,[2] under an hour's Reading, wherein I make as much use of the *Scale of Creatures* as serves my purpose. For the whole *Scale* is rather a contemplation of the wisdome of God in the Harmony of his Creatures, than an Argument for more than that proud Man is a pittyfull Thing.

Here is some news—not so much of Plotts as of Counter-plotts, and of papists prodding protestants into Plotts.[3] You know I doe not deale in News,

---

[1] Endorsed by Southwell, " Received February 24, 1678/9 ".

[2] Possibly an essay founded on the undated synopsis entitled " Religion " (*Papers*, No. 30).

[3] The ' Popish Plot ' leading to the impeachment of Danby and other Catholics had taken place in the previous year.

nor can I tell you anie extraordinary matter of fact, but wish you had my Commentaries and Inferences upon many late passages.

I had rather hear of your and your families health than of the Intrigues of the approaching Parliament;[1] and because you mencon your Godson in your last letter, I tell you of him, That he is the most thoughtful and Sollicitous Creature I know, and torments himself with Inquiries and reasonings upon all Things that come in his way. Hee has a wonderful proportion of French, his Chiefe Tallent is the History of the Scriptures and discourses upon it. I doe not find as yet That hee takes much to Numbers, But believe That, when he does, hee will pay it.

The Coppie of the Letter you write concerning dear Rupey,[2] I keep and consider'd, Though I have seem'd to have done the Contrary; for there was something to bee done upon you, which by the measures I take of myself, I did not think feizible.

'Tis late, Dear Cousin, Goodnight.

I am Yo[rs]

W. P.

35. *Petty to Southwell.*

[Petty's affray with Colonel Vernon, which seems to have been the outcome of a long-standing quarrel, has been recounted above (p. 27). His antagonist was presumably the person who is mentioned in the *Political Anatomy of Ireland*, as an intermediary who managed to secure ' per proviso ' for the Irish Papists the restitution of some of their lands which had been declared forfeited under the Cromwellian Settlement (Hull, p. 136). From the earlier mention in this Correspondence of Vernon's name in connection with that of Ormond (*supra*, p. 28), we may no doubt conclude that he was the Colonel Edward Vernon who in the year 1663 had revealed to the Lord-Lieutenant

---

[1] The Parliament which had sat since 1661 had just been dissolved (January 1679). The new Parliament met on March 6.

[2] *Supra*, p. 57.

the existence of Colonel Blood's plot against the government of Ireland (*Life of Ormond*, i. p. 65).

The ' Long Brief ' which accompanies this letter fills in some of the gaps in the history of Petty's quarrel. We are, however, left in ignorance of its ultimate issue, for there is no further reference to the matter in either *Correspondence* or *Papers*.]

Dublin, 4⁰ March 1678/9

Dear Cousin

The bearer Mr Callowe, who sollicits my buisnes of Vernon &c, will deliver you the long briefe of that Matter. Pray lay it some where where you may find it upon occasion, for I doe not desire you to read it till then. I will keep my promise in mingling nothing with this fowle stuffe, even although I saw you lolling and lazing for want of buisnes, and not groaning and teeming out contrivances for our peace and Settlement in this instant Parliament.

If I did ever write of publick affaires, I would send you my Algebra upon the Plott,[1] for my thinks I could upon that subject out doe Grant's *Bills of Mortality*.

You need our prayers this time, and I doe heartily pray God to blesse you in your proceedings and am Yoʳˢ

W. P.

[*Enclosure to preceding letter*]

THE STATE OF MATTERS BETWEEN SIR WM. PETTY AND COLL VERNON.

There never haveing been any discord between the said Persons, nor any dealings between them which might have occasioned the same, but there haveing been always as much friendship and Familiarity between them as could bee between two persons of so different humours, This Colonel—when Sir James Shaen and the present Farmers would have trapand Petty to have been bound with them, and when Petty

---

[1] *I.e.* the Popish Plot of 1678.

did give the reasons to the Lord Treasurer why hee could not bee bound with them (which was because the King had parted with his security, which was agreed to bee given him, so as the whole burthen fell upon Petty)—This Vernon comes without any reason, concernment, or provocation, and bals out in the Privy Lodgings at Whitehall before three score persons, that Petty had ever been a Rogue and a Traytor and did not shew it, &c.

Petty took little notice of this for some dayes, knowing that Vernon was generally esteemd for a foule mouth fellow of little Truth, a Coward &c. But hearing that he brag'd of what hee had said, as of a noble exploit, Petty did (by the advize of those who pretended to understand the punctillios of such affairs), in the open day and in the open street, accompanied onely with his owne Domesticks, affront this Colonel with a few blowes of a Cudgell, and thereupon drew his sword, and according to practise desired the Colonel to draw also. But the Colonel being, with the Drawers of the Blew Posts Ordinary, drawn into the house, hee did with the street dores bolted, raile out of a window taxing Petty for Cowardize for haveing so assaulted him. To which Petty in the heate of the Fray answered, That hee Vernon was a notirious Coward, and had betrayd the King's Cause by his Cowardize; meaning that Vernon had abused the King and his Trust by takeing upon a Colonel[1] &c. Vernon the next day sends one East as with a Challenge, who haveing the place appointed, declined the matter and could not bee found any where that day.

Sometime after hee gets the Duke of Monmouth to confine Petty and himself. Petty desires the matter may bee referd to the Lord Marshall as most proper for his conderačon, but Vernon declining him, flies to an Information in the King's Bench, gets a Tryall, works with the Farmers, brings witnesses to sweare not onely what they heard and saw, but whatever they

---

[1] *Sic*, ' by taking the title of Colonel ' would seem to be intended.

imagind, and when Petty and his Company were found guilty, hee begs the fines under the name of Mrs. Foules, a poore Cavaleer's widdow ; which was paid accordingly, and about 400£ paid and lost by Petty upon this occasion.

Whilst these things were in transacting, Vernon and East, and Vernon's two Servants, fall upon Mr. James Waller, being in company with a youth, Mr. Hughs, among the stones in a Stone-Cutter's yard, where Mr Waller wounded East.

When Vernon complained as aforesaid to the King's Bench, Waller also brings his Informačon in the same place, convicts the Colonel and his Complicyes of a Riott, but Vernon brings a *noli prosequi* in from the King.

Petty, because the witnesses who heard the passages at Whitehall were gone for Ireland, sues Vernon there, for saying hee had been ever a Traytor ; but contemned to prosecute it, Vernon haveing been generally laught at. And comeing back unto Ireland, comes with his Brother and his servants and of a sudden runs the Pike of his Cane into Petty's left eye who saw him not, and thereupon drawes his sword.[1] Whereupon Petty advances upon him and drove him back forty foot, hee crying out all the time, till hee got within protexion ; and afterwards used friends to diswade Petty not to fall upon him in like manner, and laboured with some of the Judges to send their Tip-staves to that purpose. And Petty, understanding that one Mr. Becket, a Lawyer, had beaten the Colonel at a Taverne for his foul mouth till the Colonel had askd him forgiveness for what hee had said, did comply with the Colonel's Intercessors, neither did he prosecute either the Bastinado or the suit at Law against the Colonel ; there being no end for either but to him rediculous and Infamous, which he had made himself by the last mentčoned action with Mr. Becket, as also by seting his Irish servants to assault one Mr. Vernon a merchant, a weakly consumptive youth upon

---

[1] This was on April 27, 1677 (*supra*, p. 27).

the exchange, whom the Colonel had treacherously cousened of an estate of 600£ a yeare; concerning which the suit now depends in Chancery.

The Colonel, finding no reliefe to his honor begins a suit in England for the damages of his being beaten in the first fray, as also for being told that hee had betray'd the King's Cause, leaving out the words by his Cowardize. For it is known the Colonel is a great brager, and by his braging perswaded somebody that hee might bee cald Colonel, but performing nothing suitable to his Title. Petty told him hee had disappointed his employers, tho the Colonel would have it thought that the King's whole Cause and Intrest in 1676 was confided in him (not between 1672 and 1676), and that Petty should say that the Intrest of the King, 16 years setled in his Throne, was betrayd by him, Vernon, whom Petty never thought worthy in the least thereof.

36. *Petty to Southwell.*

[The Popish Plot, to which Petty has referred in the previous letter, had been exposed (or invented) by the notorious Titus Oates in 1678. Amongst those who suffered death for alleged complicity in the plot was one Harcourt, a Jesuit, but suspicion was general and many were accused. The mention of " Harcourt " in the opening paragraph of this letter seems to indicate that Southwell's conduct had somehow been impugned in relation to these events, and it may be that his resignation of the office of Clerk of the Council, which took place about this time, was not unconnected with the accusations which appear to have been brought against him. He was, however, sufficiently in favour in the following year to be sent on another diplomatic mission.

A new Parliament had met on March 6, 1679; its predecessor, which had been in being since the Restoration, having been dissolved at the beginning of the year. Southwell was once again included among its members as representative of Penryn. It was about this time that he bought Kingsweston near Bristol, where from the end of 1680 he was to live in retirement until the accession of William III.

The " Kingrode " mentioned below, and again later on (p. 126) was the name by which the port of Bristol was then distinguished.]

Dublin, 8ᵗʰ Aprill 1679

Dear Cousin

To yours of the 1st instant. I received the paper which contained the 2 Monumentall pillars of your vindicacõn and meritt. It was a Scurvy Scratch in the face of your proceedings, to say you omĩtted the names of Harcourt and Benningfield, and that the time was about the 13ᵗʰ or 14ᵗʰ of October. But God be thanked You have so glewd the staffe which your Enemies broake, That tis now become stronger and fairer then the whole Wood, and I doubt not But it will hold firme for ever. This with what you say of Kingrode (putt together) is a brave piece of bread and butter.

The news wee have of the parliaments zeale to defend Ireland against the Pope and King of France is very gratefull to many, and I find there are severall Clubbs and Meetings to draw upp advices to bee sent for England upon that Accompt. I myself have just now finished a Couple of Sheets in number with measures to that purpose,[1] but am unresolved what to doe with them, for I never have been fortunate in this way—I mean not to my selfe. And Yett I verily believe That the Ayre which I have breathd upon the Coffee-houses hath been very prolifique, and soe I believe this paper will bee, soe soon as other men can vent it as their owne.

I have 2 or 3 buisinesses that pull mee for England like the tack of a Saile, and as many more which hold mee back like the Sheats of the same. I am now preparing for the assizes of Meath and the King's County.

My Lord Lieutenant does nothing upon the King's Letter ;[2] Putts mee to take a Course at Law which

[1] *Infra*, p. 77 *n.*
[2] This was a further letter from the King to the Lord-Lieutenant ' positively ordering that an end should be put to Petty's affair ' (MSS.).

(without either that Letter or him) I might have taken tenn years since. I beleive hee is as much concernd as my self to putt an end to this buisnes ; it concerns many that the Settlement of Ireland should not bee reviewd. A Shipp can stande its course, if the wind blow some 3 of the 4 points ; but in our Case If it blow either of the 3 points I have formerly named to you, Wee of Ireland shall bee driven on a Lee Shoar. Upon the whole matter, I hope things will mend. I am pretty well in my health. My Wife and Children are well and your God-sonn is sick of anxiety to learn anything which hee hears prais'd. These are the onely Matters I have to solace myself with. I heartily thank God for them, and remaine

Yours entirely

W^M PETTY

37. Petty to Southwell.

[Sir William Temple had produced a scheme to interpose a more powerful Privy Council between King and Parliament. But, as Petty here seems to anticipate, the new Parliament was dissolved before this reform could become effective. Petty had his own plans for government by ' Councils ' in various forms, some of which I have printed in the *Petty Papers* (ch. i.), but in the absence of dates there is nothing to show when they were written.

The controversy with Colonel or Sir Jerome Sankey, who had accused Petty of malpractises in connection with the Down Survey of Ireland, took place in the Parliament of 1659. Petty published an account of it anonymously in the following year in his *Reflections upon Some Persons and Things in Ireland* (Hull, *Bibliography*, p. 634).

Of his other quarrels that with Sir George Carteret, which is here mentioned for the first time, deserves some notice. Carteret, who was grandfather to the peer and wellknown statesman of the same name, had been Controller of the Navy under Charles I. After the King's execution he had energetically befriended his successor, whom he entertained for some months in exile at his castle in the Island of Jersey. When that fortress was subsequently besieged and captured by the Cromwellian forces, Carteret rejoined

King Charles II. in Holland, and returned to England with him on Restoration Day. Honours and appointments were at once showered upon him, among them the lucrative post of Treasurer of the Navy. This brought him into contact with Pepys, in whose *Diary* he is often mentioned. He came into relations with Petty about the same time. There seems to have been at the outset some form of partnership between Petty and Carteret. In the " Distribution Book ", where the grantees of forfeited lands after the Cromwellian Settlement of Ireland are shown in a column reserved for that purpose, Carteret's name constantly appears with (and sometimes without) that of Petty in respect of land which Petty is known to have afterwards enjoyed. There is nothing, however, to show what (if any) was Carteret's part in these ventures, and it may be that he was brought in by Petty rather for the sake of the protection his name would afford than as a sharer in the enterprise. The relations between the two men did not at all events long remain on a friendly basis, for Lawsuits with Carteret seem (*infra*, p. 255) to have preoccupied Petty's attention in subsequent years, and to have continued until Carteret's death, which took place in 1680.]

Dublin, 29th Apr 1679.

Dear Cousin

You did not answer my last of the 8th instant, Neither visibly nor with a lowd vapouring voice. But my Lord Duke did last weeke call upon mee of his own accord to settle the Quitrents &c, which I take to bee an effectuall answer to some Melancholy words which leakt out of my heart in my said last Letter, and for which I heartily thank you and will doe the same in Silent deeds when ever I can.

The news of the wonderfull alterãcons in the Councill hath made us all drunk with the new wine of further expectãcons. The change happened at London on the same days 20 year that I answered Colonel Sankey in the Parliament at London, being the 21st April 1659, and on the 22nd the said Parliament was dissolvd. Since which time I have been travailing in dark, dirty, crooked ways, and have been rowing against Wind and Tide. May I now come into some Smoothings with Sir George Carterrett, the farmers, Kerry Quittrents, Vernon and my 1100£ disaster ;

and as my eyes and activity doe faile, may there bee clearer weather and a Calme at Sea, that I may stand that Course for this little latter Span of my Life which my own Needle points at, and not bee dasht and tost too and fro wither the outrages of fooles and knaves do force mee. The *novaturient* world is gapeing here after the like alteracõns for Ireland. May whatever is done tend to the resisting of the French, pulling out the sting of popery, and pulling up the old acts of 17mo and 18vo Car. prim,[1] being 3 things I have feard this many yeares, and which I beleive need not bee feard if moderate and easy remedies bee timely applyed.   I consider your buisnes, wherefore bee you and you are hereby released from your Troubles

W^M PETTY

38. *Petty to Southwell.*

Dublin, 3° May 1679

Dear Cousin
        I answerd yours of the 26th past before I received it, and you have answered some of mine before I writ them, By which I think wee are both inspir'd &c.
        Concerning our Kerry buisnes.   My Lord Lieutenant hath been made beleive That the King's Letters gave him noe power to settle our arreares, But I have this day presented him a Report from the King's Councill That hee clearly hath.   Soe as now Wee have our fore topp sails loose and our anchors apeeke to Saile againe.   I hope wee shall at last find the Northeast or the Northwest passage into the Indies of Kerry, although all this while I continue sailing about the Cape of the Law, and it is the Cape of good Hope That I am now doubling.   And truely Cousin, although I have been unkindly and unequally

---

[1] 1640–1641.   The Act by which 2,500,000 acres of Irish land were pledged to the adventurers who advanced money to put down the Irish rebellion.

and absurdly dealt with, Yett I goe on without fear of the French, of popery, nor even of death itself.

I have not to this hour communicated my sheets [1] to any person, But doe now send them unto you, beleiveing you will apply them to their best and most propper ends. I have also sent you a paper concerning the vertues of a certaine booke I would have made. Our Lord Lieutenant accepted its designe kindly from mee and said the Booke it self should bee forth with made, But I heare no more of it. Though your privy Councill in England bee namd, Yett I have sent you over a List of such as I think Worthy of preferrment. They are strangers to [most] of our late statesmen, nor have they many friends ; however pray use your interrest to gett them in, and endeavour to gett yourself Clerke of that Councill and make hay therein while the Sun shineth.

These 3 papers [2] are pestered with the Indiscretions whereunto I am obnoxious ; Wherefore you must purge them when you shew them to others, Least some expression offend them that may mischiefe Mee. All I can say is that I meane well to the whole, and not ill to any person in particular. If it bee so taken, I am contented to be a martyr for my Country. Bee it how it will, I have the Vanity to think That no body else can handle this Important Matter in this way.

If you shew it, 1°. Let it bee to such as will read it 3 or 4 times over. 2°. To such as desire to have Ireland well saved from Popery and the French. 3°. To such as have some power to execute what is good, for all is practicable. You fi[nd m]any points but onely touchd, but I have treatises ready on most

---

[1] *Supra*, p. 73.

[2] The three papers enclosed were :

(1) " Consideraĉons how the protestants (or non papists) of Ireland may disable the Papists there, both for intestine Rebellion, and also for assisting a French Invasion ; as the state of both parties now standeth in this present yeare, 1679."

(2) " The uses of Sir Wm. Petty's book 1679 " (*Papers*, No. 50).

(3) " 22 Councellors 1679 : being, not the names of individuals, but 22 points concerning the government of Ireland which deserve attention."

of them and can get the rest ready before I have power to use them.   Adieu.

.W. P.

39. *Petty to Southwell.*

Dublin, 10th June 1679

Dear Cousin
    I thought to have layn downe and dyed under my Kerry Calamityes, But you, Cousin, would needs wrench open my fallen Chapps, and force in strong Spiritts to revive me.   My Lord Lieutenant upon yours and my Lady's (as I think upon my owne) Interest, I beleive would bee glad I had some reasonable reliefe.   But my Lord dreads either the Trouble or danger of doeing it—Though there bee nothing of either in the Case.   For when hee has gone about it, There comes the Chief Judges of each Bench and the King's whole Learned Counsill, All armed with prongs and pitchforks.   They all agree in a deepe sence of my sufferings, But breake upp in Irresolution and in some oblique Expedients, without anie direct remedy ; Soe as nothing is yett done.   I find your Cordiall warme in my stomack, But cañot yet lift upp my Head ; Nor don't know friends from foes, such is my Apoplexy.
    I am upon a new Expedient, as you will see by the inclosed Letter to my Lord of Essex and my other papers.   Perhaps this powder may make mee sneeze, and that sneezing may remove the Kerry humour which oppresses my brayne.   I will not trouble you with any Thing in earnest about it, for I doe not thinke it worth the talking of ; much lesse the spurring of a free horse, for such you have beene to mee.   In requitall whereof, I declare myself
                    Yo^r humble thankfull Asse

W. P.

    Did you receive the 3 papers I sent you ?   I think the apprehensions of men are changed since they were composed. The world was then full of fury, But the temper of these papers I conceive to bee such as may serve in all times, and therefore keep them till Antichrist comes.[1]

40. *Petty to Southwell.*

[Charles Petty, Southwell's godson, was now seven years old, and his father thought it was time to put him through a course of home travel. Kerry had to be frequently visited on account of Petty's iron mines and other interests in that county, so father and son travelled *via* Cork, visiting *en route* Liscaroll and Knockanoss, which had each been the scene of severe fighting during the Rebellion. Burton in the same county was the family mansion of the Percevals, the reigning baronet, Sir Philip, being succeeded in 1680 by his brother John. Sir John was married to a sister of Sir Edward Dering (of Surrenden in Kent), and was therefore brother-in-law to Southwell.]

Dublin, 18th Octobr 1679

Dear Cousin

Your Godson Charles hath made a seaven and 40 dayes travell through Ireland and is now writing a booke of his observaçons which hee intends to dedicate to his God father ; which if it take, Hee intends at Spring to continue his Travells into the North of Ireland and thence to Edinbrough in Scotland, and thence with severall intermediate excursions to terminate at London, and hopes before hee bee 8 years old to give a good account of all that is remarkable in the 3 kingdomes. I assure you hee hath already learned to ride through such ways and weathers as I dare not, To bee content with such meat, drink and lodging as comes next to hands, As also to goe to bedd and rise at cõmand &c. In our voyage wee passed through Liscarroll, saw the place thereabouts where the battle was fought, As also that of Knockanoss, But went not to Burton because Sir Phillip was then absent at Kilkenny. But in our

---

[1] *I.e.* till the Catholics become supreme.

return from Kerry, Wee went through many places
to Kinsale, where Wee were refreshed by your and
Sir Phillip's county, and are full of observac̃ons of
what wee saw there on the sea and the Land, and doe
omnes omnia bona dicere et laudere fortunas &c.[1]

Although there needs noe intercession in any Case
in the Admiralty Court of Ireland, yet I doe not
know whether the Planet of Reformac̃on has yet gone
so farr eastward, as that favor and kindness is not
still necessary in the more eastern Admiralty Courts
of the world—I mean those of Moscovia and China,
not of England.   But if you find it [better] Then I
desire you to make Sir Lionell Je[nkins] [2] very patient
and Considerate in our case of the Shipp [which] hath
been most outragiously and contumeliously carried
away out of the Marshall of the Admiraltys Custody ;
after a legall and just Condemnac̃on, and out of the
hands of the Sheriffe of the County who had attachd
her by writt out of the high Court of Chancery ;
after the pretended Master and Company had voluntarily and by mutuall consent deliverd upp her sails
to the Marshall ; after the said Master had voluntarily
sworn upon the Bible not to suffer the shipp to bee
carryed away till I were satisfied, and had likewise
given bond to the same purpose.   I say after all this,
the Master presently gets other sails on board,
resists all the officers that [tried] to stopp the shipp,
actually threw the Marshall [into] the sea, fird gunns,
beat them with their hand-S[pikes] Like to chopp off
their hands with a broad ax, Spoake most villanously
of the King's Warr and his officers and as in the
afidavits already sent may more at large appeare.

I have lost 1100£ in hard ready money with the
interest of the same for 12 months, and above 100£
lost and charges.

There is a manifest Juggle between the Merchants

_____

[1] Terence, *Andrandria*, i. 1, 69.
[2] Sir Leoline Jenkins (1623–1685), diplomatist. He had lately returned
from the Continent, where he had negotiated several treaties with Holland,
Spain, and other European countries. He was now a Privy Councillor and
Member of Parliament for Oxford, and later (1680–1684) Secretary of State.

of London (the pretended owners of the Shipp) and the Bankrupt Elliston. For before hee broake The whole Shipp was Elliston's, all the money came from Elliston, whose Agent ingaged the Shipp for my Security. But when hee was broake, Then hee had but 600£ concernment, whereas it was above 2000£ before.

All these points are visible and certaine. Wee have been certainly unlucky in these particulars. The question is whether wee shall have the luck to bee relievd—I mean the luck of the Law. What I have said is enough to cause pitty and Consideracõn upon our behalfe. But what is to bee said to the Judge in the Court, shall bee furnished from another hand.

Sir William Temple,[1] Sir William Godolphin,[2] Mr Peapys and Mr Cooke, I think have all interests in Sir Lyonell, and I hope you have likewise. For God's sake use some means that wee bee not run down violently against the Cryes and Clamours of our right.

As for the old Kerry Quitrents, Wee Jogg on through the long Lane of the Exchequer Law, and are in the same way which no body could have hindred us from takeing ten yeares ago.

Arthur Bush is too buisy to tell mee your smale domesticke of your Children &c. I would fain sweep together the dust of those diamonds without troubling you.

I imagine you are very buisy and find me in no good humor, and therefore I say no more but that I am Most affectionately yo^rs

WM PETTY

41. *Petty to Southwell.*

[Petty had come to London at the end of 1679, apparently in connection with an offer which had been made to him of

---

[1] Sir William Temple (1628–1699), the well-known statesman and author.
[2] Sir William Godolphin (1634–1696) had been ambassador at Madrid from 1671 to 1678. He afterwards became a Roman Catholic.

a seat on the new Irish Privy Council and of a peerage (Hull, xxxviii.). He was not, however, destined to obtain either of these honours, and we here find him once more in Dublin. Southwell, who, as we have seen, had resigned his clerkship of the Privy Council in December 1679, was now in Berlin, where he had been sent as Envoy Extraordinary to the Elector of Brandenburg a few months before. This letter is endorsed by him as received there on June 27, and the context of the next shows that he had returned from his mission (probably to his new home at Kingsweston) in November of the same year.]

Dubl. 15⁰ May 1680

Dr Cozⁿ

Within 3 weekes after you left London, I was forc'd for Ireland, where I feele warmth from your kind letters to my Lord Lieutenant, but far from health, tho they are onely occult qualityes that hinder it &c.

I do not write thus to wish you prosperity &c, for I do it daily ; But The very scope of this Letter to you is To presse you to do what I believe you will do in due time and Method—That is to advance Arthur Bush. And now what shall I say for it ? Shall I praise him mightily ? You know 100 times more of him than I ; but I will praise the Zeale, Care and Industry of his parents for him and the rest of their children, which should move you to some Cooperation. I also say :

Est illi indotata soror, paupercula mater[1]

And then help must come from the Sons. If hee have faults, consider onely how much they are more or lesse then others, and enter not into Narrow Judgement with thy servant, for no flesh is righteous. Remember also the difference between Merit and grace. Lastly If any Thing can bee done, I will help to thank you.

God Almighty blesse you & yours

W^M PETTY

---

[1] Horace, *Ep.* i. xvii. 46.

42. *Petty to Southwell.*

Dublin, 27 Nov. 1680

D^{re} Cousin

I was glad to heare from Mr Tisdale's of your safe returne. These are to aske how you do, and to tell you what Wee shall say to these Things, and what will the end of them bee ; or rather of what other Things will the ends of these bee the beginnings of.

I will say nothing of Kerry. The King and you have done all I could desire, but *haeret lateri lethalis arundo.*[1]

Twere a sad Thing to bee fluxd for a corne on ones Toe. What I have prophesied is now in View. Pray bee large in your next to Mee—I meane send mee an answer to all the quaeries I left with you.

Charles is your humble servant and desires his service may bee presented to his Cousens. Hee does well, but nothing prodigious.

I am as ever Y^{rs} &c.

43. *Southwell to Petty.*

[Kingsweston] 8 Deb^r 80

Dr Cousin

Tis a great addition to the contentment I here am in with my family to understand the health of yours, and that from your owne hand of the 27th past. But as to the end of these Things, you that have prophesied the beginning, must e'en prophesy agen and tell the conclusion, for I cannot. I have heard that a serene Skie, a dead calme for 3 dayes, and a sort of hissing in the bottome of wells and vaults, brings a hurricane in the Plantations. And then doe the Seamen presently Shipp Anchor, putt off from the shore, take downe their topp masts and shutt up their scupper holes.

[1] Virgil, *Æneid*, iv. 73.

I would have been here 9 monthes agoe,[1] but soe much time I have quailed after the rest (?) The obedyence therein pleased my master, and the insuccesse I beleive gratifyed others. Soe perhaps it makes a kind of burtresse to my quiett, which is the onely blessing I propose. Yett if an earthquake comes, noe man's foundation is much better than his neighbours.

As to the corne on your toe that disquietts the whole masse of blood—what shall I say? I grieve for you and grieve for others that doe not ease you. But what does nature dictate in such cases? The fox, for the sake of 3, parts with one legg, and scripture envites you to heaven even with one eye. And as you have more wisely then any man already calculated severall modells of Living (to want and to abound) as revolutions may require it, soe tis but voluntarily retrenching that expectation, and you have Paradice in all the rest. Time may perhaps alone doe therein what neither Justice, Witt, or favour have been able to effect.

My .boy was very proud to heare of his cousin Charles, but agrieved at his perfections, for I chastise him therewith. Mine has vigour, and, if he keepes his face towards Jerusalem and not Samaria, he may doe well enough. If you have the operation of the whole Sintax (?) in a short peece of latine, as according to your former advice it was, pray lett me have a Copie of it.

You see I have tyred you without Answering one of the Scheme of Queryes you gave me. That must be a worke of time and a little more settlement.

I may be in London soone after Christmas, but no longer there than needes must, and in the spring I may hope to see you where you are. With due respects to all and from the whole society of this place, I am ever, Yrs

R. S.

---

[1] Southwell had bought Kingsweston, close to Bristol, in the previous year from Sir Humphrey Hooke. This passage indicates that it was against his will that he had undertaken the Brandenburg mission, and that his negotiations there had not met with success.

44. *Petty to Southwell.*

[Southwell had just lost his wife, Elizabeth, daughter of Sir Edward Dering of Surrenden in Kent. Petty's condolences on this occasion are perhaps somewhat lacking in tact, and it is scarcely astonishing that Southwell betrayed a sense of resentment that his friend should have suggested to him a second marriage almost before he had had time to bury his first wife !]

Dublin, 31ˢᵗ Janʸ 1681

Dear Cousin

I received last Night the Ill news of a Separation between those who had been happily united, And I doe now endeavour to answer the desent Custom of Condoling with you ; and I doe it by imagining and figuring to myself what Condic̃on I my self should be in upon the like Occac̃on.

I am perswaded we are both Unison strings as to the Love of our Wives ; Wherfore you being struck, you may easily beleive That I also tremble, and really so I doe.

When your good father dyed, I told you that hee was full of years and ripe fruit, and that you had no reason to wish him longer in the paines of this world. But I cannot use the same Argument in this Case, for your Lady is taken away somewhat within half the ordinary age of Man and soon after you have been perfectly married to her ; For I cannot beleive your perfect union and assimulac̃on was made till many years after the Ceremonies at Kingsington.

What I have hitherto said Tends to aggravate rather than Mitigate your sorrow. But as the sun shining strongly upon burning Coles doth quench them, so perhaps the sadder Sentiments that I beget in you may extinguish those which now afflict you. The next Thing I shall say is, That when I myself married, I was scarce a year younger then you are now, and consequently do apprehend That you have a second Crop of Contentment and as much yet to come as ever I have had.

In the next place I beg you to divert your self by entertaining some powerfull thoughts of other kinds. I had yesterday a hopefull day in the Exchequer. I have the vanity to think That to tell you so, would a little refresh you. I wish you could hear a thousand parcells of such News from a thousand as sincere friends as is

Yours

W. P.

45. *Petty to Southwell.*

[In the following letter (for the first time in this Correspondence) we find mention of Petty's famous double-keeled ship. The ' double bottom ' or ' sluice boat ', as it was variously called, was originally planned in 1662, and at first met with considerable success. It won a sailing race open to all comers in Dublin Bay, it outsailed the Holyhead packet in a gale of wind, and apparently went through more than one edition before it was lost with all hands in the Bay of Biscay in 1666.

Petty, as this letter shows, had been somewhat sore at the lack of support accorded to him by the Royal Society and by His Majesty King Charles II. One of his grievances was that although the experiments had been made under the Society's auspices, he was not allowed to put their arms on his flag. Presumably, had this permission been accorded, he would have escaped the operations of the press-gang which, as he explains below, deprived him of two-thirds of his crew just before the final catastrophe took place.

Dr. Nehemiah Grew (1641–1712) was sometime secretary to the Royal Society, and was evidently now preparing the *Catalogue of Rarities* belonging to the Society which he published this year. In this book there is an account of a model of a double bottom 4 feet 7 inches long. There is still a model of a double bottom at Burlington House, which may well have been that which was at Gresham College in 1681, though it is much smaller than that described by Dr. Grew. It is of a single-decked boat, and no doubt represents one of the earlier trial types. There is, however, a drawing of a two-decked model in the Pepys Library at Magdalene College, Cambridge (reproduced in Fitzmaurice's *Life*), which is probably that of the boat which ultimately came to grief.

Petty, as we shall see, was soon to return with fresh zest to his double-bottom experiments, but in their final phase these proved even more disappointing than they had done before (*infra*, pp. 128-132).]

Dubl. 26 feb[r] 1680/81

D[re] Coz[n]

I owe you answers to 2 letters, as also to Dr Grewe's [1] about the Double Bottom. To which I say : That the modell at Gresham is not the Modell of the reall ship which was built : (1) That having 2 decks, whereas The Modell hath but one, (2) That the history of the Royall Society hath given already an Accompt of the fate of the Ship, (3) If wee say any more, Wee must tell how the Ship, which requird 50 men, had but 17 when shee perished. The rest being pressed out of her by the *Dragon* frigat, and might adde how little encouragment That designe had from the most Navarchall Prince[2]—with many other things.

But you have taught mee more discretion than to follow truth too nere. I might adde That the Royall Society would not suffer their armes to bee put into our Ship's Jack as a Canton.[3]

Wherefore let the dead bury the dead, But I have a Treatise ready to Vindicate the designe and the necessity of attempting it, which will make it rise againe when I am dead.

I am not well ; pardon mee dear Cousen That I onely adde my vowes of being

Yo[rs] for ever

W. P.

Pray cause Sir Leolin [4] not to forget mee.

---

[1] Nehemiah Grew (1641–1712), a vegetable physiologist. He was secretary to the Royal Society about this time.

[2] The King.

[3] A 'Jack' is, properly, a miniature flag flown from a staff at the end of the bowsprit, though the term is misused in the familiar ' Union Jack '. Arms displayed ' in canton ' would mean that they were inset or quatered in the flag.

[4] Sir Leoline Jenkins.

46. *Southwell to Petty.*

Kingsweston, 28 Feb^r 1681

Deare Couzin

You were not onely my Comforter uppon the death of an excellent father, but you exercised great skill to prevent his death. And now, by yours of the 31st past, you doe not onely condole the great loss I have sustained in a wife, but you seeme to think it reparable. As to the loss, tis true twas but of a mortall thing, and soe I must submitt. He that hath an unlimited Jurisdiction did it, for we wanted nothing that humane aydes could give. And perhaps I ought not to repine that one whoe had soe many preparations for heaven, was taken to the rewards thereof.

But when by 19 yeares conversation I knew the greate vertues of her mind, and discover since her death a more secrett corespondence with Heaven in Acts of Pietye and devotion (which before I knew not of), you will allow me, att least for my Children's sake, to lament that they have too early lost their guide.

I have had many other close tryalls since my father's death—The loss of a good mother, of an onely sister, two nephewes educated by my care, and a beloved Son who dyed three yeares before. And yet I may saye, he dyed but even now; for by what steps and motions he declined towards his grave, just the same were now gon over againe by his deare mother, to the observation and sorrow of all that beheld. Soe that a Tragedye of the greatest past affliction I ever had, was that repeated uppon me, And I leave you to judge whether I had not loade enough.

But I hope all these rugged paths will best conduct me to my Journeyes end. Tis certaine the Earth becomes less worthy for the good who leave it, and weake natures may be allowed to think Heaven the more desireable for their friends whoe are gone before.

There is but one Strong Motive in me to respite

such desires, which is the consideraĉon of 4 young
children who will hardly find soe good a friend as
my selfe in the whole world. They deserve well
from me, and with application may be lead into the
Path of a vertuous life. They are all parcells of their
Mother, acting in small different resemblances the
tenour and habitt of her life. Soe that, as to your
Expedient, I look uppon it, under Correction, but as
a meere knocking these 4 in the head ; and I cannot
think my Selfe out of the Bonds of Wedlock while
they live. Your owne Case and mine (about this age)
was quite uppon a different foote and without any
proportion.

I speake not this in sorrow, for I have wiped that
away and am cheerfully entertayning myself heere
with my Children, and cannot wish for a better
Employment of my life. My Son either walks or
rides about with me, repeateing att a time an hundred
of your verses (of the 104th Psalme [1]) with such Accent
and delight as would perhaps give you Entertainment
to heare him. The Loadestone, Mercurye, the Bees,
the 4 small animalls and so to the stars &c, are all
to him as the Mariner's Compass.[2] And would you
have me forgett this Boy, whoe remembers with pride
the kiss you gave him for demonstrating at 8 yeares
old an equilaterall triangle ? Well of this I have saide
enough to Justifie my rejection of any salve that can
ever be thought of on this side Heaven ; and I will
onely add, as to my selfe, that being wonderfully
troubled with the Scurvey in my Nerves, I am under
all the tryalls I can beare, to gett some deliverance
from it.

As to your good Sentence lately obtained in the
Exchequer, I am sure I take reall comfort in itt and
wish from my hearte that you may see a short and
prosperous event of that greate perplexitye ; that soe
the world may have the fruite and treasure which
your leisure and tranquility would afford.

---

[1] *Supra*, pp. 20-23.
[2] The allusion is to Petty's coat-of-arms, for which see *infra*, p. 222.

My blessing to my Godson and to his hearty
Brother. My Boy puts in his humble service to his
fine Cousins, and I am ever S^r Y^r most hum. ser.

R. S.

47. *Petty to Southwell.*

[Southwell, we learn elsewhere (*History of Bandon,*
Barnett), was now at Kinsale, where he had gone to meet
the Duke of Ormond, who was on a visit to County Cork.
Petty no doubt thought this a convenient opportunity to
reach through his friend the ear of the Lord-Lieutenant in
the matter of his Irish grievances. Aubrey tells us (*Lives,*
p. 149) that on July 25, 1681, Petty had given evidence
before Henry Hen, Lord Chief Baron of Ireland, as to the
' Soldier's land' which he had purchased in Kerry. The
particular ' Calamity' under which he was now suffering
appears to have been an adverse decision on the part of
the Chief Baron in regard to these lands. Petty gave vent
to his chagrin in a long and scurrilous lampoon against the
offending judge, entitled : " HENEALOGIE or the legend of
Hen-Hene and Pen-Hene in two parts. Whereof the first
doth in 24 chapters of Raillery, contain the enchantments,
metamorphoses and merry concepts relating to them. The
second part contayning (in good earnest) the foolish,
erroneous, absurd, malicious and ridiculous JUDGEMENTS
OF HEN-HENE " (Petty MSS.). Fortunately perhaps for the
repute of its author, this diatribe was never made public.]

Dublin, 2° Aug 1681

D^{re} Cousin

I received from Kilkenny your sense and
remembrance of my Calamity, and place your want of
opportunity among the rest of my many and customary
disasters. I sent you the printed affidavit the same
moment it came from the presse. I herewith send
you 4 more—God speed them well &c.

I am ashamed, Dear Cousen, That I can pay you
for these troubles with nothing but such notions as
(whatever they cost mee) are not equivalent to a
bottle of Choice Wine in the estimation of most men
and those in most power. You see That What I

solemnly clayme is restitution to Lands worth about
1500£ per annum and 30,000£ damages ; and withall
That the future quitrents may bee as easy as have
been granted to many others, or (at worst) not to
exceed the legall rigor of the reducd Collumne.[1]

And now Cousin, Why might not this matter
afford a better gratuity then what the 49 Men[2] promisd
you ? and Why should I cast unprofitable burthens
on my friends because They are my friends.—Like
the Ale-wife, who expectd that her best friends and
customers should take off her dead drinke and pay
her for good, because they were her friends ?

I do not reckon all my right and reasoning to
bee worth a straw, till I can get some powerfull
person to consider it. I compose curious peeces in
Music and play them accurately ; but all this while
my hearers are as deafe as haddocks, nor will their
eares (I feare) ever be opened with just applications,
till Wee run a Spit into them made of some convenient
Metall. I wish I could forget the whole.

Let me heare your Maine Objeĉons against what
you carryd from hence. The designe was to calme
men's minds by bringing things to reall and originall
Simplicity. Wherefore I would have it raise no
Storme in yours—rather burne the whole.

Pray lay together the Writings which concerne
my Wife.

My reall service to Sir John Percivale—other
additions are diminutions. I am his and yours

W. P.

48. *Petty to Southwell.*

Dublin, 20 Aug. 1681

Dᵣ Cozⁿ

Once more pay the postage of 4 sheetes. By
the last you saw the *quantum* of my damage, By this

---

[1] The ' Reduced Column ' was the column (in the " Book of Distribution
of Forfeited Lands in Ireland ") which showed the net amount of ' profitable '
land held by the grantee after subtracting all land scheduled as ' unprofitable '.

[2] *Supra,* p. 4.

you shall the *Quomodo* and consequently the Injury.
Oh that I could get somebody but to read my papers
&c.

There is a good Man about this towne Writing
against Atheisme, and in particular at this time
answering their Cavills against the Resurrection;
which are, That the whole Globe of the Earth will
not afford sufficient matter to the bodyes that must
rise, Much lesse will the surface thereof (say They)
afford footing to all those bodies. Now the assistances
which I have given this good Man [1] are, viz :

(1) Supposing The People in England, Scotland,
and Ireland to bee about 9 millions, those in Holland
and Zealand about 1 million, and in France 16 ; I say
That, by comparing the rest of the world therewith,
There are but between 300 and 400 Millions of Soules
now living.

(2) Upon this and Grant's measures I ascertaine
the Number that ever have dyed since the Creation,
and find that Munster would afford them all graves,
and the Mangerton [2] bodyes, or the Equivalent in
weight of earth.

Having thus helped my friend, I took occasion
to proceed, vizt : I find that the world being 5630
yeares old,[3] That Adam and Eve, doubling but every
200 yeares (as Grant also sayth), That there must
bee now 316 millions of people upon the Earth, which
answers admirably and is a brave argument against
Scripture Scoffers and Prae-Adamites.[4] Neverthelesse, upon Examination of our friend Grant's
positions, I find That People do double very differently
in every century of the World and have (as I think),

---

[1] The ' good man ' appears to have been the person referred to as a " worthy
divine" in Petty's published essay on the *Growth of the City of London* (Hull,
p. 466 and note).

[2] Mount Mangerton, a large hill near Kenmare, in the midst of the property
of which Petty had become possessed in South Kerry.

[3] Scaliger's Chronology, *De emendatione temporum*, placed the Creation
in the year 3948 B.C. It may be noted that this book is referred to, and in the
same sense, in the *London Observations* (cf. Hull, p. 388).

[4] The Pre-Adamites were the rationalist thinkers of the time who held that
people existed on the earth before Adam's time. They fortified this argument
by a reference to the perennial puzzle of Cain's wife.

rectifyd his doctrine, by making many numbers in continuall proportion &c.

I further find that the world at a Medium is at this day not much better peopld than our wretched baronyes in Kerry, nor above $\frac{1}{10}$ part so well as our poore Ireland is ; nor above $\frac{1}{100}$ part so well as Holland, which is over-peopld.

I find that in the next 1400 yeares The World, doubling its people in my correctd proportion, must bee over-peopld ; and that then there must be great Wars and Slaughters, and that the Strong must then destroy the weake, or the World must come (of necessity) to an end.

I find, by looking far back upon the paucity of people in the Assyrian, Persian, and other first Monarchyes, how easy a Thing twas for a few resolute fellowes to conquer the World as then it was ; and that (whatever the King of France may think) the Universall or Great Monarchy doth and will grow every Century more and more difficult by the Course of nature.

I conclude that, as people double faster now then they did in former ages, so the rent of Lands must also rise proportionably, and the number of yeares purchase also. Wherefore let us get possession of what the affidavit sayth is kept from us.

Thus, deare Cousin, having ended where I began, I am still Yours

W. P.

To punish you the More I send you a legible Copy with my owne scrible.

49. *Petty to Southwell.*

Dr Cousin   Dubl. 2º Sept 1681

To yours of the 20th Aug. . . . I thank you for shewing the affidavit &c, but It appeared Intricate. Yourself and others, that have read it, can better than I tell whether it bee so or not. But his Grace is made

Judge of the arrears. It is hard to understand That 19 yeares holding the lands, is a sufficient quitrent for 3 yeares enjoyment by the Grantee.

The next thing I pray from you is, Whether the discourse about the ' reduced Collume ' bee Intelligible ? In what a case am I, who suffer so much, for that Those who ought to know all things will know nothing ! I thank you for telling mee There was a Coldnes ; The Contrary hath been pretended. Next tell mee (if you can or dare) the Causes of it.

As for the Calculations &c, I use them to help faith against Scripture scoffers. As for that of Religion, I pray God to inspire you with what hee would have you to believe, and help you to do as you would bee done unto, and deliver you from vaine philosophy and the crafty traditions of interested Men and from Impracticable Lawes ; and then believe That ye most Merciful God will not reape where hee hath not sowne.   Adieu, dear Cousin, I am Yo͏ͬˢ

I expect with feare to heare you are going away.

50. *Petty to Southwell.*

[In the summer of 1681 an elephant had been accidentally burnt in Essex Street, Dublin. It was dissected and reported on by Dr. Allan Mullen (or Molines), whose account was one of the earliest written on this thesis. The pamphlet excited great interest at the time, and was later honoured by express citation in Buffon's monumental work (Gilbert, *History of Dublin*, ii. 147).]

Dublin, 24ᵗʰ Sepͬ 1681

Dear Cousin

God bless our Boys, and let us dispose them to friendship and Emulation. I have not yet spoaken with Mr Sollicitor about the Book of Money ; [1]   I

---

[1] At first sight the allusion would a⸀pear to be to Petty's *Quantulumcunque concerning Money*. It is, however, clear from the succeeding letters (pp. 100-106) that this had not yet been written, much less printed. Petty may possibly be referring to the *Treatise of Taxes*, of which an unauthorised version (reprinted from the edition of 1667) appeared in 1679 (Hull, *Bibliography*, No. 11).

guess that a Lawyer of Gray's Inn hath printed it under his own name. I and Mr Tisdell have sought it here, but cannot yet find it; however by hook or by Crook you shall have it.

The Sonn of the Hand Squeezer can alone doe our buisnes, even without the great Mathematician.[1] But if both of them faile, I shall nevertheles Trust to God and to the force of Eternall reason.

I thank you for the Abstracts of the writings. Wee have already exact coppies of what concerns my Wife, and 2000£ had been unto us without the fines and Recoveryes you mention.

As for the Sceleton of the Elephant: It is well enough set together, soe as it hath cost the poor owner 30£ between its death and this day. It is become a publick shew of the Painted picture; the Sceleton, the Trunk, Toung, gutts, Penis, Bladder and some parts of the Skin with the Anatomicall description of some other parts not now to bee shewn. The Sceleton is suspended, That it turns round about upon a Swivle fixt in the Beam of the House and at its just heighth. The particulars remarkable in the Sceleton are these, vizt:

1. The Ivory Tusks are not Teeth, but Horns; there being other Teeth besides, like those of other great Animails.

2. There be 20 Ribbs of a side.

3. The bones of the Ulna and Radius, as also of the Tibia and fibula, do cross each other, as if they were Twisted—very different from other Animalls.

4. The Lower Jaw is far greater and thicker than that of any other Animall I know.

5. The bones of the foot have a generall correspondence with those of other Creatures, but very diferent in their proportions.

6. The Trunck hath a broad footing and insertion about and upon the Bones, which make the Nose.

Dear Cousin, I wish the wind and you could agree

---

[1] I am unable to identify these potential advocates of Petty's cause.

to stay longer here ; but if it must be otherwise, I submit to your Interest and conveniences and remaine Yo^{rs}

W. P.

51. *Petty to Southwell.*

Dubl. 4 Octob. 1681

Dr Coz^n

    To yours of the 30th past.   God restore health to the relations you mention and preserve it in the rest, and in all other things reward the Care you have of Mee.   The Glympse you mention was good, Let It but blaze out and the work is done.

My Busines now is to shew That I have not abusd you in the many discourses I have troilld (?) you in this Matter ; nor the world in the late printed Case, accusd of important omissions.   To which purpose I say : . . .

I now returne to tell you, That the Shew of the Elephant will in some measure repaire the poore man's losses, for they get sometimes 20s a day, neither doth the Sceleton eate oates &c.

Sir John Temple [1] hath sent mee 6 London and 14 Dublin yearly bills of Mortality,[2] with some few scatterd quarterly bills.   By the next you shall have my Observaçons upon them, by which (among Other Things) you shall see what a shame it is, that these and many other accompts are no better kept. There are great discontents in the Government, but mine is this : Let good accompts bee but kept, and you secure mee against Mutiny.

I conclude with praying That God would make us all do and beleive what best pleaseth him, and bee our Light in this dark world.

I am and shall ever bee Yo^{rs} &c

---

[1] Sir John Temple (1632–1704), Speaker of the Irish Parliament and Solicitor-General for Ireland, 1660–1689.

[2] *Infra*, p. 110.

The world do feare and therefore hate that Things should bee tryed by Number, Weight and Measure. I cannot bring the Farmers to any accompt.

52. *Petty to Southwell.*

[It seems that Petty had again been urging his friend to console himself for the loss of his wife by a second marriage, and that Southwell had resented this advice even more emphatically than before. The letter to which the following is a reply is, however, no longer extant.

Petty was again in London, primarily (as he himself states) in relation to his 'wrongs'. He improved the occasion by taking part in a general discussion which was now in progress before the Privy Council as to the reorganisation of the Irish Revenue, as well as by making proposals thereon on his own account.

Two of his papers, a draft *Commission for the Survey of the Lands, People, Trade and Revenue in Ireland* (*Petty Papers*, No. 29), dated July 28, 1682, and a *Colloquium between A B and C concerning a New Instrument of Government* (*ibid.* No. 30), indicate not obscurely that Petty was prepared to undertake, and hoped to be given, the post in question. The newspapers went so far as to announce his appointment (*infra*, p. 99), but his hopes were dashed by the appointment of a new set of Commissioners, amongst whom he did not find a place (p. 100).]

London, 10 Junii 1682

D{re} Cosen

The last of your letters had deep marks of resentment, so deep as I could not hope to rub them out with anything I could say ; and the Truth is I am ashamed to perswade my friends to what neither can nor ought to bee done, such as is the blotting out of your memory what ought to live eternally in it. Wherefore I pray God not so much to take away your just resentments, as to counterpoise them with some other felicity, which I guesse will bee by the extra vertues of your children. I hinted to you that your Godson did not continue to do so well as hee began, but wee have since discovered a leake in the

Ship, which was his Tutor's being desparately in love [1] and the Consequences thereof.

I am here by a letter sent from the Commissioners of the Treasury to stop our proceedings in the Exchequer, and as I suppose to examine the matter here. I do not care where it bee examined and hope the King will descend to heare my wrong. It now lyes in Sir Edward's [2] way to help mee, for God knowes how and when the rest may understand the matter. I know in your next to him you will say what you think fit. As for newes, I tell you That the Portsmouth Yacht wherein I came over came fowle of her owne Anchor just as shee dropt it, and so bilgd her That in an hower shee was all coverd with water, but I beleive is since recovered without much damage. I was the first that got into the boate ; nobody was lost or dampnified, so neere the shoare did this accident happen.[3]

Pray let mee now and then heare from you, and I hope to answer with what smells lesse selfish than this doth.

I am, d^re Cousen, perfectly yours,

W. P.

My wife gives you her humble service and has been these two months ill from her ague. Shee hopes your daughters have lost theirs.

53. Southwell to Petty.

Kingsweston, 21 Jun. 1682

Deare Cousin

I was the last post told by a good friend [4] that you had beene to see him, and that he desired an

---

[1] Mr. Mesnil, Charles Petty's tutor, had, as we learn elsewhere, fallen in love with " Lady Clancarty's French Woman " [MSS., Petty to Ly. Petty, March 25, 1682].

[2] Sir Edward Dering (supra, p. 43 n.).

[3] A full account of this adventure (which happened at Neston on June 5) is given in a letter from Petty to his wife of that date.

[4] Probably Ormond.

abstract from you of all that had past.   That, in a petition given in, you take little notice of hardship or obstruction from the Treasury, which surely if made out would be redrest.   That you passe to an other point, which is so firmely settled as seames next to Impossible for you to shake it.[1]

I know not if this small hint may be of any use to you.   I hope on Saturday night to be in London.

I am ever Y^{rs}

R. S.

54. *Southwell to Petty.*

Kingsweston, 28 Augt 1682

Deare Cousin

I have been Rouleing of late between this and Bath, and am tomorrow carrying my little fry to compliment the Company there, of which I had a coachfull of the Ladyes here on Wenesday last.

So I come slow to the acknowledgeing yours of the 17th, which came with a valuable Cargo to me. For tho I had noe concerne in the subject matter of any paper you writt, yet all of them are to me as soe many modells to worke by, and of like force as the five Powers in the meckanicks.   Wherefore lett me not want copies of what you can spare, for they shall not dye, if I or Neddy can helpe it.

The Prints doe constitute you one of the 3 Governours of his Majesty's Irish Revenue, but a word from your selfe would be more authentick.   I wish for his Majesty's sake it were the worst newes I could have concerning Ireland.

Rejoyce at the happy arrival of your two brave Boyes.   Neddy will be at leisure ere long to try his cousin's patience.   Happinesse to all is the constant wish of

Yours

R. SOUTHWELL

---

[1] Southwell is no doubt here alluding to Petty's proposal that the " Farm " should be abolished and that he should be made responsible for the Collection of Taxes in Ireland (cf. Hull, xxix.).

55. *Petty to Southwell.*

[Disappointed in his hopes of obtaining the management to the Irish Revenue, Petty now found solace in other directions. His children were showing aptitude in arithmetic—though not, it may be supposed, as yet in the 'political' variety of that science. He speaks of a paper on Logic, which is no longer extant, and of another "concerning money". The latter is the *Quantulumcunque concerning Money*, written in 1682 but not printed till 1695 (Hull, *Bibliography*, p. 638). It may be noted, however, that the book as published contains 32, and not 31, questions and answers. The 'Paper about Building' mentioned in this letter was no doubt that on *Taxation of Buildings* which is printed in the *Papers* (No. 143)]

London, ye 5⁰ Sep^br 1682

Deare Cosen

Yesterday came to Town what was declard on Sunday night at Windsor, vizt, That the Revenue of Ireland is to bee managed by the Ld Longford,[1] Lem Kingdon, one Mr Strong of the Excise, Mr Dixon[2] of the Customes of London, and Captain Bridges of Dublin, who as tis thought did but represent Mr Trant. By good Lucke I never sollicitated any body in the Case, I onely putt in 3 severall papers of proposalls before you went hence, which I think did the service no harme. As for my selfe, my work hath ever been my wages in this world. My owne buisnesse sticks in the Bog where you left it. I have much to say, but I have nobody to heare mee.

I will review the specimen of *Logick*, and perhaps send it inlargd as well as explaind. Wee are all in health here. Charles and his sister are in daily emulation about Arithmetick; That spirit doth begin to rise and appeare in Charles upon the Charmes and Conjurations of his sister. The Latin also joggs on, so as I hope you shall ere long bee redy to receive

---

[1] Francis Lord Aungier (*d.* 1700), who had recently been created Lord Longford by Charles II., was at this time a Commissioner of Revenue. He subsequently held several other appointments.
[2] *Recte* Dickinson (*infra*, p. 110).

Cosen Neddy's Arrows.   As for news : it is said that
the Duke of Hanover [1] is to have my Ld Lowther-
dell's Garter.[2]

I have writ 3 sheets in answer to 31 questions
concerning mony.   If it take (for I renounce all
Judgement of my owne) you shall have a Coppy.
But laying all these things aside, lett mee here that
you and your family are well, for that will best please

Yoⁿ

W. P.

S^r   *Postscript*

Sir William's head has been so perplext with
the Ill success of his buisness that hee could not turne it
to the explanation of the Paper about Building.   But
you see hee intends both to explaine and inlarge it,
which I will bee sure to putt him in mind of.

I am S^r Y^r most humble serv^t

J. W.[3]

56. *Southwell to Petty.*

Kingsweston, 11 Sepr 1682

Deare Cousin

By yours of the 5th Instant I see the 5
Commissioners of the Revenue of Ireland.   The first
I easily guesse at, but who lanched the other 4 into
this Bethesda I want to know ?   You say nothing
of their Sallary ; nor of their subordination to the
Treasury here ;   nor if those 2 points (which soe
indeared the former prosecution) doe still subsist, as
to Tanger [4] and the Shipps, wherein as a Kingsale
man I am a little concernd.

---

[1] Ernest Augustus, Duke of Hanover, the husband of the Electress Sophia
and father of George I.

[2] *Sic*, but Lord Lauderdale is evidently intended.   The Duke of Lauderdale, who had been in high favour with the King since the Restoration, had
died in August of this year.

[3] The initials are those of Petty's brother-in-law, James Waller.

[4] Tangier (with Bombay) had come to Charles II. as part of Catherine of
Braganza's dowry.   Large sums had been spent there with a view to securing
the Mediterranean Trade, but in 1683 all was abandoned and the garrison
were brought away [Burnet, *History of His Own Time* (1897), i. 306].

But I confesse I am much more, to see that when the Citty is delivered, yett noebody reguards the wise man. I will believe that your papers had more effect than you are told of ; and seeing they turne you noe better to Account, lett me at least have the Transcript of what you gave in. For I shrine all up, and fancy that in after times I shall be resorted too for your workes, as Mr Hedges is for the true Opo-balsamum.[1]

I see alsoe as to your particular affaire, that you stick fast as before, and scarce know where with benefitt to expose your doleance. I would advise better if I knew how ; but surely it can do no hurt if you take Sir Edward Dering fresh at his arrivall from Kent and explain to him that by him alone you can hope to be understood. The proposall which by my Lord Hyde's [2] incouragement he soe laboured in, being quite layed by, and new things done (wherein as being absent he has noe share), I am apt to think he will not be unwilling to learn and know the extent of your case, and afterwards to act as faire opportunityes shall be offered him.

I take notice that all your clouds are only without dores, for at the same time you can think and turne your mind to the instruction of the unkind world. Your 3 sheetes about money shall be much more welcome to me than money itselfe.

And then to have the specimen of Logick enlarged, as well as explained, is a matter I really take to heart. For my chiefe businesse is now growne a sollicitude for my son's education, and soe I am chawing over every thing that I judge usefull in order to his easier digestion. Neddy remembers you advysed him to gather Tooles, as Hammer, saw, pincers, gimblett &c ; and he calls the arts and sciences

---

[1] William Hedges was a rich Eastern trader who was subsequently knighted and became Governor of Bengal. ὁποβάλσαμον: " That licour most excellent, which for his excellency and mervealous effects is called Balsamo . . . made of a tree greater than the Powngarned Tree. It carrieth leaves like to nettles. The Indians do call it Xilo, and we do call the same Balsamo" [*Joyful Newes of the New Found Worlde*, by Nicolas Monardes, sixteenth century].

[2] Lawrence Hyde (1641–1711), second son of Lord Clarendon, had been created Lord Hyde in the previous year, but was now Earl of Rochester.

already by these nick-names, and meanes to value them noe more than as they really proove such. And as he passes for the top-artisan that invents a new Toole, soe Neddy meanes to throng in among your admirers ; not onely for this *Logick*, but for all other Tooles, which either for the Sake of his cousin Charles or the Publick you shall vouchsafe to frame or invent. He hopes also you will cause the 104th Psalme to be printed anew.

You have alsoe within dores the sunshine of this new and profitable emulation betweene Charles and his sister. I see that tis she ferments Arithmetick in him, but how you levened her (unlesse *ex traduce*) pray let us know. I have gott Dr Wallis [1] by the end touching this subject ; for I would faine by comprehending the reason retaine the practice, which else vanisheth as I have found for want of frequent use.

All my young ones are well and afford me much content ; tis the most sensible share of worldly happinesse we can have. I doe heartily congratulate your part, and am ever Yours

R. SOUTHWELL

57. *Petty to Southwell.*

London, ye 16⁰ Sepbʳ 1682.

Deare Cosen

Tis said the Managers [2] are to have 1000£ per annum without any obligation whatsoever, and I suppose they may treat how and with whom they please concerning Tangeer and the ships, whereas I did in a manner undertake for the whole, by Demonstraçon, by Oath, and a wager of 2000£. But I am represented (as the Duke of Ormond told mee this day) by some to be a Conjurer, by others to bee

---

[1] John Wallis (1616–1703), celebrated in mathematics and theology. He wrote many works on both subjects.
[2] Of the Irish Revenue (p. 100).

notionall and fancy-full neer up to madness, and also a Fanatick.

Sir Edward Deering is come to Towne.   Before his comeing the Lords of the Treasury made an Order to withdraw their stop in the Exchequer of Ireland.   But I aime to have my grand Accompt examined, which his grace hath this day promised to gett done—being unwilling to doe any thing for mee upon all the King's former Letters, Reports, &c made thereupon,—and this before the King goes to Newmarket.   I do not see that Edward Deering needs any spuring, nevertheless you must conjure him to consider mee thoroly, for hee onely can doe me good. My Lady Dutches[1] is very harty for mee.   On Tuesday next will bee a great transaction about the Sherrifs which I suppose affects and takes up our great men's thoughts.

I this day delivered the 3 sheets conteyning the whole Doctrine of Mony to Mr Blathwight[2] who wanted illumination in this matter.   I wish it bee truely written and well painted.

I have perused the *logick* paper,[3] but cannot much explaine it, for the scope of it is.   1°. To pick out the principle words of the question, and then to sett downe and number all the meanings you can fancy of every word, and then to new state your question according to the precise signification of each word as you intend it.   2°. When that is done, to find out your *data* or *media probationis*, and then to ratiocinate (in what Rediculous manner you know of) and that will bring you to a Sollid conclusion.

Remember mee to dear Nedy, bid him study moderately, and not burn his fingers with his tongs nor pinch them in his vice.   I say cram into him

---

[1] Elizabeth Preston, sole daughter and heiress of Richard (Preston), Earl of Desmond, in whose favour the title had been revived in 1619.   She had married the Duke of Ormond in 1629 and died in 1685.

[2] William Blathwayt (1649–1717), secretary to Sir William Temple, and afterwards Clerk to the Privy Council and Secretary at War.

[3] See *infra*, p. 309, where it appears that this paper was not strictly one on logic, but had reference to the size of London treated in Petty's logical manner by 'ratiocination'.

some lattin, some mathematicks, some drawing and some Law (which is almost all done already), and then lett nature worke, and let him follow his owne Inclinations. For further forceing him to learne what you like and not what hee chooses himself, will come to no great matter. But when you see what he thrives and prospers in, provide him a Course of Life, whereby hee may make the best market of his owne naturall wares.

I will be ever Yo^{rs} &c.

58. *Southwell to Petty.*

Kingsweston, 27 Sept 1682

Deare Cousin

I had sooner payd you hearty thankes for yours of the 16th, but I have lately beene at Longleete to see Sir Thomas Thinn in his new gloryes.[1] There I mett Sir Thomas Clergis[2] who has for you under his Thumb a purchase of 4 or 500£ per annum, reaching up on the Sumersettsheir syde to the Gates of Bristoll. He told me alsoe of a merchant that brings with him an estate of 80 thousand pounds, pickt up in the East Indies by the sole trafique of diamonds. You will find him if you desire it in London, and try if his experience can confirme or give any varyation to your Theory on the subject of diamonds. I confesse I often rave in my thoughts after that *Dialogue*[3] you made at Dunstable, and shall not be quiett till I have it.

Mr Blathwayt has lately sent me your *Quan-tulumcunque*. I read it with great delight, being

---

[1] Sir Thomas Thynne, shortly to be created Viscount Weymouth, had just succeeded to Longleat on the death of his cousin.

[2] Sir Thomas Clarges (*d.* 1695), the politician who had acted as inter-mediary between the Commonwealth and Royalist leaders.

[3] The *Dialogue of Diamonds* (published by Hull, p. 624) was found among the philosophical papers collected by Abraham Hill, one of the original members of the Royal Society (British Museum, Sloane MS. 2903).

able thereby to range with some method all the wild notions which in some points have occurrd to my thoughts, and to store up others of great moment whereof I never had thought at all. I have sent back 3 or 4 queryes to Mr Blathwayt which I suspect to be mistakes in the coppying.[1]

I thank you for what you say as to your *Logick* paper, altho' formerly you had thought of enlarging as well as explaining the same. Neddy takes deep impression of all you say or vouchsafe to advise in his behalfe.

From what you say as concerning the Irish Revenue, I must needes admire the Malignity of your Starrs; that while you would have secured the maine, by oath, wager, and demonstration, you are told (as formerly in the play) 'consideration is our foe'. Well may you get your owne Grand Account Stated, which it seemes you have a promise of, and I will excite Sir Edward all I can to take it to heart. But be sure you instill early some easy expedient of Recompense; for else the terrour of such a debt and the injustice susteyned, will bring to passe the saying in an other case, that ' in seeing they will neither see nor understand '.

By the next convenyency I will send my Lady the small picture of the lady Harris of Corneworthy which I promised, and with heapes of good wishes to the little ones, I am ever Sᵣ, Your most affect cousin & most humble servant

ROBERT SOUTHWELL

59. *Petty to Southwell.*

London, 10 Octob. 1682.

Dʳᵉ Cosin

A pretty indifferent letter [2] was agreed to bee signed by the Lords of the Treasury, but when Sir

---

[1] The *Quantulumcunque* was evidently not yet printed (cf. Hull, p. 438).
[2] On the eternal dispute about Petty's Quit-rents. The law officers of the Crown disagreeing, Petty had been once more disappointed of a settlement.

Edward Dering came home, It was alleged with a
great Byas ; which seemd to honour the Sollicitor's
opinion as more for the King's service.   How much
hee consented to it I know not, but [he] seemes still
very kind &c.

My Wife and I go for Ireland and leave our
children.   I have found my Lady Southwell's [1] poems,
tell mee to whom you would have them delivered.
I am much out of order and out of love with my
studyes.

God blesse you all, for that would bee some
amends to
Yors
W. P.

60. Southwell to Petty.

Kingsweston, 14 Oct 1682
Deare Cousin

I received yours of the 10th with sorrow.   I
see you are hastning with my Lady at an unseasonable
time to Ireland ; that you leave your children behind ;
that you were much out of order, and out of love with
your Studyes.   I see alsoe how you resent the Byas
that is given to your businesse, and how from better,
it became worse after the arrivall of one who yett
seemes kind ; and soe you are doubtfull whence the
hurt hath hapned.   I can at this distance say nothing
to any matter of Fact, but should it come that way,
I am sure I must resent it alsoe as contradiction
to all my entreatyes and concerne.   I can the lesse
beleive it soe, because in every other thing I feele
the effects of kindnesse in whatsoever I appeare to
affect.   What shall I say or what can I doe more in
this matter, than to wish you ease ?

I confesse I often reflect uppon this businesse [2]

---

[1] An aunt of Sir Robert's who had married Sir Thomas Southwell of
Spineworth in Norfolk.   The Lady Harris referred to in the preceding letter
was her mother.

[2] *I.e.* Petty's quarrel with the Farmers.

as the onely Incumbrence of your life. You have
a chaine of blessings in all other Respects—of wife,
children and other fortune sufficient ; onely this single
Linck, and the rust and canker of it pulls back the
Joyes and Contemplation of all the Rest. I consider
that you have for 20 yeares contended in this quarrell
with noe small cost, but perhaps with as many good
thoughts and Laborious contrivances as might have
servd to establish a Kingdome. Judge Hale was
noe Superstition man, but I had it lately from his
Daughter, that if he had undertaken anything, and
prepared for it with all the wisdom and contrivance
that lay in his power, yett if he found a run of crosse
accidents to the contrary, he gave off and reckoned
as if he had some superior advertisment in that Matter.
This was his Rule in all his owne affaires.

When you and I were in 1663 in our great Storme,[1]
which of us would not have flung over board a very
deare Jewell to have been at Rest ?   Your troubles
since in this affaire makes up more than that Storme,
and you are still in Agitation. Would to God you
would resolve to run the vessell into some Bay and
there lett her Lodge. The time will come when your
son may find your impossible worke a worke of ease.
One cannot still endure a stone in one's foot, tho
it were a Diamond. Such a Resolution as this : to
forgett past toyles and oppression, and to leave true
Modells of all unto your son and to the wonderfull
operations of Time—this would add unto your life
length of dayes, suffer you to enjoy the pleasure of
educating your Children in your owne way, seeing
God has made them capable of it. And for once,
seeing you cannot conquer the World, E'ene conquer
yourselfe, which is perhaps a more blessed part of
courage.

You have been so good as alwayes to allow me

---

[1] Southwell is evidently here referring to the period succeeding the Act of
Settlement (1662), when through the claims of alleged ' Innocents ' many
Cromwellian settlers were in danger of losing the land which had been allotted
to them.

liberty of speaking, and I use it ; because in my time I have seene great resolutions taken from weake advisers, especially when knowne that they have spoaken from their Hearts.

If you and my lady goe, My best wishes shall attend you. You may send any papers for me to Mr Madox.[1]

I am ever Sʳ Your most affect Cousin & most humble servant

ROBERT SOUTHWELL

61. *Southwell to Petty.*

Kingsweston. Thursday 19 Oct 1682

Deare Cousin

. . . I now write to Sir John Werden to procure an Instruction to the new Commissioners for Ireland, that the Vice-Admiralls officers when they seize floating goods may be allowed to keepe them in their Custody, Whereas the late Farmour's officers have still Refused them for the duty; and I putt that point to be now determined wheather such goods shall be lyable to duty or not. I received a complaint of this nature from Mr Richard Chute, my deputy for Kerry, who says alsoe that the people run away with all they can seize, because there is noe court nigh at hand to complaine too and keepe them in Awe.

I suppose when you have established Mr William Fitzgerald by your commission, He may lay about him, and turne his abilityes to grow considerable in this Jurisdiction. For if some body doe not take the matter to heart, and in truth take some sort of pride to appeare in it, what betweene the ill nature of the Comon lawyers and the injustice of others, twill quick be trampled under foot.

[1] Subsequent references show that this was one Philip Madox, a lawyer, who acted as Southwell's correspondent in London.

I will tire you noe more but with the constant assurance that I am Sʳ Your most affecᵗ Cousin & most humble servant

ROBERT SOUTHWELL

I have old acquaintance with Mr Dickinson one of the Commissioners, and newer with Mr Ellis [1] their secretary.   If you value my recomendation of you or your Concernes to their friendshipp, I am ready to prouve all I have for you.

62. *Petty to Southwell.*

[Petty had given up for the time being the intention which he had expressed of returning to Ireland, and (in spite of undertakings to the contrary) had plunged once more into ' ratiocination ' and ' political arithmetic '.

In the letters which follow we find an important piece of evidence in favour of his authorship of ' Graunt's ' *Observations on the London Bills of Mortality.*

The pamphlet concerning Dublin which he sent Southwell on November 25, 1682, was an advance copy of his *Observations on the Dublin Bills of Mortality*, which were published " by Mark Pardoe at the sign of the Black Raven, over against Bedford House in the Strand " in the following year.   The title-page gives the book as written " by the Observator on the London Bills of Mortality ", though there was no secret that it came from Petty's pen —Graunt having been for eight years in his grave.

The confession by Petty in print that he was himself the author of the London *Observations* evidently gave great pleasure to Southwell, who explains (*infra*, p. 112) that he, like others, had long suspected it.   But Petty's reply to his felicitations, which might have clinched the matter once and for all, is unfortunately no longer extant.

It still remains a matter for surprise that Petty, who seems never to have admitted explicitly that he had written this book, should on this one occasion have allowed the secret to be given away by implication.   (See " The Disputed Authorship," *Petty Papers*, ch. xxii. and Introduction, *supra*.)]

---

[1] John Ellis (1643–1738). He had been secretary to Sir Leoline Jenkins and was afterwards Under-Secretary of State.

London, ye 25 Novb^r 82

Dr Cosen

    I told you in my last that I would meddle no more with Politicall Arithmetic nor with Ratiocinations &c, but would turne Beast and grow absurd as the Glorious Men of the world are. Wherefore I desire you not to look upon the inclosed Pamphlet[1] as a startting from my Resolutions; For it was put a printing when I first came to towne, and hath been kept in hand ever since by my Brother Beast, Mark Pardo the Stationer. And I doe now pursue my Beastship by goreing you and Cosen Neddy with these my hornes; and I would have you run at the Citty of Bristoll with the same, and bore their sculs with the same advice which is here given for Dublin.

    You see Cosen, That I am fully bent upon mischief, by troubling you and my best friends with these pestilent Computations; and am so absurd, that not withstanding the hurt I am doing you, I do neverthelesse subscribe my self

    Yo^r most Affec^t friend Kinsman & serv^t

W^M PETTY

63. *Southwell to Petty.*

Kingsweston, 28 No^{br} 1682.

Deare Cousin

    When by yours of the 24th past[2] I understood your putting off the evill day of a dirty and dangerous Journey, I became much more sedate than before; but when you concluded your letter with an Interdiction to your selfe, and such a Reverse as to say ' lett there be darknesse ', I fell into griefe and you may think stupidity (by my long silence); and this for many Accounts. First that the world should be soe wicked as to give you provocation, but chiefly

---

[1] *The Observations on the Dublin Bills of Mortality.*
[2] The letter referred to is not extant.

that you should take it.   For has Sir Walter Raleigh added to his character by burning halfe the World ? [1] Had he not been even more revenged, in heaping up coales and obleiging the ungratefull age ?   Besydes how preposterous is it for the Iniquity of the present bystanders (which are but a handfull) to bespite the inoffensive generations that are to come ?   And how well did Ben Johnson defy their hissings when he declared that what he had written was for Posterity. A prophet has no honour in his owne time.

I have now the favour of yours of the 25th Instant, and in it some of the Rich Ore of the same old mine. Herein I first congratulate that you take home the prodigall son (I should indeed have sayd it of the Father) and that you lett the world see plaine, what they still suspected, that the spiritt of Sir William Petty and not of John Graunt presided in those Bills of Mortality.   Poore John, tho in his purgatory, can hardly drive such points as (by your allowance) he ventured on while here, in his State of fudling and of frailty.   The good man was herein like a dwarfe mounted on an Elephant.

But altho, to keepe gravity, you will needs excuse this new eruption and that still you are for unthinking and unobleiging too ;   I can but smile, as I would doe to heare naturall agents such as the sun, moone, and starrs talke at the same rate.   Wherefore tis but weakely done to say you will not think ; and tho you *must* think, to say you will not Ratiocinate, is to sever heate from Light, which will not doe—or to say again that tho' you do Ratiocinate we shall noe more heare on't.   You may better say soe much touching Gunpowder, for tis a child when borne that cannot be murtherd.   Light when generated will shine out and wisdome must still crye alowd in the streetes.   Wherefore, deare Cousin, make a virtue of Necessity, and

---

[1] Raleigh was credited with the burning of Cadiz, though this was done after he had been wounded in the assault.   Beyond this he seems to have been responsible for nothing more than the burning of a Spanish village on the Orinoco in 1616.   Possibly Southwell is here confusing him with Drake.

what you cannot Resist or suppresse, lett us have it with a good Grace, and as it were, have amongst you blind Harpers.[1]

While I was too credulous of your first anger (which yett I congratulate), I went to ransack all my papers, and have putt together in one Treasure all that ever I had from you, and which shall lye together an Heire-loom not only for this Neddy, but all the Neddyes that may come hereafter.

As to your present worke ; the very Patterne is Admirable—to teach men how to present to the World with vitalls, and not with long Haire and Nailes which comonly make up the bulke. But Cousin, this Herb is a peculiar of your owne Garden, and be not angry if it springs not up in every soyle. For me to attempt to propagate This method in my Neighbourhood as you propose,[2] would be to destroy it. I am not their favorite, which I really congratulate, as much as I prefer Philosophy before drinking.

I can truly tell you that tis neere a month that I writt to Mr Dickinson and Mr John Ellis in termes of as much concerne for you as I could expresse.

My small puggs are all well and very Joviall, for I have got them a blind Harper. I hope the like with my Godson and all his good company, being ever
Sr Your most affect Kinsman & most humble
servant
ROBERT SOUTHWELL

I am glad you have speeded orders about our old friend Wm Fitzgerald.

64. *Petty to Southwell.*

[The *Observations on the Dublin Bills of Mortality* were followed by *Another Essay in Political Arithmetic concerning the Growth of the City of London*, similarly published

---

[1] *I.e.* musicians who produced their music almost unconsciously.
[2] *I.e.* by collecting the vital statistics of Bristol.

for Mark Pardoe in 1683 (Hull, *Bibliography*, No. 13, p. 641).

In its original edition a note was inserted at the commencement of this book explaining to the reader that it had been called "Another Essay" because it had been originally intended as a sequel to an essay on the broader question of the "Growth, Encrease and Multiplication of Mankind". The first essay, however, had not been forthcoming at the time of going to press, so that part only which related to the growth of London came to be published.

Petty had sent Southwell both essays in manuscript, but Southwell's criticisms (which are met by Petty in this letter in a jocular strain) had evidently been directed rather to the missing essay on the "Multiplication of Mankind" than to the second on the "Growth of London".

Petty's theories on this subject of Multiplication, though perhaps not intended to be taken *au pied de la lettre*, were (as we shall see later on) the subject of fresh strictures on the part of his correspondent, and it was no doubt owing to these criticisms that the ' Multiplication ' essay was never published.]

London, ye 17° Feb^r 1682/3

Dr Cosen

You have in words applauded my late Discourse *Of the Growth of London*, But have indeed damned the same by intimating that the two great points (vizt, of the time wherein the world will bee fully peopled, and the sufficiency of Ireland to furnish graves and Boddys for all that have died since the Creation) are not examinable, [but] onely asserted in the same manner that Tho. Mall and Mrs Pipho [1] might have avered themselves to be Adam and Eve. Wherefore this trouble is to raise you and Mr Alcock back from runing into such an error.

To which purpose I say (1) That any man by measuring a Globe, may find that the contents of the dry Land is under 50 thousand millions of acres. (2) I know no nation in the world that hath one head to two acres and a half of Land ; and therefore 20 thousand millions of people must fully stock 50 thousand millions of acres. (3) If there bee 320

---

[1] I have been unable to discover who are the characters here alluded to.

millions of people now upon the face of the Earth (for which there is very good grounds) ; then 360 years hence (or Anno 2042) there will bee 640, and Anno 3842 there will bee 20480 millions.[1]

As for the other great point. You must take the table which conteyns the severall Periods of doubling the People from the ffloud to this day, to bee a good estimate of the same, Because it solves all the Phenomena of Scripture upon ground Experimentally true. And, that a fortyeth part dye per annum, depends upon the experience of one in 50 dying per annum in the Country, and one out of 30 in the Citty,—the medium whereof is 40 ; and then it follows that 12,570 millions have dyed since the floud.

That there are 28 thousand square miles in Ireland may be tryed by the map ; and that a mile square will afford 4 millions of graves, at a medium between the Boddyes of full grown men and Infants, is also true by computation. Wherefore the whole ascertion is not onely true, but examineable also ; and that Thom Mall and Mrs Pipho were Adam and Eve is examinably false, for that it is impossible they should have had 320 millions of children.

And now Cosen, by paying the additionall Postage of this Letter, take heed how you provoke mee any more ! Present my service to Dear Neddy and all your Little ones, whose noise in my howse shall bee as the melody of a chest of Viols, especially if wee can get any Right or beleif of Demonstration from the Grandees.
                              I am Yrs

                                             W. P.

65. *Southwell to Petty.*

[Thomas Thynne of Longleat, " Tom of Ten Thousand ", who had married Elizabeth, the heiress of the Percy estates, had been murdered by her lover, Konigsmark, in 1682. He was succeeded by his cousin Sir Thomas Thynne, the Viscount Weymouth mentioned in this letter.

[1] *I.e.* 64 times 320 millions.

The subject of Bankers was exciting a good deal of public attention. It had been discussed in a pamphlet entitled *The Case of Bankers and their Creditors more fully stated and explained*, published a few years before. It was perhaps this brochure which had excited Lord Weymouth's enquiry. Petty's reply, "Wherein the Lamb may wade and the Elephant may swim", may be found in his paper *On Bankrupts* (*Papers*, No 76).]

Kingsweston, 16 Aprill 1683

Deare Cousin

Your last demonstration was soe killing, and in a matter of that bulke and importance, that I have remayned ever since as one that had seene a miracle.

My Lord Weymouth, who is in the Role of your admirers, was lately here with me. We shall both meet by the end of this month in London, and are not to be long from your House. He was wishing he had your thoughts on the great catastrophe of Banquers ; wheather land will Rise, or what may be the most probable consequences thereof.

But, deare cousin, must you have [had] a fortunate hearing in the Treasury uppon Saturday last,[1] and must I owe the glad tydings rather to one of your Judges than your selfe ? Well ! *Laus Deo*, which I heartily pronounced first in consideration of Kerry, and then of nature and Philosophy. For if the World will but give you Rest, I am sure you will be Teeming.

My 3 Girles have beene coughing till quite tyred out, but the approach of a London Journey seemes very restorative.

With true Service to my lady, my godson, and the Rest

I am ever, Sr Your most affect Cousin & most humble servant

Robert Southwell

---

[1] The allusion is to a decision of the Lords of the Treasury to remove the land claimed by Petty in County Kerry from the ' custodium ' of his enemies the ' Farmers ' (Petty MSS.).

66. *Petty to Southwell.*

London, ye 19⁰ Aprill 1683

Dʳ Cosen

To yours of the 16⁰. I say nothing of my Demonstrations about the Growth of London. When you come, in reference to my Lord Waymouth's questions concerning Bankrupts, I will shew you a scheme of a Bankrupt wherein the Lamb may wade, and the Elephant may swim &c.

I had a little opium [1] given mee on Saturday last, of which I said nothing, as doubting it might be corrected with Castorium and other strong Ingredients,—as it hath been. But I being dosd and Stupifyed, can make no Judgement of it, but am sqird back like the weavers shuttle into Ireland, there to endure time and chance.

The fitts of the Double-Bottome do returne very fiercely upon mee. [2] I cannot bee diswaded but that it conteynes most glorious, usefull and pleasant things. My happiness lyes in being mad. I wish I were grown up to that Degree as to beleive I were fairly dealt with. I doe not attribute my wrongs to much hatred of my Person, as to other internall motions within the lucky Men of Power. Wee long here to see how wan the 3 girls will bee when they come to their cosens hither.

I am Yoʳˢ

W. P.

I desire you to get mee an Account of some Parishes according to the Method enclosed. [3]

---

[1] Evidently the "favourable hearing in the Treasury" to which Southwell alluded in the previous letter.

[2] Petty's third double-bottom ship was put in hand in the following year (*vide infra*, p. 128 foll.).

[3] The "Method enclosed" was no doubt that given in tabulated form in the *Petty Papers* (vol. i. p. 180).

67. *Petty to Southwell.*

[Petty had returned to Ireland in the summer of 1683. He had failed to secure the administration of the Irish Revenue, but had been so far successful as to obtain a promise from the King of one-fifth of any additional revenue accruing to the Irish Exchequer as a result of the advice which he had given. The promise (of which there is a copy among the MSS.) is dated May 24, 1683, and is certified by the Lord Privy Seal (Halifax), the Lord-Lieutenant (Ormond) and the Lord Treasurer (Rochester).]

Dublin, 25th Feb^r 1683/4

Cousin

To yours of the 16th. I am just now going to Trym upon a charitable account, But must stay till I have made you some small answer, in order to stop the violent bleeding of our Wound.

As for the ship Experiments, I have used them as Opium to stupify the sense of my sufferings; nor would I have any friends doe himself harme raising or pressing them.

Concerning Kerry, my peculiar Misery is That it is grown soe vast that no man understands the whole, Though some of late have studied some parts or shares of it. Wherefore I doe again tell you, That my Printed Papers, the Auditors' account lodged with the Lords of the Treasury, the King's Letters of April 1676, Decem^{er} 1677, and the 9th March 1679,[1] and the Papers I sent you a little before this Expedient, doe sufficiently comprehend the whole; and he that hath an ear to hear, may hear from them my Lamentable Condi͠con.

*   *   *   *   *   *

God Almighty bless you and your Brood and reward to [you the kindness] you show me. As for my own Children, you have heard that Twas my

---

[1] These were letters addressed to the Lord-Lieutenant in reply to the constant petitions lodged by Petty for relief in the matter of Quit-rents (*supra*). He appears to have derived little advantage from them.

ambiĉon to be their Schooll Master, but [they will] not suffer it. Wherefore They must grope out a [way] and follow such a Course of Life as the Genius which God has [put] in them doth best incline them to

I need not say I [am] yrs

W. P.

Just at taking Coach I made experiment upon 4 Bodys which did jointly and severally justify the highest Rants that ever I made in this matter.[1] Nevertheless be as sparing as you please about it—

Res nolunt male administrari.

68. *Southwell to Petty.*

London, 10 Aprill. 1684

Deare Cousin

Tis houres agoe that I was sitting downe to write, when in came 4 long winded visitants who have successively wasted the day.

I meant to have acknowledged yours of the 22nd past,[2] which is a descant uppon that Report of Mr Sollicitour's which is Inclosed, and which in conclusion seemes onely to affect the clearing of Marshall's Lands from Arrears by the King's allowing 1680£ to those who owe him thousands and may never pay a grote.

*   *   *   *   *   *

I will say noe more of the land, but as to sea affaires. Here is Mr Pepys come who will bee the proper object of your navall addresses in the future.[3] He beggs what I relate unto him, and he shall have

---

[1] This is an allusion to the experiments with modells of double-bottom ships in which Petty was deeply engaged at this time.

[2] This letter is no longer extant.

[3] Pepys was now reinstated as Secretary to the Navy and continued in that office till the end of James II.'s reign.

the papers I copyed which at this houre are with Sir Anthony Deane.[1]

As for the other hand you addrest too before,[2] his genius strikes not soe high and you are not to wonder if he flaggs, but if you tell him of an easy Coach or Chariot you bring him to bedd.

I read with delight your last to my lady and your sonn's, and of the legacy you leave them. The proposed great improvment in Navigation shall goe (by my ladyes favour) to Mr Pepys. But as to your Poetry,[3] I shall make bold to putt in a Caveat that it goe noe further. It may 20 yeares hence be read with admiration, but now it would destroy the very thing that it applaudes. Lett the babe be content with swaddling clothes; for tho the oracle whispers to the Parent 'It will proove a Heroe'; yett if the Speare, Launce, & Targett be presently bought, the young swordmen will goe neere to mutiny and stifle him.

Deare Cousin, you see the liberty I take. I am the next weeke going with my little ones into the country, which in your behalfe I regrett the lesse because I think your businisse will cheifily lye on that syde.

But if you would have my friend see on some particular occasions how things stand, you may yett write to me under cover to Mr Madox at the Councill office, and leaving your letter open, he shall have direction to shew it.

I have only roome to add that I am Y[rs]

R. S.

---

[1] Sir Anthony Deane (1638–1721), shipbuilder and commissioner of the navy. The papers in question were no doubt some of Petty's long dissertations on the improvement of shipping (by the use of double-bottom boats) which survive in MS. The correspondence on this subject shows that Petty made constant efforts to secure Government support for his invention, through the instrumentality of Pepys and Deane, though he got nothing out of them but a series of wagers against the success of his boat (*infra*, p. 132).

[2] Sir John Worden, who has been already mentioned in connection with Petty's travelling chariot.

[3] Apparently a poem on the double bottom.

69. *Petty to Southwell.*

Dublin, 19 April 1684

Cousin

To yours of the 10th. I have sent the *Dialogue of Devills*, written at Aylesbury whilst my shoulder of Mutton was roasting. It is a subtile and spirituall subject; and therefore wonder not that it is not brought fully under sence and reason. Enquire who hath done more, and keep it to yourselfe till you find that.

I have written to Sir John Werden very hopefull news of the Carriage hee longs for; viz, which contemns the asperity of any way wherein horses can tread. I have also sent him the scheme of Enquieries I made concerning this whole matter, and a few principall Experiments already made uppon the same matter.[1] I concur with you about the poetry. T'is too early and *ante victoriam triumphum canere*;[2] besides the last verses hath a botch in it, which is since well mended, or may be time enough.

Your answer to the 2 points of my intended petition is an answer to my manny prayers: viz. that God should bring those who have erred and are deceived into the way of truth. In the enquiry into the 4 points you mention is the way of truth, which I hope will bring [us] to truth itself. What you say of the ' Scraps ' is suitable to the present methods, but those scraps (at little quit rent) was part of the price for which I submitted to the Lord of Essex. Gods will be done! You have done your part; and now you mention charges, discharges, and surcharges, I could, like Dol Common in the ' Alchemist ',[3] run out into a new ocean of complaints that much of this hath been done, and other parts I have many times begged to have done. " Let's look forward " &c.

I have written to Mr Pepys to wellcome him home (after) the Many Conflicts they have had with

---

[1] Cf. *supra*, p. 13, and *Papers*, Nos. 124 and 125.
[2] *Ante victoriam ne canas triumphum*, proverb.
[3] By Ben Jonson.

fire and water,[1] not to importune him to presse on
the Shipping Experiments. I can have partners
enough here, when I am sure that the King would
have it take effect; wherein wee erred before. We
have conquerd the Ridicule part, so as there remaynd
but one objection, viz, whether it would do in salt
water as in fresh. Whereunto was answered: That
since there was a way to make salt water fresh, it
was but our makeing the whole ocean so &c.

Pray thank on my behalfe these friends who keep
Kerry business afloate, so as wee may be ready to
saile if wind presents.

O Cousin, wee want a wind! This rowing at
oares against wind and tide breakes my heart. The
best rights and reason are but oares, favour and
kindnes are the wind, and I am but a Galley slave
&c. I should scarce beare your departure from
London, but that I think you may be back againe
before we have on this side gott through the 4 points
and Scraps. Kiss Neddy and all my cosens for me.

Yrs

W. P.

70. *Petty to Southwell.*

Dublin, 28 Junii. 1684

D[re] Cousin

I have defered answering yours of—till now.
I can assure you our Money, Materialls, Master,
Modell are all fixt to begin on Monday the 30 instant
upon the Sluice building. Wee heare of politicall
Objecōns, but cannot see them. Mr Pepys hath
answered neither of my 2 letters—perhaps upon this
accompt. God help us and save us from suffering
for our good deeds.

I am glad the dialogue of [Devils] pleased you.
Let the last distich of the Epigram bee mended thus:

" Si Veteres geminis conferes ab inertibus istas
    Daedaleo has factum Rege putabis opus."

---

[1] Pepys had accompanied Lord Dartmouth on his expedition for demolishing
Tangier, whence he had just returned (*Pepys Correspondence*, Aug. 7, 1683).

The Commissioners of Grace [1] are very busy.   I
see nothing yet to quarrell at and, If I did, will not.
Sed sinam mundum vadere sicut vult.   My reference
lying before the Commissioners of the Revenue
creepes sadly on, but the 608£ per annum losse to
the King is already shrunk to 329£ &c.   Oh, I could
run on for 10 sheetes upon this tack ; but I here anchor
on the stiff ground of being

Yours and Neddyes &c most honest kinsman &
humble servant

W^M PETTY

Postscript

If I had anything worth troubling you Sir, this
paper should not goe without another, tho it be only
to assure you that we are all your most humble
servants.

E. P.[2]

71. *Petty to Southwell.*

Dublyn, ye 12th July 84

Dear Cousen

Tis but Late since we have heard the certainty of Sir Edward Deering's [3] death ; but now
finding it too true, we heartily Condole with you
therein and bewail our-selves, that we are therby put
out of that way which we hoped would have brought
us to quiet. If Sir Edward Deering had been as
much above 70 as he was above 50, we should have
thought his death to have been a deliverance from
many Irksome Inconveniencys ; but dying at about
57 years of age, we must resent that his friends have
lost 20 years usu-fruit of his Excellent Talents ; and
therefore we do again heartily Condole with you and

---

[1] The ' Commission of Grace ' had been appointed in the previous year,
with the object of confirming the titles of those in possession of Irish land, and
of granting manorial and other privileges to such as were prepared to pay for
them.

[2] Elizabeth Petty. She had joined her husband in Dublin during the
previous month.   The two letters which follow are in her hand.

[3] Southwell's father-in-law.

Lament our Loss in him, praying God to repair it some other way.

We are now ready to transmit several reports and accounts about our business, so we are like to be Like sheep without a Shephard, and perhaps Led to the Slaughter.

The Sluice Shipe hath been 12 days in hand and goes on at the usuall Rate. A Chariott is now also goeing from hence for England, which will Cary a Rider and the Rideing Driver, with about 20 lb weight of Necessarys, with one horse, as farr and as well as the same horse would cary one Man upon his backe. Moreover one man without any horse at all can draw one Rider up and down the streets, with halfe the Labour that a chair-man takes.[1] These Chariots doe a Little stupyfie the sence of our sufferings—we wish this relation of them may divert you.

Charles is now learning Virgile's Georgicks, as pure Latine and excelent Poem, and the best Rules for the old and most honest Trade of Husbandry. Before we write more, Let us hear from you how you have digested the smart of your Blow, that we may not be impertinent or importune, for our desires are much the contrary ; being, dear Cousen

Yr most affect huble serv[ts]

W[M] PETTY. E. PETTY

72. *Petty to Southwell.*

Dublyn, ye 9 Aug 84

Dear Cousin

I have yours from Astrop [2] of the 28th past and expect another from London, at your Condolement there, but fear you will be gone from thence before this reach you.

---

[1] Cf. *Of Calashes*, 1686 (*Papers*, No. 124).
[2] ? Adlestrop, near Chipping Norton.

On the 17 past bundles of Reports were sent from hence on my behalfe, even from Mr Solicitor and the Commissioners of the Revenue. I'm allso forceing the understandings of the Commissioners of Grace to the same purpose, but Can't Learn with Certainty what effect it had on the Lords of the Treasury. Tis a sad thing to grope in the darke as I doe. Pray learn some answer to this question if you can, and what end is really made with Ld Rannelagh, the Forths,[1] and Sir James Shaen ; for their friends say all is Concluded, but I do not hear it from others.

The Chariott is done, and so as I verily beleive can never be much improv'd. This day ends the 6th weeke of the Sluice being a Building. The objection which I make is, that the workmanshipe is mean, Clouterly [2] and very dear, but in all other points very hopefull. And I say, and say again Dear Cousin, she will be the strongest vessell I ever saw ;—Big enough to goe Round the World, and smale enough to goe from the Key of Dublyn to the Key of Chester ; and able to goe to sea in all Winds and Weathers, and Cary Saile when noe other vessell can. The next month's full moon will tell you more.

Dear Cousin Neddy Can't Loose his time in Learning so much of the Georgicks by heart as Containe the pure Rules of Husbandry. I'm heartily sorry for what you tell me of your sister Jane ; we must give Nature Leave to Worke. I thank you for the account of Sir Edward's Exit, for he Dyed with that serenity of mind and moderate pains that I my self pray for.

I strain hard to be at London in Michaelmas Terme, in the mean time God preserve you and yours. We are well in health, I prais God, and with all respect and affection are

Yrs &c.

---

[1] Alderman John Forth was one of the Farmers of the Revenue.
[2] ? Clumsy.

73. *Southwell to Petty.*

Kingsweston, 20 Sept. 1684

Deare Cousin

I had not till the last night yours of the 31st past,[1] which I have read over and over, for the great kindnesse as well as varyety of it.

I see the Vulture is still knawing in Kirry, when at the same time a man child is borne to make you forgett that sorrow. Surely this new shipp has stupifyed that other anguish ; and you might be exalted too much, but for that other dead weight that keepes your life in ballance. In the Life of Paulus Emilius by Plutark there are these words :

" It seemes the province of some God to lessen that hapinesse which is too great and inordinate, and soe mingle the affaires of human life that noe one should be entirely free and exempt from Calamitys, but (as it is in Homer) that those should think themselves truly blest to whom fortune has given an equall share of good and evill." [2]

But as to the shipp, you forgett to inclose the Catalogue of wagers,[3] which I lament. If she take into Kingrode on her way about, I will be answerable for her good reception here.

As to Kirry, I now write and lend your letter to Mr Pepys, not onely for his Entertainment, but that he excite Mr Guy [4] to all that is friendly ; and in particular that Mr Dickinson may be called uppon, not only to ease the Patient, but the Doctors alsoe, who confesse they know not what to make of the Case.

But I am at some stand how to thinke of all that

---

[1] This letter is not extant.

[2] Plutarch's reflection was induced by the fact that Paulus Aemilius lost two of his sons at the very moment when he was celebrating his ' triumph '.

[3] A list of fifteen ' propositions ' or points on which Petty was prepared to back his double-bottom ship is among the Petty MSS. His challenges were in December taken up by Sir Anthony Deane and Mr. Pepys (*infra*, p. 132 ; Fitzmaurice, p. 266).

[4] ? Henry Guy (1631–1710), politician. He was Secretary to the Treasury from 1679 to 1688, and a boon companion of Charles II.

is past, and what the Reports now depending may signify, if you are (as you say) beginning all anew under the new Commission. Nor doe I heare you presse on Judgment for the Reduced Collumn, or wheather it be already done or not, whereas in this great point seemed formerly to consist your antidote [to] the Thunderbolt.

I would have repeated my visitt to my deare Cousins in London, but that I hurry'd away on the sickness of my 2 eldest Daughters, who attending their Grandmother at Bath, mett with this new feavour which hath humbled them ; For they are still but creeping towards the health and vigour which they formerly had. And this alsoe makes our resolution of a quiett wintering in the Country the more needfull, while between the Apple Roaster and the Blind Harper (who is sent for), we shall forgett the long and blustering nights.

I rejoyce exceedingly that my Cousin Charles is in the Carreere you like, and tis enough to make my Grumett [1] proud that you enquire how he climbes his ropes. He is very strong ; a stout rider—110 [miles] in 2 days and $\frac{1}{2}$—going 46 the first day (when I lately sent him home from Peterbrough) all on the trott, and one day thunder and rayne to the skin. He will Learne anything on Horseback, and if repeated by his Tutour, in half the time he can doe it from the booke. Formerly his worke was to gett many of the finest passages that lay about in verse and Prose, which I reckon he will never forgett, but serve hereafter as good materialls when he has judgment to spinn them out. He is now chiefly intent to be absolute master of Caesar's Comentarys, and is learning his Greeke Grammer, in order to some sprinkling onely of that tongue. There are Virgill's Georgicks, Plutark's Lives (as newly translated) and other like things for the by. But wee are now going seriously into Arithmetick, Geometry, Astronomy and Cosmography, or some tincture or Instruction towards

---

[1] *Grummet* or *gromet* = a cabin-boy (Skeate).

them, by the helpe of one Ferfaix who is coming downe and to stay this winter at Least amongst us.

I have never prest or Strayned on the Boy to his booke, being content to lett him grow att the same time in other things; which his going about with me does bring in, As an acquaintance with all my friends and the Business that is depending between us. He reads all my Letters and all the Answers I make, and sometimes he answers some for me, and will write a Letter passing well. He designes and has a Musicall Voyce; but when all is done, he loves play in his Heart. I have here sayd enough for 7 yeares; with all duty to my Lady and love to Charles

I am ever

74. *Petty to Southwell.*

[" The Fits of the Double Bottom " which had assailed Petty during the previous year (*supra*, p. 117) had led to the building of yet another ' sluice boat ' on a larger scale than any of her predecessors. She was named *St. Michael the Archangel*. The new ship had been commenced in June and successfully launched, though not without dis-agreements between the ' partners ' whom Petty had pre-vailed upon to put up the money for her construction. The next two letters record her failure, which when she was tried under sail was definite and complete. " She performed so abominably as if built on purpose to disappoint in the highest degree in every particular that was expected of her," while the seamen swore they would not venture over the bar in her for £1000 a piece (Molyneux to Ashton, *Petty MSS.*).

But Petty was entirely unrepentant. In a long letter addressed to Samuel Pepys and Sir Anthony Deane about the middle of December 1684, he goes over the whole ground, explaining the motives by which he had been impelled to " pursue the improvement of shipping upon new principles " and how the fates (as well as the King) had always been against him. He suggests that " it is better for myself that the same should terminate in disaster and disappointment, so as the King may be justified in all he hath said and have such a victory as himself desires—that my follies may be the foil of his wisdom and that I may be his Scaramouch ". His letter concludes with this characteristic peroration : " Wherefore in the name of God—instead of these wages, instead of raising contentions, invidious and dangerous emulations—if the improvement of shipping be desirable, do some better thing towards it. If you think the new principle desperate (whereas we think that what hath happened is but a bowpeep of Fortune), refute it by the same methods that we have asserted it. If you think it difficult and glorious if effected, offer some proportionable helps and rewards, suitable to all the great circumstances of the matter. Do not dishearten us by offering only Rigging to one small vessel as a full reward for blessing the whole world to the world's end " (Petty MSS.).]

Dublyn, ye 4 Decem^{br} 84

To yours, Dear Cousen, of the 13th past. I never recevd any Letter from Mr Pepyes, Mr Hewer, or Mr Houblon [1] Concerning the Ship—Be pleas'd to enquir the reason of it. I had a kind one from Sir Anthony Dean, wherin he aproves of 5 principal Points, but doubteth of another more Certain than any of the rest.

I hear from good hands that the King cometh about, but like a ship that carieth much dead Water, for I find he hath never been enformd by a friend that understood the matter. The severall accounts which you have had of Experiments, together with what Sir John Percevall Lately had, is more than you need, and I Nausiate the harpeing Longer on that string. Wherefore I pass to another sort of account of the same matters, viz : The Mutiny that arose amongst the Partners 14 days before the Launching, was not apeasd till a month after, nor was any worke done in that time. We were so abusd in the Building, the Management wherof I ever declind, that the Charge therof amounted to 3 times the Comon Market

---

[1] Hewer was Pepys' clerk, and Houblon a merchant, mentioned in his *Diary*—probably the John Houblon who later became the first Governor of the Bank of England and died in 1712.

Rate—the mischiefe wherof they would have cast upon me, for haveing made not only an erronious, but also (as I think they meant) a fraudulent Computation of the matter.[1]   From whence, Let Dear Cousin Neddy Learn how to trust multitudes with his Merite, be his Cause and Cariage never so good.   I hope noe better from some other hands; but my Worke is my Wages, and my Expence is my Profite, and I hope my Wrongs will prove my Recreations.   And for this I thank God.

The New Accounts of the Ship which I meant are no more of Models, but the History of the Ship '*Archangell*' itself, not extending my discourse or Conjectures any further : saying hence-forward ' Let you who are a Cold Blow the Fire ', ' Let the Blind Lead the Blind ', ' Let the Dead Bury the Dead ', knowing that after all this *Res nolunt male adminis-trari*, and that things which are of God will stand.

The account of this Ship is thus :

1°. At her Launching she drew 40 Inches Water astern and 50 ahead.

2°. That the weight of two Deckes and Masts, sogging in the water for about 5 weeks time, encreased this draught 4 inches at each end.

3°. Having setled the Knowledge of her Draught, we added two Triangular false Keeles, wherby we now swime upon a Levell Keele, intending to Trime her with stones, that is to adapt her swiming to the Quantity of Canvass Charged upon each Mast, and the distance of the said Masts.   Which is the next Peece of Art to be performed, before she saileth in Earnest.

4°. We have sett her Maine Mast, which is 55 foot high, above her Upper Decke, and her fore-mast 48 foot above the same, at which the Faith of my New Disciples began to Stagger.   But to Clear this, we brought her upon the Carine, and (to be short) did find that 9 men, at a double Tackle fastend 29 foot

---

[1] Some of Petty's original partners in the undertaking had ' run out ' owing to the high costs of building.

above the Decke, were required to bring her down, and that 4 men more, weighing 600 weight, Runing out to the Extremity of her Mast, were not felt by her. All which with her violent Riseing, which the Sea-men Terme very angryly, have Convinct the World that she will bear saile to the full of my Calculations.

5°. Within the time of this Carining, the Tides fell out very Irregularly which caused our vessell to Lye Aground upon one Keele and one Bilge, so as 20 Tun Weight strain'd upon the Sliuce and its Beams without makeing her Leaky in the Least, which is a mighty Argument of her strength.

6°. She was Towed down from Lazy Hill[1] to Rings-End with a Boat of 4 oares, with double the speed expected.

Haveing done with these important matters, we come to the Bawbles our Children, viz : I do not know how you could have educated my Cousin Neddy better than you have, and hope that one day Arith-meticke and Accountantshipe will adorne a Young Woman better than a suit of Rubands, and keepe her Warmer than a Damnable dear Manto.

If God-son Charles grows Like a Weede without much Culture or help of the Gardiners, perhaps it may be never the worse. For the Race will not be to the swift, nor the Batle to the Strong ; nor will favor goe to the Men of Skill, or Bread to the Men of Understanding.

As to Kerry, it Lyes before the Commissioners of the Revenue here, and the Commissioners of Grace, the Lord Lieutenant, the Court of Exchequer and the Lords of the Treasury in England. God grant that all this Riging may Run well through the severall Blocks ! What effect the Change will have I know not. 'Tis said that when things are at worst they

---

[1] ' Lazar's Hill ', which was afterwards corrupted into ' Lazy ' or ' Lowsy Hill, was not far from Trinity College at the termination of Townsend Street. It was so called from the fact that a leper hospital had formerly stood there. Ringsend is the port of Dublin.

will mend—a poor encouragement for the pains I
have taken. In pitty to you, we will say noe more,
but that we are all Yr Most affect hūble serv^{ts} [1]

75. *Petty to Southwell.*

Dublin, 23° Xbr. 1684

Dear Cosen
Tho I am not upon my oath, yet for the
Honor of Eternall Truth, whom I have ever sought
and adoard, I will tell you the whole Truth, and
nothing but the Truth, concerning our Navall Experiments. Upon the 15th and 16th of this month,
wee got her out, to try her sailing &c, which did not
answer expectaĉon. The main fault (unto which all
the rest were Consequences) was not bearing sufficient
Saile, which the Careening I menĉoned in my last
seemed to secure our Gravest Ship-wrights and Seamen against; and is a fault the more easily remedyed
upon our Principle, which all our Modells do still
justify. But what is all that?—Wee have suffered a
Publiq disappointment!
Just now I received a joynt Letter from Mr Pepys
and Sir Anthony Deane, contayning severall wagers,
with a proposall That I must bee personally a board
upon all their trialls; with a proposall a little before
that if wee did excell all the King's yachts, that then
the Charge of our Rigging should be boaren. The
Consideraĉon of all which doth lessen my trouble
concerning this matter. I will calmly and gravely
spend the remainder of my days in diging for Truth
in this matter; and being conscious of no willfull
miscarriage therein, will courageously indure the
Reproches and derisions of the Vulgar; remaining
with my service to all of your family.
Yo^{rs} most intirely

W^M PETTY

---

[1] The letter is in Lady Petty's hand.

PART II

UNDER KING JAMES II

1685–1687

76. *Petty to Southwell.*

[KING CHARLES II. died in February 1685. One of the first acts of his successor was to recall the Duke of Ormond, and it soon became apparent that the Settlement was in jeopardy under the new monarch. Petty decided to return to England, where he no doubt hoped that he might do something to stem the torrent which was threatening to engulf his concerns in Ireland.

The Dublin Philosophical Society had been inaugurated by Molyneux and Petty during the previous year on lines similar to those of the Royal Society. Petty was its first president and Molyneux its secretary. The Rules of the Society and some ' Advertisements ', containing proposals for modelling its future progress, appear to be Petty's handiwork and are printed in the *Papers* (Nos. 105 and 106). The Dublin Society was soon to wither in the unfavourable atmosphere which preceded the Revolution, though it was revived in a somewhat altered form during the following century.]

Dublin, 17 March 1684/5

Deare Cousin

I long since receved yours with the enclosed from Mr Pepys, but by reason of my sorenes with the blowes of Misfortune (now pretty well cured in the beliefe of my principles), and the great changes which have hapned since (and which will bring mee and my family shortly for England), I have not answered you. Nor had I now, but that I heard yesterday by chance that you are in London, where I presume you will stay till my Lord of Ormond's coming thither.

And now I have begun, I know not what to write that may be gratefull to you, without offerring you drink that stinks of the pot fumed with my owne concernments : Viz. (1) I will bring over two great chests of Modells and other apparatus for Experiments, which shall exercise the talents of your Sophie.   (2) I intend to bring over The Specimen of the *Survey of Ireland*—in Countyes, Baronyes, parishes and town-lands.[1]   (3) The Auditor's accompts of 40 m. wrongs done mee in Kery, which hath now past the view of all my adversaryes here and in England.   (4) Your Godson—a garden of weeds, wherein are tall Thistles, Nettles, and hemlock with other *sponte creata*.   Hee would beare other things, but I am not qualifyed to plant him or gett him planted.

Having thus troubled you at the old rate with my owne concerns, what shall I say of yours, But that you would stay my stomack with Down-Survey of my Cozen Neddy's proceeding, nor of the arrable, meadow, pasture, gardens, timber, groves, fisheryes &c, planted upon him, as also of the Arithmeticall Achievements performed by my pretty shee Cousens. Tell me also in grosse how the great pendulum vibrates, how long you intend to stay at London, and what you are doing ?

Our Dublin Society is pretty well thriven.   They have already as much Contribution as they need spend. Their number is above 30, whereof the greater part are very sufficient men.

Our protestant churches are thronged with extra-ordinary numbers ;[2] whose the cause is I do not clearly see.   My Lord Duke, on whom I waited this Morning, took notice of it to me without any hint given him.   I propounded to him That in the expected apportionment of the poll-charge upon the severall parts of his Majesty's dominions, That Ireland (who not having the tenth part of the Wealth of England) may bee chargd with a full tenth and no more of whatever England payes.   I bid you

---

[1] *I.e.* the maps of the Down Survey, which it was Petty's intention to have printed in large as well as in small scale.   The county and provincial maps were however the only ones published.

[2] In order to show their sympathy with the Duke of Ormond on his recall (*Life of the Duke of Ormonde*, Lady Burghclere, ii. 703).

think of 6 lines from the parlment (?) of England to conforme things in Ireland.

I have just now yours of the 7th. As for the Sliuce Built [I mean] to leave it to time and Chance, and hope my Endeavour have been no Crime against the Government. I heartily wishe you may be of the Parliament.[1] We hope the next Month to come to give you thanks for your favors to our Little family.

We are Dear S^r Y^r affec^t hūble serv^{ts}

77. *Petty to Southwell.*

Dr Coz
Dublin, 20 March, between 2 & 3 in ye afternoon [1685]

Just now my Lord Duke is going on board. In my last to you I declined all mencõn of Kery, In this I make nothing else. Our Lords of the revenue did yesterday write to my Lord Treasurer Rochester to declare his pleasure upon the many Letters and reports sent to the Lords of the Treasury about July last and since. I beg you to desire Mr Guy to look them all out and present them to his Lordship, and presse his Lordship to do something upon them. The Reduced Collumn is far best for the King, but Let his Lordship do what hee pleases. I'll say no more— Let nature worke. Adieu

W. P.

78. *Petty to Southwell.*

Dr Coz
Dublin, 23 Aprill 1685

I thank you for your 2 letters purely about my buisines; I dare not appear much for it myself, for feare of the Breeden's[2] Freinds. My Wife and

---

A new Parliament was about to be elected following the death of Charles II. Southwell was returned member for Lostwithiel.

[2] John Breden was one of the Farmers of the Revenue.

your Godson, with Jemy Waller, intend to ship for
England to morrow, and myselfe about 10 dayes
after, or according to what I shall heare of the arrivall
of my goods already sent to London, which with what
I have to bring, will bee entertainment to some.   I
have rumaged and Methodized my papers which
amount to 53 chests, and are so many monuments of
my Labours and Misfortunes.

I will ad no more, but that I am Yours &c

W. P.

79. *Petty to Southwell.*

[Petty, as may be seen by the concluding paragraph of
this letter, had still hopes of King James should His Majesty
be well advised.   But it was not very safe to write about
politics at this time, so he talks about other things.

" His Majesty's forces at Hounslow," which Charles
had been to see, were the 30,000 men which, after the suppression of the Monmouth rebellion, King James insisted
on keeping as a standing army—for the purpose of overawing
the capital.

The news from the Continent concerned the fighting
between the Emperor and the Turks.   Charles, Duke of
Lorraine, who had married the Emperor's sister and commanded his forces, had recently obtained some notable
successes.   The siege of Vienna had been raised and Gran
in Hungary taken in 1683, and more recently the town of
Neuhäusel had been recaptured from the Turks.   The victory of the Christian army over that of the Infidels excited
great enthusiasm, and numerous pamphlets on the subject
were printed in London about this time.]

London, 22 Augt 1685

Dear Cosen

When my wife and I had taken the ayre
and water at Epsom about 12 days, and were in the
coach comeing away, wee had a terrible overthrough,
which hurt most of us more or lesse, but my wife so
terribly that for the first 3 days we doubted of her
Life.   After a full months suffering under her bruises,

wee brought her home last night, past fear (as we believe) of any irrepareable hurt.

Charles &c have been this day at Hounslo Heath, and seen the noble appearances of his Majesties forces ; and have also heard, at the second hand from the King himself, That New Leusell is taken by Storme, and that all the Forces in it were put to the sword ; and also That, in releiving of Gran, 4000 Janisarys were cut off and the Duke of Lorrain in pursute of the Rest.

Your Book of Maps[1] is collourd. The thoughts not onely of Kerry, but of all Ireland, are now in my head. God send them well out.

Will you bee at London by the 9th of October when the Parliament sits, and help to do such things for the com̃on good, that no King since the Conquest besides His present Majesty can so easily effect ?

Wee are all here your very humble servants,

So am I

W[M] PETTY

80. *Southwell to Petty.*

Kingsweston, 25 Augst 1685

Deare Cousin

I am bound to thanke you for the good newes of ill Tydings, that is to say that I heare of recovery at the same time you tell me of the disease. I lament the misfortune of all and most particularly to my lady, who it seemes has sufferd as if she had fallen from a Steeple ! Pray putt me into good temper againe by assuring me that her Ladyship is not onely past danger, but past all payne or the least symptome of this unhappy affaire.

I am glad my Godson Charles has been making his Campayne at Hounslow and brought home soe signall a Victory against the Turks. The Newes is very good in itselfe and may have consequences in

---

[1] A copy of Petty's maps of Ireland (*Hiberniae Delineatio*) which had recently been printed.

it—I meane to encouraging in time the Duke of Loraine to looke after his owne.[1]

I perceive as to your owne particular, the thoughts of Ireland begin to drowne those of Kerry. Soe you have formerly noted that one evill is cured by an other—as the Heckup, by a fright. But pray have you any particular Instances as to the danger of the Settlement, more than what you gather from the Clouds, and some alterations in other things? Perhaps you remember the attempt in 1670, and the Commission of Inspection,[2] and the unextinguishable desire in many to unravell all. But do you discover any marks that the Government is fond of a new Scramble, or to be pestered with some yeares tinkering to frame a new Settlement, and putt all Trade, Improvement and Exchange in the meane time to a stand? I am here at a distance and therefore must be uppon the enquiring hand, and only know *Bonum est timere.*

I shall, God willing, be in London at or before the 9th of November, and wish I could help to sow the seedes of soe much good as you could dictate for his Majesty's Glory and the Comon Improvement. But among all your meditations and Contrivances, why might not you in a good way putt me in at the window and then I will open the dore for you? I meane that you contrive how I may strike into My Lord Treasurer's [3] favour and then you shall be call'd in next. It would be worth him ten yeares purchase of his Staff (?) that he but thought of you as I doe.

Shall I now tell you somewhat of the Country? I and my 3 spinsters spent a weeke at Badminton to take share in the nuptialls of my Lord Ossory [4] and

---

[1] *I.e.* to obtain possession of his own principality of Lorraine, which had been taken from him by the French.

[2] This Commission had been appointed in 1672 for the purpose of enquiring generally into the working of the Acts of Settlement and Explanation.

[3] Rochester, who was shortly to be dismissed in favour of Lord Bellasis.

[4] James Butler (1665–1745), afterwards second Duke of Ormond, eldest surviving son of Thomas, Earl of Ossory, who had died in 1680, and grandson of the first duke. He had married first (in 1682), Anne, the daughter of Lord Hyde, Earl of Rochester, and now secondly, Lady Mary Somerset, daughter of Henry, first Duke of Beaufort. The marriage was arranged by Southwell (cf. *Life of the Duke of Ormonde,* by Lady Burghclere).

we had our share of the Solemnity.   There is doubtlesse as great a prospect of happinesse as in wedlock
I ever saw.   There is Age, quality, fortune, principles,
and disposition, that run all in lines parallel, and they
sett forth at the greatest rate of kindlyness that you
can imagine.   Everybody is contented that has but
relation unto them.   The young lady is rich in vertue,
good Housewifery and great Civility ; and I'le assure
you the young lord will make bold to disappoint the
blades and give them short allowance of what they
formerly enjoyd.   They were here with us and the
Duke of Beaufort the other day, but they are shortly
comeing for a weeke.   And thus you have our Rurall
Gazette, and nothing to add but that my 3 girles are
well pleasd with the fields and like the Country aire,
yett in point of good manners are sensible they want
some what of the aire of the Towne.

'Tis welcome newes that your kind present of the
Mapps are coloured.   I will appoint Neddy to looke
after them.   My few Acres in and neere Kingsale
lye all in the Baronyes of Kinalea and Coursyes,
and in the Parishes following : St Multes (which is
Kingsale), Rincorran Parish, Clantead Parish, Texax
Parish, Kinure Parish and Brimy Parish.[1]   If I had
these 2 Baronyes and these 6 Parishes, I should think
I were very well fitted with mapps, but that shall be
a new Petition in November.

In the meane time I often think of your Advice
about the method for our young ones to read the
Bible.   I have now in my hand those hasty notes
I tooke, but pray when you have time to compleat
your Essay uppon that subject, lett me be soe happy
as to have a copy of It.

I hope my son will pay his duty now you and
my lady and his cousins are come to towne, and as
you make any mad versions [2] on him—I meane the

---

[1] These were the forfeited lands of Philip Barry Oge, which had been
granted to Southwell's father at the Restoration and subsequently (1666)
confirmed to him by letters patent.

[2] *Sic*, but ' animadversions ' is of course intended !

desiderata—pray lett me know them and I will drive the nailes up to the head.

I wish you and yours all happinesse, and am ever Sʳ Yʳ most affect & most humble servant

ROBERT SOUTHWELL

81. *Petty to Southwell.*

London, 29th August 1685

Dʳᵉ Coᶻ

To yours of the 25th. As to my wife's perfect Recovery, wee must have patience, but do not doubt it.

I agree with you in Hopes that the Duke of Lorrain may bee able to take downe the great Troubler of the World,[1] of whom Ireland ought to be jealous. I am also cleere that if men will but consider, our terrors concerning Ireland are not well grounded. I only feare what men drunk with Rage and Revenge may doe of harm to Themselves and others.

I congratulate what you say of the pretty Spinsters and the Rest of your Rurall Gazette.

I hope wee may answer your desires in the 2 Barrony Maps of land neere Kingsale when you come to Towne.

I think there needs be no formall Essay about what I hinted for reading the Scriptures, for (1st) We hold all equally canonised. (2) Tis Manifest that St Luke and the Acts are the best History of Christ and the Apostles. (3) The Epistles of Peter, James, John and Jude, are stiled Catholiq or Generall Epistles, directed to the whole world, and not to Particular Churches upon speciall occasions.[2] (4) They do manifestly containe the whole Christian Doctrine. I only add that the 2 Bookes of the Chronicles is the like Epitome of the History of the Jewish nation and Church.

---

[1] Louis XIV.
[2] Cf. " Church Service " (*Papers*, No. 39).

What you say of My Lord Treasurer[1] pleases me well, and I hope tis not an Embryon, but a *foetus prope partum*. Gett but into that organ loft and I will blow your bellowes, having wind enough for all your Pipes—I say Wind.

For further impositions about Neddy, I think them needless. You have planted all necessarys in his ground, you have led him through all the shops and warehouses of other things. Let nature now work. See what he will choose and learn of himself. What is crāmed in by much teaching will never come to much, but parch away when the Teachers are gone. Within a yeare or two you will have a crisis on him ;— let's mark that.

I am contented you will be here about the Parliament's sitting. What shall We say more, but the old assertion that I am Yours

W^M P.

Tell the spinsters what fine wooll and flax I wish them to work upon, and how good a market for their weares.

Postscript

I am angry that you did not speake a word, neither of Reason or Ridicule, uppon the Paper *for the Multiplication of Mankind*; as if that Desideratum were frivolous which I take to be equall to all the Projects which have been these many yeares for the advantage of the World. Pray send it back with an affidavit on the back of itt That you have neither shewne it to any fortunate fop, nor taken any copie of itt. In dudgeon : Adieu.

[The succeeding letters show that Petty was obsessed at this period by his schemes for the " Multiplication of Mankind ", and that his theories thereon provoked warm criticisms on the part of Southwell. The subject had already been mooted between the correspondents in 1683 (*supra*, pp. 114-115), but we have evidently here to do with a new paper, which was followed by others in a similar strain.

[1] As to the possibility of Southwell making interest for Petty in that quarter.

There can be no doubt that these various "Multiplication" papers went to form the introductory "Essay" which should have been, but was not, forthcoming when "Another Essay" (on the growth of London) went to press, and in place of which a synopsis only of the intended essay was given. (See Hull, pp. 454-455.)

The principal argument, however, between Petty and Southwell developed, as we shall see, round the tenth heading in that synopsis, *e.g.* whether the speedy peopling of the earth was for the good of mankind, according to the will of God and advantageous to the King of England.]

82. *Southwell to Petty.*

Kingsweston, 5 Sept 1685

Dear Cousin

I have yours in your own ill hand of the 29th past, but what you say of my Lady's Recovery makes ample compensation. Soe alsoe does your kind mention of the Spinsters, and the faire opineon of their Brother Neddy, and your Inculcateing the Method of reading the Holy Writt, which are all favours of Weight.

But you come off at last with a Biting Postscript. You chide that I say nothing of your Calculation, as if it were soe small a matter to speak Skilfully of Mankind, and to discourse in this Great Case (of) the Effects and power of Generation, as it were the putting of a dowsen of Eggs under a Henn!

Your Great Demonstration is first the Defect, then the Art, and lastly the value of *Multiplication*. And since you will force me to object, pray answer me this : Mankind must by your method become at last as thick as grasse—not 3 acres to a man, but 3 men to an acre, and what not! Nay the Sea alsoe must be covered as farr as timber can be gotten for stages and ships.

And now that I speak of a Shipp, What if your proposall had been made to those on the Arck, and the Deluge were to have lasted ? If getting children had not been restrained, the Shipp at last must have sunk or the Surplus gone over-board. Wherefore if the Tower you build, — how beautiful soever in the progress—must by its own heighth or weight fall at last, what need we rayse it higher then it is?

Then your Great art cannot remain a Secret, as the Philosopher's Stone, or be monopolized by Letters Patent; for all Men are become Philosophers in this Science. And if the noise that one Kingdom (by adding a Law to Generation) is likely to Infect and devour his neighbour, be but heard, that Neighbour will presently make Resistance by the same Engine; and it will soone goe about, since the practice will be more easy to the Latter than it was to the first. Yett they surely who begin with the greatest numbers will have the greatest advantage in this Experiment, tho at the last a superfoetation of mankind, since our Space is Limited, must produce either Laws or Blood-shed for their necessary Reducing. Soe I have seen in Germany most Stately Trees for a great space Burnt downe, to gett a little Arable to live by. Soe you knew the Hebrew Children were drownd on account of Multiplication, and somewhere in Greece the old men were by Law to be tumbled over a Bridge.

Now if the Success of the Project be Ruinous, what need I speake of the Meanes towards it—as to putt a Girle at 16 and a Ladd at 18 to gett Children, before they know how to maintain them, or have served out halfe their Apprentiseshipps?

If a whole Country of poore Labourers should have more Children than honest labour can maintaine (as may presently bee, if one may have 25 children, and the first 12 be helpless), it follows that they must be maintained by the State. And consequently the State will be owners and disposers of the Children begotten, and soe introduce a vasilage which leaves the Parents noe other Right to their Children than the Earth hath to its Plants. How to gett new Lawes and fitt Judges for such a Constitution will in this our Climate be somewhat hard.

Then whereas you fix the value of a man's Labour at 83£,[1] and soe multiply the value with the increase of men, this my thinks would have a quite Contrary Effect; for if Diamonds grew as comõn as pebbles, they would be but of the same account.

Soe in the case of mortality, if in London it exceede that in the Country, the multiplication of other Cittys will doe the like. For if there be more men, there will be and must be more communitys; and the more London is populous the more will the Rule of Mortality increase. And soe the future Throngs will somewhat impayre the numbers you impute to the career of generaçon.

But why do I meddle in these matters? You know Calculation is not a Herb of my Garden—tis a peculiar of your owne. I can only write captiously and, as they say 'turne the Tables', because you will have me write.

However to make you some amends. I will conclude with a story: There is a Province in China where by the constitution, all of the comõn sort who desired to marry, were twice a yeare to send up their names to the Capitall Citty and to some Senatours who presided for That End. Six of these took Care of the Males, and six more of the Females, and at the day of appearance each of the numbers were marshalled into 3 Squadrons. The men into the most Rich, the most Poore, and those who were indifferent. Alsoe the women into the most Fair, the most ugly, and those alsoe who were indifferent. These indifferents were matcht up on equall termes. The most beautifull were at high and valuable rates payd for by the most Rich; and at last the most Poore marryed the most Ugly. Yett they had this satisfaction: to have all the money devided among them which the most rich had given for the most fair. After this the magistrates lead them to the Nuptiall

---

[1] Cf. *Papers*, i. 182, where Petty takes the value per head of the people at this figure. In other parts of his writings the calculation varies between £69 (in the *Verbum Sapienti*) and £90 in his *Magnalia Regni* (*Papers*, i. 265).

House, where at the publick charges they had fiddles and sack possett for that night, and the next morning they had leave to depart.

I have shewne your Paper to Mr Pepys, who is but one of all mankind who are concerned in itt; And I doe hereby make affidavit that I have taken a copy of it.

Yrs

R. S.

83. *Petty to Southwell.*

[Petty was now established in Piccadilly, in a house of which he had bought the lease from one Robert Chip in 1673. The deed of purchase is still extant and shows its situation to have been at the corner of Portugal Street (now Piccadilly) and Chip (now Sackville) Street.

In the letter which follows, reference is made to two pamphlets which were exciting considerable interest at the time—the first entitled *Twelve Quaeries relating to the Interest of Ireland*, the second *A Narrative of the Sale and Settlement of Ireland*. Both were intended, by impugning the Settlement and its principal authors, to prepare the way for a general reversal of policy in Ireland, and were believed to have been inspired from high quarters. The pamphlets were published anonymously, though the *Quaeries* (of which there is a copy among the Petty MSS.) appeared over the initials G. F. D. These letters, as Petty somewhere remarks, " for ought anybody knows signify David Fitzgerald, who has already appeared pro and con in publiq matters of importance ", and the pamphlet was generally attributed to this man. The *Narrative* (or another paper of the same description) had, according to Hull, been originally published at Louvain by Nicholas French, titular archbishop of Ferns, in 1668. Hull therefore supposes the document now in question to have been a reprint (Hull, p. 613).

Petty was pressed by Southwell to write an answer to both pamphlets, and there are among the papers several draft replies to the *Quaeries*, one of which he proposed to adorn with the following title-page : " Maurice O'Ferkall, An Irish operator lately come from beyond Seas, Lodging over and against Mr. David Fitzgerald's in Plott Alley, undertakes (without trepaning the skull) to cure his countrymen's understanding expressed in their 12 Quaeries ", etc.

It seems doubtful, however, whether he showed these answers even to Southwell, since he writes to him a few months later: " Concerning the Quaeries, let the Divell take them for me " (*infra*, p. 172).

In 1687 he produced a reply to the second pamphlet under the title *Another more true and calm Narrative of the Settlement and Sale of Ireland* (*infra*, p. 273). There are two copies of this essay, one among the Nelligan MS. in the British Museum, and another in the Petty MSS. I have used the second in the *Papers* (No. 18). The substance of his argument reappears (in a somewhat different form) in the Essay *Speculum Hiberniae* (B.M. and Petty MSS.), as also in the *Treatise of Ireland* (Hull, p. 545 foll.).]

Piccadilly, 8 Septemb^r 1685

Dear Cous^n

I now find twas tenderness and indulgence towards me that made you silent to my paper, and I find that I have not now roused a roreing Lyon against it. Nevertheless I reply to yours of the 5th Instant in these following positions, vizt :

1°. It is for the honor of God and the advantage of mankind that the world should be fully and speedily peopled, and that objections against the same may be deferred till a thousand years hence.

2°. That the more People there are in any Country, the greater is the value of each of them, as the more Pilchards the greater price.

3°. There is no need of careing how to provide for children, as long as there bee three acres of Land for every head, which I call sufficient peopleing.[1]

4°. To say that other nations may use the same expedient as well as wee, is an objection to all proposers for the good of mankind.

I like your haveing shewn the paper to Mr Pepys, for he is no fop though fortunate. You needed not to have taken a coppy of the paper, for I feele you have transcribed it into your mind.

I thank you for Monsr Paschall's Thoughts.[2] The Author and the Subject invited me to read them

---

[1] Cf. *Papers*, Introduction, xxxvi.
[2] *Infra*, pp. 157-159.

over and over, but I except against most of his expressions, so as I could not draw any clear nočon or science out of it.

As to my answering the *Quaeries*, I say that my Lord of Ormond and Lord Chancellor Clarendon's [1] family are much concerned to satisfy the World as to the said *Quaeryes*, and also to the substance of that Scandalous Treatise called *The Sale and Settlement of Ireland*, and that therefore it should be done by such hands as they think sufficient for it : vizt, by Lawyers best skilld in Parliamentary and Prerogative Law, and such as are well versd in the history of the Warr of Ireland and in all the Transactions between Phelym O'Nealians, Owen O'Nealians, Renucinions (*sic*) and Cherocratians (?) on the one side ; and Ormondians, Insiqueenians, Jonesians and the Oliverians of the other side.[2] Or in other words between those who changed the Government, Rebelled against the same, and would have extirpated the English name and Religion,—whom we may in one Word call *Rebells*,—of the one side ; and those who endeavored to revenge the wrongs and crueltys done to their King, Countrymen, and Religion under the best Captains and Conductors which they could from time to time find, in direct pursuance of the Act made 17 Carol I for that purpose,—whom in one other word wee call *Patriots*,—of the other side. I ad that these answers will be most vigourously made by those unto whom the Settlement and execučon thereof hath been most propitious and favourable. I say the most proper answerers of these quaeries must be through friends to the Lord of Ormond and Clarendon, men skilld in the Parliamentary and Prerogative Law, well versed in the transactions

---

[1] Edward Hyde, first Earl of Clarendon (1608–1674), Lord High Chancellor after the Restoration, but ultimately banished from England. His son was now Lord-Lieutenant of Ireland.

[2] Sir Phelim O'Neill, Colonel Owen O'Neill (Owen Roe), Rinuccini (Archbishop of Fermo and Nuncio to Pope Innocent X.) had all taken part in the Irish Rebellion between 1641 and 1648 ; while the Duke of Ormond, Lord Inchiquin, Colonel Michael Jones and finally Cromwell had been instrumental in its suppression.

between the Rebells and Patriots, as also Beneficiaryes and favourites of the Settlement itself and the Present Interest.

These *Quaeries* are owned by that David Fitz-Gerald who was so troublesome to Sir Thomas Southwell.[1] I know him not, but here that he giveth out in speeches that I have endeavoured to answer his quaeries but find it impossible.

Cousin, you carp at my ill writing, but I protest That if you write any dangerous matter to mee I cannot conceale it, but shall have alwayes 3 witnesses against you ; for so many are necessary to the reading of your Letters, how finely soever you think you write !

Your most humble servant and affectionate kinsman
WᴹPETTY

Cosen Neddy dined with us this day and is well. The Duke of Ormond whom I visited this morning is also well. My wife mends every day and will card a reel for the spinsters, as their and your humble servant &c.

84. *Southwell to Petty.*

Kingsweston, 15 Sept 1685

Deare Cousin

I have yours of the 8ᵗʰ and find my account in It, for whereas by censuring your paper I have only a gentle Reprimand, I know if I had flattered you it had been more severe. You compare me to a Roring Lyon, but alas I can neither roare nor bite as a Lyon—I can only knaw as a little Mouse !

But that you may know what men of my Scantling will say, as well as those of the deeper dye, I will presume to touch uppon somewhat of your Answers :

You say that Objections against a Surplus of men in the world may be spoke of a thousand yeare hence.

---

[1] Sir Thomas Southwell was brother to Anthony Southwell (Sir Robert's grandfather). They came to Munster as ' undertakers ' in the reign of James I.

Now if in Great Brittaine and Ireland there were 10 millions and 60 millions of Acres, then by your standard of 3 Acres to a head, the Land would be halfe peopled. But you say that by your method there would in 12 yeares be 20 millions of men in these Dominions, so in 12 yeares they would be fully peopled. Then by the same rule in 24 yeares there would be 40 millions, which would be but 3 acres to 4 men, vizt, a very great overplus.

Now if all this Increase comes in 3 Redoubles of the number 12 (which is 80 times in one thousand), I suppose your method would in this time produce more men than there be now haires uppon mankind, which surely would be an overstock, and so neither to God's honour or the advantage of mankind as you affirme.

But I wish I had figures enough to stepp from these Dominions to the whole Earth. Tis somewhere sayd that mankind may make 350 millions. Now if we knew the acres of the Earth, one might see how many Acres to a Man, and in how many revolutions of the number 12, men might soe Increase as to have onely 3 acres to a man.

If at a Ventur I may suppose that these Dominions are 12 times better stockt than the whole rest of the Earth ; then, if 12 yeares will give us a full stock, 124 yeares will fully stock the Earth, and therefore the danger I spoke of is not soe distant as 1000 yeares off.

As to your comparison of Men to Pilchards, I have some reason to know this Fish, and ever found that the fewer taken the greater the Price. But you say the Contrary, which I can hardly believe ; unless all in the sea were taken and soe men might give much for what they were never to taste of more. I confesse if your valuing the greater Numbers of Men In a Country depend uppon this Illustration, I am yett to seeke ; and soe I should have been had you named Diamonds instead of Pilchards, tho' the eye be bigger than the Belly.

But I have done as to figures, and enough to make you confesse one errour in shewing your paper to a Fop, And even this had been more pardonable if it had been to a fortunate one.

As to Mr Paschall's paper, I will sett Sir John Louther uppon you, who admires it. If there be noe foundation of Truth in his position, then all the fine Stroakes uppon the diversity of Witts are quite besydes the marke; but because Sir John Louther is not a single man that is deluded with this fancy, I wish you would generally bestowe one halfe sheete to undeceive Them.

As to the *Queryes*, I like very well your manner of giving them a Gripe. Mr Boyle [1] told a friend of mine they would be substantially answered. I wish he had only said that Sir William Petty had undertaken it, that soe the author might change his note.

If the sequestered Lands were 5 millions of Irish Acres, I would gladly know how much of this the Irish now have. I think I have heard you say before the Explanatory Bill,[2] that they had gott one quarter of that Land, tho but one 16th, vizt, 500 of 8000 Claymants, were restored. I agree with you that it lyes uppon the 2 great familyes you mention to have these papers well answered, and whoever they may make use of yett I know you could doe it best.

I must end, since without help (as you object) you cannot read my Scrawle; yett how 3 other such blind men as your self come to read more than one, unlesse by Art Magick, I cannot tell!

Neque negativis recte concludere si vis.

Deare Cozin, I torment you with fustion, but call to Neddy and beat him into better manners that he may hereafter keep out of harmes way.

I congratulate my Lady's Recovery and soe of

[1] The Hon. Robert Boyle (1627–1691), son of Richard Boyle, first Earl of Cork : a natural philosopher of great repute and one of the founders of the Royal Society.
[2] *I.e.* the Act of Explanation (1665).

the Duke of Ormond, and am ever your most affect
cousin and humble servant

ROBERT SOUTHWELL

85. *Petty to Southwell.*

London, 19 Sepb^r 1685

Dr Cosen
      I find I must take some pains with you, as
I did with Wat Waller 32 years since, at the dissecting
of a Sturgeon.   I say about this matter of *Multiplication of mankind,* concerning which I must Rebuke
you for these faults, viz :

1°. That you say the speedy peopling of the Earth
is an Evill Designe—whereas I say It tends greatly
to the honor of God and the benefit of all Mankind.

2°. I say that endeavors to people the Earth may
slacken, when every 3 acres thereof hath one head
of mankind to till and enjoy them, which will not
bee these 1000 years.   But you (That you may bee
the sooner allowed to raile) say twil bee—by my
method — within 124 years ; which I wish were
true, as makeing for us, tho you were let loose to
morrow.

3°. I say that the more Pilchards (I meant at
Killmare ¹) were taken, the better price they yield ;
And I say again tis true.   For when they bee few,
merchants will not come to fetch them ; and when we
have not enough of them to load a ship, nor other
goods to make up a freight, our Pilchards are undervalued.   But quitting the Instance of Pilchards, I
say that in Holland and Zeeland (the thickest peopled
Countrys I know), the worth of men and of their
days labour is greater than in Kerry and Connaught,
and there also are fewer beggars.

Having thus chargd you in 3 points, I returne to
the 2 first, vizt, that the speedy peopling of the Earth

---

¹ Kenmare in County Kerry, where Petty had established a colony of
fishermen and iron workers.

is an honor to God and benefit to mankind. (1) To honor God is really (and not in specious words onely) to acknowledge his Power, Wisdome &c. Wee comonly say that the whole Earth, and the fixed stars too, was made for the use of man. But till we see the Earth peopled (as perhaps ¾ is not), wee may doubt it ; and not knowing to what other use it was designd, may stumble into the Error of Its haveing been made by Chance, and not by the designe of an Infinite wisdome—I would rather say of the greatest Wisdome. Wherefore the sooner this stumbling block is removed the better. I ad that Hee who shall give the reason and use of what lyes in the 8000 miles space between the 2 poles of the Earth, and of the use of the fixed stars to man, shall honor God more than by singing his *Te Deum* every day. (2) I say that as in great Cittys and Cohabitations of men art and sciences are better cultivated than in Deserts ; so I say That if there were as many men on Earth as It could bear, the works and wonders of God's Wisdome would bee the sooner discoverd and God the sooner honored really and heartily. (3) I say that God's first and greatest comand to Man and Beast was *to encrease and multiply to replenish the Earth*. Why therefore should this duty bee put off ? (4) The not doing this duty (That is when half the teeming women are neglected) is the Cawse of Rapes, Incest, Sodomyes, Adulterys, Fornications &c, with pox and duells about misses and whores. I should ad to my last head that, it being probable That the world shall not be destroyed, nor the Day of Judgement come till the whole Earth bee peopled, if we pray that God would hasten the full number of his elect, and If the blisse of the blessed cannot be perfect till the Soule and Body are united, Then we must wish the speedy peopling the Earth.

As to the benefit of mankind :

(1) It is a benefit and satisfaction to man that hee can worship and praise God with understanding. For to pray in an unknowne tongue is more

tollerable than to speak in generall and grosely of the Wisdome of God in his works, when wee know little or nothing of them. To which I ad that as People encrease, so will Philosophers encrease proportionally — that is Enquirers into the works and Wisdome of God.

(2) The King of England hath a greater share of the unpeopled Earth (viz, from Nova Scotia and the entrance into Hudson's Bay to Florida) than most other Princes ; wherefore when the whole shall bee peopled, Hee will have a greater share than he hath now.

(3) To come nearer the point (Good Cozen) our Lands in Ireland may 12 years hence bee double in value to what they are now ; that is wee shall have double the hands to serve us as wee have now.

The 2^d Main point is that, till the Earth bee peopled with an head for every 3 acres, there is no cause for obstructing the designe. Wherefore if you cannot forbeare 1000 years, do it 100 years. In the mean time I'le hold you 5 pounds That, do what you can, the whole Earth will not be fully peopled as aforesaid these 1000 years. You know wagers are good reasoning, because all unexpected accidents and the obliq endeavors of partys concerned against the new proposall, do help the wagerer. Mr Pen [1] is overjoyd to heare that it is your opinion the Earth will bee fully peopld in 124 years and desires it may not bee contradicted.

As to Monsr Paschall's paper, let it alone till you come to Towne and then I will roast Sir John Lowther and your self both upon one Spitt.

As to the greater point of answering the narrative of *the Settlement and Sale of Ireland* and the 12 *Quaeries* signed G. F. D. :—I concur with you that the Familys of Ormond and Clarendon are chiefly concernd therein. For the author charges : 1°. The Lord Clarendon with swearing that the Irish ought to bee extirpated root and branch. 2°. That Hee

---

[1] William Penn (see *infra*, p. 165).

hindred my Lord Robert [1] going chief Governor
(whom he presumes would have done the contrary),
and got the Lord Ormond to bee sent in his stead,
who got them exempted in the English Act of Pardon.
By all which tis sayd they got great rewards.   3°.
They charge my Lord of Ormond (i.) With getting
them exempted from Pardon as aforesaid, (ii.) That
the Act for barring their Innocence was in his Government, and that hee got by the same as much Lands
over and above what hee had anno 1641, as would
have fully satisfyed the Adventurers ; which I think
to bee 595^m Irish Acres, now worth about 139^m pound
per annum.

Now who should answer these charges but themselves and confidents ?   Who should dare meddle with
it for feare of erring but whom they entrust ? who
can do this well who hath not the history and the
Law ?

For my part—(1) Whereas the *Narrative* and
Quaeries says That no people upon the Face of the
Earth are in so wretchd and deploreable a condition
as the Irish, nor have been so unchristianly and
inhumanely dealt with as they ; I could onely describe
their Condition about the years 1655, 1665, and 1685,
and perhaps shew that in the very worst of these 3
epoches, their condition was (in the bulk) better than
that of the Subjects of the neighboring kingdomes ;
and that If any particular men have suffer'd It hath
been by the Iniquity of the rest.

(2) If they object against the Parliament which
made the Acts of Settlement and Explanacõn, I
could onely justify that Parliament by mathematicall
demonstrations, and that the King hath above 10
millions by it.

(3) When they complaine of their wrongs, I should
onely say that they gayned (by plundering the
personall and usurping the reall estates of the Pro-

---

[1] John, Lord Robartes or Roberts (1606–1685), a Commonwealth officer,
who found favour at the Restoration, becoming Lord Privy Seal in 1661. He
succeeded Ormond as Lord-Lieutenant in 1668, but was recalled in 1670. The
Observations on the London Bills of Mortality were dedicated to him.

testants within the Rebellion) 10 times as much as all the Land which they had anno 1641 were worth anno 1653, when the Rebellion ended ; and that the Lands which they have now are also now worth 10 times the same.[1]

(4) I might also say that the Guilts for which they are not toucht in those Acts, do require above 30 millions for their expiation, besides the sin of their massacres.

And now Cosen, Let mee have one quaery, viz : If the Irish bee now to the Brittish as 8 to one ; and if they should bee all armd as an army and militia, and the English disarmed ; and if the Irish should bee the predominant party in all Corporations,[2] may not the kingdome bee delivered up to the French ? And that It would bee, depends upon the motives on each side to do the same—which I leave to the Consideration of our superiors, whom God direct.

86. *Petty to Southwell.*

[Pascal died in 1662. His *Pensées* were posthumously published in 1669, and had been sent to Petty a fortnight before this letter was written (*supra*, p. 148). Petty had then ' excepted against most of Pascal's expressions ', and he now states his objections to them in greater detail ; giving at the same time his own receipt for producing ' transcendental men ' in all walks of life. Petty's criticisms of Pascal are apparently directed, not towards the *Pensées* themselves, but to one of the ' Opuscules ' which follow them entitled *Différence entre l'esprit de Géométrie et l'esprit de finesse.*

I have published elsewhere a short document dealing with this subject which was found among the Petty MSS. under the title " Wit Enlarged " (*Papers*, No. 137). A close comparison between this tract and Pascal's paper reveals

---

[1] Land in Ireland was of course almost valueless at the termination of the Rebellion.

[2] This was, in fact, being accomplished by the practice of annulling the Charters, while the Irish militia, consisting mainly of Protestants, was in process of being disbanded.

the fact that *Wit Enlarged* is little more than a précis by Petty of the Opuscule in question.

It was Pascal's paper, no doubt, which led him on to his subsequent exploration of the subjects of wit, mimics and ridicule (*infra*, p. 191 foll.).]

Extract

[21 September 1685]

As to Mr Paschall's paper, whose name I honour, I must say as followeth vizt :—

1°. That there be many words, Phrases, and sentences in it which have no certain, sensible signification, and therefore cannot beget any clear notion, sence, or science in the Reader.

2°. He distinguisheth witts only by their aptitude either for Geometry or Sagacity ; whereas I think that the best Geometricians were the most Sagacious men, or that the most Sagacious men did ever make the Best Geometricians. Wherefore the distinction of Witts is not well made by these words, which are but the cause and effect and consequently the same.

3°. He maketh the difference of great Atchievements (made by the severall great men undernamed) to have depended uppon either their making use of many or few principles ; whereas the very words 'many' and 'few' have noe reall difference, no man being able to say whether the number 10 be many or few, or be a small or great number.

Those I would name among the ancient are : Archimedes, Aristotle, Hippocrates, Homer, Julius Caesar, Cicero, Varro, Tacitus. Among the modern : Moliere, Swarez, Galileo, Sir Thos Moore, Sir Fra Bacon, Dr Donne, Mr Hobbs, Des Cartes.

Whereas the good parts of men are in Generall :

(1) Good Sences,

(2) Tenacious memory of figures, colors, sounds, names &c,

(3) A quickness in finding out, matching and compareing, as alsoe in adding and substracting the *sensata* layd up in the memory,

(4) A good method of thinking,
(5) The true use of words,
(6) Good organs of speech and voice,
(7) Strength, Agility, and Health of Body and of
all its parts.

The severall atchievements of the severall great
persons above named have proceeded from the just
and proportionable applications of these last menčoned
facultys to severall matters and ends.

I have now given you a description of what I
call ' good parts ', which I ressemble to the severall
colours upon a Painter's Pallet, out of which any
colour may be made by composition ; and I say
that I can, out of the Ingredients aforementioned,
make you an Archimedes, an Homer, a Julius Caesar,
a Cicero, a chess-player, a musitian, a Painter, a
dancer of the Ropes, a couragious Spark, a fighting
fool, a Metaphysicall Swarez[1] &c. And I would
faine see how, out of Monsʳ Paschall's grounds
(vizt, of aptitude for Geometry or Sagacity, and the
use of many or few Principles), the same can bee
performed ; and how thereby all the above mentioned
species of Transcendentall Men can be produced.

87. *Southwell to Petty.*

Kingsweston, 24 Sept 1685

Deare Cousin
        The Inclosed is to one part of your kind
letter of the 19ᵗʰ. As to the other, about the Irish
Settlement, I must have a little time to ruminate on
those master Stroakes you give, which in the meane
time I very heartily thank you for.

I use my servant's hand in the Inclosed, because
you have complayned that my owne is not always
current.

[1] Francisco Suarez (1548–1617), the Spanish Jesuit, philosopher and
writer. He was prominent in the great controversy between the Jesuits and
' Molinists '.

I hope my lady and the little ones are as I wish them. Myne here I thank God are soe. Neddy braggs of your Favours and the fine Mapps he has in custody. My 2 daughters think they have gott all the mathematicks because they can demonstrate an equilaterall Tryangle.

Neddy has gott from Caspar (?) a cleare plaine Stile in all his Letters, soe that I never have one hard word from him, which I am pleased with.

I have nothing more to add concerning Hobby Horses, and therefore remayne

Sr, Your most affect Kinsman & humble serv^t

ROBERT SOUTHWELL

88. *Southwell to Petty.*

Kingsweston, 24 Sept 1685

Deare Cozin

I have the honour of yours of the 19th which is rich in particulars of great weight; in favour especially, that you conferr such things on me. Soe, Regarding you as a great Master of Deffence who keepes open Schoole, and letts all Beginners push at your impenetrable Breast, I will reply confusedly as my weakness will permitt.

For your Divine authority of " encrease and multiply and replenish the Earth ", you know at what time and day those orders were given, when 2 only were in the old world, and but 8 in the new. Yett Moses when he comes to write that story, says that by the 3 sons of Noah the whole Earth was overspread, and makes no mention of defect in his dayes.

Why should you make the Glory of God soe highly to consist in the multiplicity of mankind, when at one stroake God thought fitt to drown all but eight ? How many plagues and extirpations of men (as in Canaan &c) have there hapned, and all to God's glory ? If your assertion can hold hereafter that where there are multitudes there will still be severall Philosophers and admirers of God's works, why were there not some of these admirers in the old world, that when Noah escaped they alsoe might have embarkt? You remember in the Cityes that were desolated, there was but one Single Lott, and among the multitudes found in America we read little of Philosophers. Wherefore it does not follow that the more acres, the more Wheate; since this is a peculiar care and Culture by Itself. And truly if some security be not given herein, The Earth would but groane under a burden of men, as once before when it repented God to have made man at all and it grieved him at his Heart.

Why should wee think that the multiplication of so fraile a Creature adds to God's Glory at the rate you mention, when we see that even the Angells doe not multiply? Perhaps the Earth was much less peopled than now, when it had the highest blessing, of our Saviour's presence, that this or any other Orb could be capable of. He vouchsafed to live among men for their Instruction, yet wee doe not find that either by Praecept, and much less by Example, he ever soe much as toucht upon this point. His great apostle St Paul declares that he that does not marry does better. You also read that some were Eunuchs for the Kingdome of Heaven; and that not onely father and mother, but wife alsoe, was to be forsaken if occasion required.

You think it makes for your Proposall to say it brings on the Day of Judgment and soe hastens the full number of the Elect. If it bee soe indeed, it may not be an unspirituall, but it seemes to be a very unnaturall designe; for menkind are not to seek their own dissolution, but rather to cherish themselves and take care of Posterity. Soe that to say there shall be an end of all when the Earth is fully peopled, is to deterr all men from the thing you would have them bee att. Besydes as to God's part herein, to putt off that Great Day to a thousand years hence for certain, of whose certainty the very angells are ignorant, seemes quite out of our commission. Nay if you putt that Day off till the unhabitable parts of the Earth have a man to three acres, you will be much more [than] a millenary, as I conceive.

You believe that $\frac{1}{4}$ of the earth is not yett fully peopled. I alsoe believe that $\frac{1}{4}$ part can never be. If one would give me for the portion of a younger child a whole Region in Greenland, or a Barony in Nova Zembla, how should one doe for Tenants ?— White Beares and black devills would pay no Rent.

I take notice that after you inculcate full peopling of the Earth in order to a Pious Dissolution, and the fulle happiness unto man by the Reunion of soul and body; yett there seemes a little reluctance at that *nunc dimittis*, since to obviate my objection to over peopling, you say that when it comes to be 1 to 3 acres, then your Rule may be slackned. Why is it in men's power to slacken that which contributes, as you think, to the great period that God hath setled ? And should there bee nothing but of meere men in the case, how can you expect that any Rule of Restriction now to be given, but not executed till a thousand yeares hence, shall be then observed ? They will doubtless plead the prescription of 1000 yeares, and thinke they are as much intituled to what you now quote of Encrease and Multiplying as your selfe; and should they be restrained, why might not they as justly then complaine of Rapes, Pox, and Duels as you doe now ?

You seeme fearfull of Epicurean atheism, and that if men still observe soe much of the Earth neglected as useless, they might fancy it came by chance. I doe not thinke becoming more sensuall in Practice will make any the less Epicurean in doctrine; nor that our present Ignorance about the fixed starrs is ever to be mended. For if there were as many Philosophers on Earth as there be of those starrs in Heaven, I doe not think they ever could make out to all curious enquirys how farr forth those starrs were created for man,—nor is it very dangerous to leave it omitted.   Lett such Scepticks rather content themselves to know That the earth and its creatures were by divine Commission made over to the Dominion of man, and conclude that the fewer the men the larger this Dominion, and that there never was soe great a Potentate as Adam.

What you say to interest me in the Cause—that in 12 years Ireland would be double in value, because of double Hands,—I doe not understand enough in the Duplicate proportion [1] (as things may goe) to know whether a double of the few English would be as equall as now to the double of the numerous Irish. For I have heard you say That in building of shipps, the price of Tonnage is vastly different after a certain Pitch. But for peopling our Dominions from Hudson's Bay to Cape Florida, this indeed might encrease our numbers, but it is a Question wither it would encrease our Power—I mean not for feare of Bostoners [2] in the way.   But since your proposall lyes common to all mankind, and [is] noe more a secret or an invention than eating and drinking, I say all men may goe to it as well as Wee ; and everywhere to add as every-where to diminish, leaves things (if done equally) at the same stand they are.   Nay if you would count by acres, the Spanyards and perhaps the Portugeses too would outdoe us.

As to your wager of five pound (without saying who should hold stakes till the game be up), if that proove not a stronger argument than the comparison of Pilchers, which you still insist on, it will yett cost you paines to sett me to rights.   Why, because a single Barill of Pilchers at Kilmare is not worth the fetching, can you infer as if this single Barill would sell cheaper at Legorn than any one barill of 500 which they had the yeare before ?   I might as fairely say that, because for want of Shipps and Salt, the

---

[1] An allusion to Petty's Discourse made before the Royal Society some years before, *Concerning the Uses of Duplicate Proportion.*

[2] Seamen from the port of Boston who were apparently already showing an independent spirit.

Scotchmen doe sometimes dung their Lands with Herrings, therefore plenty of Herring is useless. This I say would not candidly refute your assertion, ' The more Pilchers the greater the Price ' ; but surely it would be a fair answer to tell you that Plenty is a blessing, but if Plenty should make things the dearer, it would be a curse. If Wat Waller's sturgeon were caught in the Thames, I dare say it was worth more than 5 taken in the Elbe, or 15 taken at ArchAngel. And as for your high wages in Holland and Zeeland where men abound, this is not because of the many hands, but of the many mouthes, and that eggs are not there sold at 20 a penny. For if a labourer in Kerry or Connaught is able for his groat a Day to buy more eating than the 12d in Holland, this ought to be the Standard. In Gerzy and Gernesey they are undone by their numbers ; for first, half their lands are Ditches and Partitions, and those who have noe property are poore knitters of stockins. Here the Begars are numerous, and if they be not soe in Holland, Tis from their government that can employ good Leggs to work for bad hands, and good hands for bad Leggs, soe as to leave noe sound faculty Idle.

Tis high time to conclude, if I knew how to come off—Shall I end with doubting whether more men would produce more philosophers, and whether more philosophers would mend the World ? This I say wee doe not always observe, that those who know most doe adore most, (unless perhaps among the Doctors). Solomon, a very great philosopher, does not so much insist on this *summum bonum* of Multiplication. He gott little by his share that way. His great Epilogue is " Feare God and keepe his Commandments ". Our Saviour did noe way inculcate this doctrine, he was more for the *Te Deum Laudamus*, and the beatitudes expressed by his Sermon on the Mount. He came in with peace and good will towards men ; and went out with bequeathing peace as his last and best Legacy. Now whether multitudes are more peaceable or more unruly, I leave to your

consideration.   Lastly wee doe not see that in Countrys
where nature has wholly governd and no unexpected
accidents or oblique endeavors of Partys could inter-
vene, that this Institution of yours has taken Root.
Soe that I am afraid that you must lett the World
Jogg on, and govern Itself as it has done and will
doe, in spite of all Philosophy.

Now Cozin, I expect you will serve me as my
Lord Chief Justice [1] an obstinate or Ignorant Jury,
in sending them out again for a better verdict ; and
truly if you will but allow me candle light, perhaps
I may alsoe change.   One thing there is in which
a little hinders me from being over hasty or Credulous,
and that is the News you mention of two very honest
gentlemen [2] who in November next are to be rosted
uppon one Spitt, and this for believing too easily the
most celebrated and mathematical Thinker of France.
I am ever & c.

89. *Petty to Southwell.*

[William Penn, already mentioned above (p. 155) as one
who would rejoice in the *Multiplication of mankind*, is here
again referred to in the same connection.   Penn had been
granted the concession of Pennsylvania four years before,
and in 1683 had founded the city of Philadelphia.   He was
now back in England.

Penn and Petty had been for some time on friendly terms,
while Petty's papers show that he was not only prepared
with advice as to the best means of developing the new
colony, but that in 1686 he actually took up a share in the
enterprise, to be unsuccessfully claimed a hundred years
later by his descendants (*Papers*, Nos. 110 to 115).

Penn required ' Hands ' for the development of his
' Lands ' in America, as Petty required them in Ireland.
They could thus make common cause in the matter of
' Multiplication ', though it must be more than doubtful
whether the eminent Quaker would have approved of Petty's
suggested means to this end.]

---

[1] The notorious Lord Jeffreys who had been Lord Chief Justice since 1683,
and was afterwards Lord Chancellor till the downfall of James II.
[2] Sir John Lowther and Southwell (*supra*, p. 155).

London, 26 Sept. 1685

To S^r R Southewell

I have shewn : 1°. That the Generation of Men may go on faster than it now doth.   2°. That the speedy replenishing the Earth is God's command and honor.   3°. That the same is for the good of Mankind in generall, for The King of England more than for other Princes, and for yours and my benefit in Ireland.   4°. That there needs no objecting against it there bee a head for every 3 acres, which I sayd at random will not bee these 1000 yeares, and offerd a wager of 5£ upon it.   Whereas you say twill bee within 124 yeares, whereby you have much honord the proposall and rejoycd Mr Pen.

If the Controversy between you and I had been onely whether The Earth would be replenishd in 1000 or in 124 yeares, you have the better of mee upon these grounds :   1°. That there are already about 320 millions of men upon the Earth.   2°. That these may bee double 12 yeares hence and quadruple 24 yeares hence, and so on by progression to the 80th period ;   there being above 80 times 12 in 1000, and there being above 48,000 millions of acres in the habitable part of the Earth.   And yet, dear Cousen, I will hold my wager for the 1000 yeares notwithstanding.

For besides the many Impediments of this brave encrease which I cannot foresee, I do foresee these that follow, vizt :

1. In the book of Mortality Bills, twas plainly set forth in Tables that in a certaine parish,[1] 5 were borne for 4 buried, which would double 100 men in 100 yeares ;   whereas The Author pitches upon 200 yeares for the time of doubling.[2]

2. In the Essay upon the growth of London, The time of doubling is made much slower ;[3] grounding the Calculation upon lesse fruitfull and healthy parishes.

---

[1] *Observations upon the Bills of Mortality* (Hull, p. 390).   The parish in question was Romsey, Petty's birthplace.
[2] *Ibid.* ch. xii. (Hull, p. 394).   [3] Viz. 360 years (Hull, p. 463).

3. I must confesse That, tho The accompt of maryd teeming women in my first paper [1] was but 32 of the 100, Yet in other parishes I find the maryed Teemers to bee above halfe. Of which I gave notice in the first paper you had, in order to a better Examination.

4. When Brittaine and Ireland shall, 12 yeares hence, have their full complement of 20 millions, and that then wee must either stop or ship our surplus for America, I foresee That Mr Pen and the Lords proprietors may not bee ready to take them off and to give us good returnes for them.

5. Altho all beggary and thieving bee the fault of the Magistrate till the Land bee overpeopld, yet I feare That such fault will not bee remedied by the Introduction of a Method for feeding and employing our new encrease.

6. I believe All Countryes will not take up this New Method of encrease tho they see it Succeed, but will either neglect it or reject it as an Innovation, or as Contrary to Custome or religion. For some Religionarys persuade and force *Caelibat*, and to such give their greatest preferments.

7. I have not yet concluded by what Lawes or other Meanes This project may be put in practise, and therefore believe That much water will go by the Mill.

8. The Unforseen Impediments may bee more than those above mencõnd. Wherefore, dear Cousen, Notwithstanding your demonstration I will still stick to my wager That, do what you can, The Earth will not bee fully peopld these 1000 yeares. But the sooner the better.

Now Though Huntsmen allow their hounds to lick the blood of the Hare they have killed, yet they must not eate it quite up ; nor must you quite devower mee by reason of your demonstration, but bee contented to lick &c. In the Meanetime Mr Pen and I trymph That The Earth and Pensylvania may bee

[1] Cf. ' Concerning Marriages " (*Papers*, No. 91).

fully emprovd within these 124 next yeares, and That
Blind I have led the blind world into the notion of it.

As to the *Narrative* and *Quaeries*, I doubt not
but that out of the many Peeres, prelates, Privy
Counsellors, Judges, Church dignitaryes, Officers of
the army and other creatures, which these 2 concernd
familyes have made, There will bee found enough who
can clere the charges against them mencõnd in that
scandalous narrative, by shewing :

(1) That tho the Irish might in rigor deserve to
bee extirpatd, yet that in truth they have not been
punishd at all for their greatest Miscariages.

(2) That tho The Irish were justly and prudently
exceptd from pardon, yet in Truth they have not
been punishd, *ut supra.*

(3) That (i) they never had right to a particular
tryall of persons, (ii) That they abusd it, (iii) and
have since sold it away.

(4) That whatever a few unlucky particulars
amongst them have suffered may and ought to bee
rectifyed by themselves.

I also hope That those whom they have wronged
or suppressd, will bee so far foolish and fearfull as
not to gainsay the same.

90. *Southwell to Petty.*

Kingsweston, 3rd Octr 1685

Deare Cozin
I have the honour of yours of the 21st, which
was by way of supplement to that of the 19th preceding;
and I have one of the 26th, which gave cover to that
of the 21st, and all of them of the month past.

I had presumed to write you a long one of the
24th past which I perceive was not then come to your
hand, soe I shall be silent now in what relates to
the *Multiplication of Mankind*—and in truth Silence
becomes me best in soe arduous a thing.

Neither shall I trouble the Points of the *Irish Settlement*, since you say that matter seemes to sleep, and it were very hard to add weapons of more execution than what you have scored down uppon that subject. ' Genoa the Proud ' was hardly better bombd.[1]

But I must take notice and thankfully acknowledge what you sett forth on Mr Paschall's *Thoughts*. I am convinced that his Path is narrow and incompetent. That he lays down for a Generall Definition of Witt, That which in Truth is but a fine description of two particular Characters ; and I confesse alsoe that he makes those things opposite which are promiscuous. For when I think of Judge Hale, Sir W.P., and a few others, I see how Geometry and sagacity consist, and how unnaturall it is to divide them. Soe that he did rather consider Severall of his friends, some that were wholly plunged in Mathematicks without meddling with the World, Others that were all World, Sagacity, and noe Mathematicks ; and thereupon pronounced them as Jew and Samaritan, and that they were each of them incapable of mixing in the Business of the other.

Noe, Cozin, your Painter's Pallet is a more generous offspring of Colours and Ingredients to build up Heros of every sort. The various fountains you assigne afford all that is necessary, and I am even charm'd with considering how I am buoy'd up aloft from the Errour I was in.

The subjects of this Nature doe the more excite and entertaine me because of carving (as it is your Phrase) a figure uppon our Neddy ; and lett me take leave to interrogate you on your Epistle dedicatory of the *Duplicate Proportion*.[2] You there recommend some Mathematicks, which are Chiefly, as I suppose, Arithmetick and Geometry, because afterwards you speak of Political Arithmetick and Geometricall

---

[1] ' Genes la superbe ' had been bombarded by the French in the previous year.

[2] *Concerning the Uses of Duplicate Proportion*, a paper read before the Royal Society by Petty in 1674.

Justice. And you alsoe inculcate that the young men be stockt with varyety of Matter, Data, and Phaenomina, to exercise Lines and Numbers uppon.

Now I would be glad to know what Data, what Phaenomina, and what variety of matter you must approve? For these things and Ingredients, as I suppose, are those *Sensata* layd up in the Memory, of which your late letter makes mention; and for the finding out, matching, and comparing whereof, as for the adding to and substracting from them, a quickness or sagacity you say is needfull.

Wherefore, if the Memory must be the Exchequer, it were good to know what should there be lock't up in the Iron Chest as things of most rich and Intrisic value, and what to leave there in the outward Roomes as most Extrinsic. It seemes there must be a great Medley by what you enumerate—as figures, Colours, Sounds, names &c. I have heard you say that Sir Audly Mervin[1] was as a Paper Scribled over, and in a farr worse Estate than if the Paper had been left quite blank, for then some words of Sence might have been inserted.

Wherefore tell us, Deare Cozin, how this *scribling* may be avoyded, and teach me to doe by this Boy as I doe by Kingsweston, where my neighbours say that nothing done is alterd or repented of, but that all the Charge and Contrivance makes for hereafter. Wee are now uppon Brewing, therefore pray throw in your handfull of Wholesome Hearbs, and those Ingredients that may doe best for the whole course of Life.

Lett us but have a Duplicate of all your Recepies for Cozen Charles, and soe you may roast two joynts uppon the same Spitt.

I now write to Neddy to show his Cozen what I lately sent him touching a Quaker's Cyder Mill;

---

[1] Sir Audley Mervin (*d*. 1675) was a pompous person, who had been much mixed up in Irish affairs before and after the Commonwealth. He was Speaker of the Irish House of Commons from 1660 to 1666.

I meane thereby that these Grummets may begin to communicate, tho it be but as Beades for Gould.

With all duty to my Lady and affection to the little ones,

I am ever S^r, Your most humble servant

ROBERT SOUTHWELL

91. *Petty to Southwell.*

[The *Multiplication* essay was now ready for publication, but (owing no doubt to Southwell's criticisms) it was not allowed to appear, and only the synopsis, to which reference has already been made, was printed at the beginning of the new edition of the pamphlet on the *Growth of the City of London* (*infra*, p. 182, and Hull, pp. 454-455).

Meanwhile Petty's pen was not otherwise idle. Both the enclosures to the letter which follows will be found in the *Papers* : the *Catechisme*, which is really an attempt to find an undenominational basis for the Christian Religion, is in Latin as well as in English. I have printed the English version "The Christian Religion of Little Children" (*Papers*, No. 35). The 'two sheets' written by Petty in reply to "A Papist misrepresented" are in the form of a tract headed "A Papist or Roman Catholic represented," 1685 (*Papers*, No. 34).]

London, 10 October 1685

Dear Cousen

Let mee tack on a tip to the tayle of our *Multiplication* businesse. I have yours of the 24th past. I have out of it and all your other letters pickt out what properly belongs to that matter. I have out of my first garble again pick't out what was wit, ornament, and Raillery, from the rest. In which finding (tho good) objections against what was not in my first essay, I have added such matter to the Essay as is a fit anvile for your heavy hamers. That what you have ingeniously written may not bee lost, I have made men to bee kild by your Armes. And all this I am importun'd to print, wherefore make hast up hither. To conclude (Cousen), If I find that you have done mee or my Essay any harme, I will satisfy my Justice upon you onely by telling all the women of between 16 and 41 years old that you hinder their haveing husbands &c. Concerning the *Quaeries*, Let the Divell take them for mee.

In consequence of what I said to Monsr Paschall's paper, you would have mee do by deare Neddye's head as my Lady Duches of Ormond did to the round tower in Kilkenny; that is make his wall thiner, breake out Lights, make partitions, set up Shelves, bring in furniture, new Frame the staires, make new passages &c. To all which I will make no answer till you come. I see tis better and easier to bee banged or beaten by you, than to write anything that pleases you.

Neverthelesse to begin the furnishing of Neddyes Tower, I send you the shortest Catichisme I can frame, and suitable to our Comon prayer Catichisme. I call it *Religio Christiana puerilis*—I might ad *Et quae etiam est mea senilis.*

Here is come out a book of note *A Papist misrepresented and represented* written by J.L. I object that Hee ought to have put nothing in his Collumne of ‘ Misrepresented ’, but what is found in authentic non-papist authors ; and nothing into his Collumne of ‘ Represented ’ but the very words of the Councill of Trent. So have you this mighty book answer'd. When you come up, I will shew you 2 sheets written by W P. to the said purpose.

I do not know what you meant by ‘ Brewing ’— Explaine it, and your operations upon Kings-Weston.
Adieu
W. P.

92. *Southwell to Petty.*

Kingsweston, 15 Oct. 1685
Deare Cousin
I am much obliged by yours of the 10th, and the *Catechysme* you enclosed shall go not onely into

Neddy's Tower but into my owne. Both of us are
now reading the Holy Booke by that particular
method you prescribed, Soe that tis want of braines
when any thing you bestow on us is lost.

I will hasten up with more keenesse to see the
2 sheetes of W.P., as after your further enlargements
of Monsr Paschall's materials of Ability, I have
done my best to drive in those 7 spikes into our
young man's Scull which you have already Assigned,
and am convincd those 7 Ingredients made up the
7 wise men of Greece.[1]

As to the word ' Brewing ', my meaning was that
we were Teaching of Neddy and giving him Instructions to doe well. And as in Brewing a wise Phisitian
will, besides the Mault and Hopps, throw in a handfull
of wholesome Herbs, and so call it a Dyett drink, my
desire was to have these Herbs from your Garden
(that is to say fitt and usefull Instructions for life),
while our young man was now in fermentation. For
tis as easy to learne those good things that ought
never to be forgott, as those which will be uselesse
hereafter. And uppon this I was so vayne as to
say that all the Improvements I had made at Kingsweston were in things permanent and of which my
Grandson might have more pleasure than I.

I see your *Multiplication* worke is looking towards
the Presse. When you talke of my objections I am
sure you smile. But if you doe not, 'tis certaine I
doe, since I had onely in mind Seneca's saying to an
humble friend or flatterer that perpetually sayd as he
did.—Soe that Seneca told him *quaeso dic aliud ut
duo simus.*[2]

Deare Cousin, when you informe the unmarryed
marrigiable of my ill will, pray lett them know alsoe
that it was not out of enmity to the sexe, for that I
doe at this day entertayne 3 misses.[3]

---

[1] *Vide* Petty's " Seven good parts of men in General " (*supra*, p. 158).

[2] Southwell evidently intends to quote from Seneca, Fifth Dialogue, " de
Ira ", Lib. iii. 8, but the actual passage runs " Caelius . . . exclamavit, Die
aliquid contra, ut duo simus ".

[3] *I.e.* his three daughters.

All happinesse to you and yours whom I hope ere long to see, and still to remayne, S^r Y^r most affect & most humble servant

ROBERT SOUTHWELL

93. *Petty to Southwell.*

[London] Oct 1685

D^r Co^z

I love you because you like the *Catechisme*, wherein God, the 3 persons, their attributes and offices, The grace of God, faith in God, The 2 Sacraments, Prayer, The Commandements, The dutyes of man to God and men, The revealed law and the Law written in the heart and the state of man after death— are all so described, That I say God hath not been so well served since Catechismes have been so much enlargd beyond our small modell, which exactly agreeth with that of the Church of England.

I suspend doing any thing upon the *Multiplication* Essay till you come. Your objeĉons are an honor and buttresse to it. The Scope is to see whether any practicible thing might bee done in the King's dominions against the paucity of subjects. I have already told you That tis the duty of a good man, instead of disputing the K[ing]'s power, to cast it up and to contrive how It may bee all applyed to the designe of God who gave it.

Concerning our panterpulla (?), Neddyes Tower, your Mysticall ' brewing ', Kings-Weston futurities &c, Wee will say more when you come. Arme yourself with charity and Courage to help me out of the Kery business, which is like the asse fasten'd by some wags to a Guernsey man's bark, whereby shee could neither saile nor steere.

Wee are all in pretty good health, nor much discomposed otherwise, a callus being now growne over my heart, who am

Y^{rs} as ever

W-P.

Our service to the pretty Spinsters, who are all under the age of the Ladyes you maligne. My spinster Nany [1] shall make you an extemporary Comoedy by acting the French gouvernante in a new and singular method. Your godson Charles does the same in the Fingallian [2] [manner].

94. *Southwell to Petty.*

Kingsweston, 31 Oct. 1685

Deare Cousin

Although I am preparing by this day Sevenight to kisse your hand, yett in the meane time I will thanke you for your last, and the Character therin of your short Cathechisme, which I annex alsoe to the Text and send it now to our Neddy to doe the like.

Whatever enemy you think me to *Multiplication*, I have this day planted above 40 faire Trees, and I hope they will produce their like, and soe on *in Secula Seculorum.* O that I could but help to plant one Cedar in Kerry, and have the same prospect of duration! But how my Charity or Courage shall avayle herein, unlesse you have some white powder or other, that can putt any man forward like a Prince Credentiall! Doe but you take care of this part and I'le warrant you for following Instructions.

I long to see the pretty Governante and our Fingallian uppon the Stage. My 3 Spinsters charge me strictly to bring them downe an exact account of all performance therein.

I see you allow me when I come up to talke of stuffing out our *puccane* (?) I meane Neddy. One point I resolve shall be to know wheather you ever writt down a Sett of Cases in the way of Politicall

---

[1] Anne Petty.

[2] By Fingalian (descendants of Fingal or Finn McCumhall, the legendary Gaelic hero of the third century) Petty appears to mean 'Irish' or 'Celtic'. It is curious to note, however, that in the *Political Economy* he distinguishes 'Fingalians' as those who "speak neither English, Irish, or Welsh" (Hull p. 206).

Arithmetick, in order to instruct and settle the present Age in the method, for this you once did Intend.

I hope my lady is in perfect health and all the little ones.   Myne are merry and content, which is as good as being wise.

I am ever, S^r, Your most affect & most humble servant

ROBERT SOUTHWELL

95. *Petty to Southwell.*

Piccadilly 25 Nov. 1685

Dr Coz^n

I have mist you 2 mornings and consequently discussion how [to] go through my Wildernes.   Pray send it me in a letter.

I am thinking of publishing the Essay for *Multiplication* and many other matters with it. Sir Peter [1] told me you were willing to adorne it with your animadversions ;   pray a word to that also. The questions wherein you are concernd are : 1°. Whether the speedy peopling of Earth bee for the good of mankind ?   2°. Whether it best answers the reveald will and designe of God ?   3°. To what Prince or State the same will be most advantageous ?

Some other thoughts are within my heart, but an abundance of others flutter about it.   Adieu.

W. P.

96. *Southwell to Petty.*

[The new Parliament (to be dissolved almost immediately by the King) had met in the previous month, and Southwell had come up to London for the occasion.   There had been an important debate on November 19 with reference to the Sovereign's policy.   Hull suggests that it was this ·discussion that inspired Petty to write the paper which he prints from a British Museum MS., on the *Powers of the King of England* (Hull, pp. 630-632).   It is evidently that to which Southwell refers below as " Instances of Regal Authority ".

For the *Engine of Salt and Fresh Water* I must refer my

[1] Pett.

readers once more to the *Papers*. An invention by which it was claimed that salt water could be turned into fresh had been made by one Fitzgerald in 1684, and a patent was granted him in this year. Petty and his friends were possibly wondering whether the project was worthy of financial support; at all events he wrote several sets of observations thereon in English (see "The Sweetening of Sea Water", *Papers*, Nos. 121, 122, 123), as well as others in Latin verse (*Epigramma in machinam dulcificam. Ad Clarissimum Geraldinum in machinam maris dulcificam*, etc.), all of which he was soon to send to Southwell.]

Deare Cousin   Kingsweston, 7 Dec[br]. 1685

    To you I pay the first tydings of my getting home on Saturday night. Here I found the spinsters in health, and all full of humility till I told them how often you and my lady had enquired after them.

    I am already teaching them the *Prestigia* you told me, and I assure them you will send more when their brother Neddy comes downe, who is to leave London on the 17th Instant. Soe by that time pray lett me alsoe have your *Observations on the Engine of Salt and Fresh Water*, and the *Instances of Regall Authority* which you showed me. I will send you back your owne originalls, as I did honestly returne you your Heads of a *Compleat Treatise of Sea and Navall affaires*.

    I write now to Mr Gwyn,[1] conjuring him to be mindfull of you, and to Mr Blathwayt that he may Spurr up Mr Gwyn.

    I am here entertaining my small compagnons with a Repetition of the Governante and performances of the Fingalian Hero. Pray lett us know all the Rules and Instructions you give and all the progresse and advancements they make, that soe we may strive to copy after the best Originalls.

    All the good wishes I have doe attend my lady and the little ones. I am ever S[r], your most affect Kinsman & humble servant

ROBERT SOUTHWELL

---

[1] ? Francis Gwyn (1648–1734), Member of Parliament and Under-Secretary of State.

97. *Petty to Southwell.*

Lond. December 1685

Dr Coz[n]

        I send by Neddy :

1°. an abstract of the King's powers.

2°. A Judgment on the art and designe of sweetning Sea-water.

3°. Some epigrams and Mottos on the Same.

4°. A pretty Arithmeticall trick, which is so to place the 9 digits, as of them to make 15 in 8 severall wayes :—

8	1	6		h	a	f
4	9	2		d	i	b
3	5	7		c	e	g

Another : Ad as many numbers as you please together and set downe the sum in the usuall manner as at C :

Ⓒ	Ⓓ	Ⓔ	Ⓕ	
36	3	2	1	9)44(4
49	6	9	7	36
98	4	6	–	—
102	9	—	8	8
11	9	17	Ⓑ	Ⓐ
—	8			
296	1			
	0			
	2			
	1			
	1			
	—			
	44			

Then add all numbers in C (as in D)—making 44.

Then add the sum 296 (as in E)—making 17.

Then ad the number 17 (as in F)—making 8.

Then divide 44 by 9.

The remainder shall be 8 (as in A)—equall to 8 (as in B). (The Rule is That any scatterd numbers (as C) and their totall (as E) being divided by 9, The remainders shall bee equall, as A and B—each being 8.)

And so I wish you a Mery Christmas.

98. *Southwell to Petty.*

Kingsweston, 23. Dec 1685

Deare Cousin

Our Neddy is come, and what between him and Christmas, the Girls think they may be romps by authority. Tis only Mr Kneller [1] that keepes them to any rules of proportion.

Your 3 Papers that he brought me, and your letter—the mother that wrapt them all—are welcome more than Christmas it selfe. I must say as old Dr Clayton, that you brought 3 quarters of these things into the world with you. [2] *Non vox hominum sonat.* Your Branches of Regall authority show all the extent of that magnificent Pallace at once.

Your judgment about the Art of *Sweetening Sea Water* makes me but wish that I had a list of all those thoughts and estimates which produced those few but effectual and mighty determinations.

The Epigrams and Mottos on that Subject shew what numberlesse thoughts you have had, and a method how to imploy the Chipps, after you have hewed out the Mayne Timbers and beames for use.

The two stratagems of Arithmetick in your letter are very pleasing to us. We admire at the hidden affinity that lyes in numbers, and breakes out as water that runns sometimes underground and some-

---

[1] Godfrey Kneller (1646–1723) was perhaps at this time painting the portrait of Southwell which is reproduced in this volume. The original belongs to the Royal Society.

[2] Dr. Thomas Clayton. He was professor of Anatomy at Oxford, where Petty, soon after his arrival there in 1648, was made his deputy. In 1650 Petty succeeded him, " Dr. Clayton resigning his interest purposely to serve him ".

times above.   This I say in reference to the second trick about scattered numbers and their Totalls.   As to the first, by placing the digitts 15 just is made in 6 places, but more in the other 2 places.

These matters were the more seasonable for that we had already plungd into a french booke of Mathematical Revelations, and poor Neddy's head was almost cloven by hard questions which the girls had prepared for him.   They are now reconciled, and all of them your votaryes ; and doe pay all duty to my Lady, and wish all manner of happinesse to their Cousins.

I have my share in all these things, and will, as the time requires, conclude with a happy Christmas to you ; and am ever with great acknowledgements Your most affect kinsman & most humble servant

ROBERT SOUTHWELL

99. *Petty to Southwell.*

[Petty's sons, Charles and Henry, were now respectively aged thirteen and ten. *Reinecke Fuchs*, the famous beast-epic, had first been translated from the German and published by Caxton in 1481. As the *History of Renard the Fox* it very soon gained, and has ever since enjoyed, immense popularity. The characters mentioned in this letter will be easily recognised by those who know the book, even if they are somewhat disguised under the strange orthography of the writer.

It may be noted that Petty had remarked a curious inconsistency in the book as written. In the first part it is stated that the Rape of Erswynd took place *before* her marriage with Isegrim the wolf, while in the second part this outrage is referred to as having happened *after* the marriage. Hence the problem which Petty had set his sons to solve in the sixth paragraph of this letter.]

Piccadilly, 31º Decemb 1685

Dᴿᵉ Coᶻⁿ

As you tell us what excellent exercises Neddy and the faire Spinsters are employed upon, So I tell you that My 2 sons are busy upon the Law.   Henry is the Lion's Attorney Generall and Counsell with most of them whom Reynard has wrongd, and Charles is of Counsell with Reynard to defend him against all accusaçons.   I will not prejudice you to bee of either Side, but will onely give you a list of the principall points that will come in question, Vizt :

(1) Whether Reynard conspir'd with the Carpenter that Wedgd Sir Bruen into the Hollow Tree.

(2) About the Murder of Dame Coppell, and whether shee was a sorceresse and intended to poyson Reynard.

(3) About the great Trepan upon Kyward, so as hee lost his life.

(4) What kind of action Curtis may bring against Reynard for the pudding taken from her.

(5) What Remedy Isegrim hath against the mare which smote him in the forehead, when hee came but to read what was written in her foot.

(6) Whether what Reynard did to Dame Arswind upon the Ice was a Rape or an Adultery.

(7) Whether Isegrim may be divorcd from Dame Arswind for that fact.

(8) Whether the Castle of Malepardus bee a privileged place, and whether a Replevin doth not lye for the goods which Reynard hath lodged in it.

(9) About the Treasure hidden in Crekenpit and the right of those that pretended unto it.

(10) About the Excellent looking glasse and the frame of it, and whether It doth not containe some Plot against the Lion.

(11) Whether Dame Rewkner hath not been accessory to many of Reynard's crimes.

(12) Of the severall Sacrileges chargd. upon Reynard.

(13) What right Renardin hath to Reynard's Estate and Dame Ermeline to her dower.

There bee many more, But by the decisions which shall bee given unto these few, you may judge of the rest.   Harry advises his Cousin Neddy not to deale with Reynard upon any accompt, for Hee hath fowle things in his papers against him.   Much lesse let the Spinsters hearken to any Treaty with Renardin.

[Endorsed " Copia Vera : Cha. Petty " with the following postscript in Petty's hand] :

2⁰ Janʳʸ 1685/6

The otherside contaynes the attested Coppy of what I had Illegibly writ concerning Reynard.   I wish you all a happy New yeare and am Yʳˢ &c

W. P.

100. *Petty to Southwell.*

[The ' Extract of his Letters ' to which Petty here alludes was evidently that to which I have already referred (*supra*, p. 171).   It was printed in place of the essay on *The Multipli-cation of Mankind* (which the publisher explains was not then ' to be found ') at the commencement of the 1685 edition of the pamphlet *Concerning the Growth of the City of London* (Hull, pp. 452-455).   We now see that the anonymous corre-spondent who gave the extract to Mark Pardoe was Southwell. Meanwhile, Petty had apparently completed the ' Essay (on Multiplication) Itself', but he never printed it in spite of Southwell's importunities that he should do so.]

[London] 9⁰ febʳ 1685/6

Dr Coz.
          I have writt nothing since that of Reynard. You gave Mark Pardo some Extract of my Letters which I here return to you Printed.   The Essay itself is ready.

Mr Wyn ¹ tells mee my Ld Treasurer will not medle with my busines till somewhat (I know not what) bee returnd out of Ireland.

About 12 of us meet every Monday night at Sir Joseph Wᵐson's.²   Wee talk somewhat [at] random, but as well as at most other places.

---

¹ *Sic*, but Mr. Gwyn (*supra*, p. 177) is probably intended.
² Sir Joseph Williamson.

Tis sayd the Lady Dorchester [1] goes for Ireland.
Sir James Shaen is still in the clowdes.
I cannot tell what to adde, but that I am Yrs
W. P.

101. *Southwell to Petty.*

[Kingsweston] 13 Feb. 1685/6

Deare Cousin
　　　　I cannot delay my acknowledgment to yours
of the 9th, tho I have now for a whole month beene
perplexed with a sore throat and am not yett quite
freed.　However I have swallowed your kind present,
and wish I could as well digest it—I meane, shew
Reasons why I admire it, since true honour comes
from the Knowing and not from the Ignorant.　But
to see Things, not onely present but the Past and
those to come, to be handled at this Rate, makes me
conclude that had you beene within Reach of Archimedes, that old Projectour, you would have found
for him a place to fasten his Engine.　I have already
sent the Booke to my Lord Weymouth, and tho but
lent him, I feare you must send me a new one.　I tell
him alsoe that the Essay itselfe is ready ; and surely
if I had it, Marke Pardo should be my Confessour,
and you must ene make him yours, that you be not
trampled downe with Importunity.　I see there are
additions I never dreamed of, not onely of the noble
apartment above the fixed Starrs, but the cold or
hott vaulted cellar within the Shell we tread on &c.
I fancy these thoughts are as the Turkish opium
against the fitts of Kerry or the inexorable exchequer
that is soe deaf and dumb.
　　You have alsoe as I see an other weekly Expedient
with a douzin of the Royall Society in your neighbourhood.　I wish I knew Their names that I might pitch
on him that has most pick (?) and time to spare to

---

[1] Catherine Sedley (1657–1717), mistress of King James II., who created
her Countess of Dorchester.　She was sent away by desire of the Queen, but
very soon returned to England.

send me thence the *Nouvelles de la Republique des lettres.*[1]

I thank you for your female newes.   It putts me in mind that Ireland was once calld *Insula Sanctorum.* I am glad tis now againe thought equall to a Nunnery in France.

I see the great Sir James is still in the Clouds— but are you sure tis soe ? for he may then discend in a benigne rayne or in some goulden shower; whereas if now up among the meteors his fall may be worse, and we may heare of him in hayle stones and fire.   Lett Roslin and Renardine have a care, and lett old Renard instruct them in what has past.[2]

To the Ladyes and all about you I am a perfect servant, and alwayes

Yours

102. Petty to Southwell.

[The *Further Observations upon the Dublin Bills* (*Bibliography*, Hull, p. 643) were published this year (1686). In sending the book to Southwell, Petty calls it " empty " in the sense that it was merely a correction and amplification of the original *Observations on the Dublin Bills* published three years before.   The two points in which, as the author explains, he had seen reason to amend his former estimates will be found in Hull's print of this brochure (Hull, p. 498).]

Pickadilly, 27th Feb^{ry} 1685/6

Dear Cosen

I defered writing tell now, That you might not say I sent you empty Letters, for I have fild this with an empty Book, which has nothing in it new, but to correct what I ever thought to bee a fault; vizt, That the Inhabitants of Dublin were but about

---

[1] Pierre Bayle in this periodical had been discussing questions akin to those dealt with by Petty.   He afterwards (*infra*, p. 244) came into direct conflict with some of Petty's conclusions.

[2] In allusion to Petty's letter (*supra*).   By Renard, Southwell here means Petty, and by Renardine and Roslin (*recte* Rossel) Petty's sons Charles and Henry.

32,000, whereas I have now better grounds to believe there are above 50^m.

The other point is to shew that the Roman Catholiq Inhabitants of Dublin are encreased within these 11 years from 2 to 5, which is performd in 6 Pages ; the rest being as it was before.

I wish your patience under the postage of this Pacquet, and remaine Yo^{rs} most heartily

W^M PETTY

103. *Southwell to Petty.*

Kingsweston, 10 March 1685/6

Deare Cousin

After more than a fortnights absence I gott here on Saturday night, but soe overwhelmed with a cold that it kept me waking severall nights, and I am still discomposed by It. I was for ten dayes at Cornebury,[1] and the rest at the Assizes at Gloucester.

My Lord of Ormond spends his time in exercise or in reading as the weather will allow, and I suppose has little thoughts of any other kind of life.

Here I found yours of the 27th past and your kind present therein of your *Dublin Observations.* I have but looked into It, as not yett fitt to read any thing, but I see you putt the worke of volumes into a little Roome, and when all is done you think fitt to call it an ' Empty Booke '. I wish a Philosopher that you and I know, would write at this rate and prevent some future well wisher to the publick the Labour of Condensation.

I have good things of our Neddy and that he cracks Euclides propositions as an Ape would Crack Nutts.

Sure I have heard you say that one time or other

---

[1] Cornbury, Lord Clarendon's seat in Oxfordshire, which he had lent or leased to the Duke of Ormond on the termination (in 1685) of his third term of office as Lord-Lieutenant of Ireland.

you would publish a sett of Cases stated in your way of Politicall Arithmetic [1] (which shall passe by the name of Pettyes *Reports*) Lett me but once more have your word for this, and I will never leave dunning till Mark Pardo be gratifyed.

The Spinsters are all well and at their country divertisments, while I scribble and cough, and can hardly tell what I write. Soe tis best to conclude with all duty to my lady and good wishes to the little ones, and telling you that I am ever, S^r, y^r most affec^t kinsman & humble servant

ROBERT SOUTHWELL

104. Petty to Southwell.

[Religious questions were now very much to the fore and prompted Petty to attempt the definition of some of the terms in dispute. This took the form of a paper called *The Explication of Twelve Theological Words*, which is referred to in the following letter. It was afterwards sent to Southwell, who betrayed some anxiety at the notion of his friends meddling with so dangerous a subject. I have printed the document in question in the *Papers* (No. 48), where another of Petty's efforts towards correct terminology will be found (*The Dictionary of Sensible Words*, No. 46).]

London, 1° Aprill 1686

Dear Cousen

I know no use you can have of my Letters, and for that Neddy is very well is the cause of my silence,—that is of my not waking you from the rest you were in with your Country affairs.

Pamphlets are very rife pro and contra concerning Religion. The Clergy also of all Partys are very busy concerning the same, so as all the Service I hope to do you is the following advice, vizt :

When any Boddy would have you to bee a Roman

---

[1] This is the second time Southwell has referred to this " Set of Cases " (cf. *supra*). They might possibly be the incomplete " Observations " which I have published in the *Petty Papers* (No. 148).

Catholiq, a Papist, a Protestant, a Church of England man, a Presbiterian, Annabaptist, Quaker, fanatick &c, or even Whig or Tory, Let them quit all those giberish denominaçons and uncertaine phrases, but make you a list of *Credenda* and *Agenda* necessary for your Eternall happinesse, and give you their reasons for the same.

This being done Let them give you a clear and senseible explanaçon of these words, vizt: God, Omnipotent, Soule of Man, Soule of Beast, Church, Christian, Pope, Spirituall, Substance, Scriptures, Reason and Sence. For without these words you cannot touch these matters, much lesse ever come unto any conclusion. This is all from

Yo^r affec^t Kinsman & humble serv^t

W^M PETTY

I am disposd forthwith to send Charles abroad. Give me your owne Routier, Remarques and Advices, with allowance for the present face of things.

105. *Petty to Southwell.*

Piccadilly, 8 Aprill 1686

Dr Coz^n

To yours of the 5th instant [1] I am to write of 3 points :

1°. of the 12 Theologicall Words.
2°. of Charles his Travells.
3°. of his mimicall faculty.

The Explication of the 12 words will be ready before you need it, and is a Toole wherewith to open many locks without a burdensome bunch of keyes.

The end of Charles his Travells are not to learne French, Latine, nor Arts and Sciences, but to learne a Competency of Teutonic and Italian. To see *mores*

---

[1] This letter is missing.

et urbes multorum hominum. To shift among dangerous men.   To be a frugall accomptant and manager *Reipublicae suae.*   To distinguish betweene friendship, Civility and flattery.   And lastly *ad faciendum populum,* and make fools believe he is more than he is, [so] as to appeare something at the University after he comes home.   Wee doe not hope he shall make an Interest with the great men abroad, but are content if he know their persons and can talk of Them, and have their names in his album, and wee approove of and thank you for every word in your letter about this matter.

As for the Mimicall faculty, I say that it was never planted by me, but one of the Weeds mencõned in some of my former letters and which I cant pluck up by the Rootes.   I never sent him to the Play House to be instructed either in Tragick or Comicall Recitations, or Acting ; nor is he a frequent Spectator there. But when he is, he doth oftner offer to correct than applaud their performances.   I doe neither indulge him in it, nor doth he value himself uppon itt, Tho I am much pleased : (1) That he decerneth the Persons who are fitt matter for the stage, (2) That he readily picks out the genius, words, action, voice and tone of any mimicable man, and can turne his to sample them, (3) That when he sees anything written, he can without Art or Industry, but by Nature or Instinct, adapt an Action, Tred, voice and tone suitable to the matter and scope thereof, (4) That he can execute a just and judicious punishment and Revenge upon his enemyes by this faculty, and (5) make himself loved by women and feared by men at once.   N.B. He is taught to bee careful in Ridiculing Nations, great parts of men and Coxcombs in Commission, without a Stake proportionable to the hazard thereof ; and must prepare Himself to justify by his Sword what he justly does in the way.

His sister hath a dash of the same, but Henry is more for the Barr than for the Stage.   His talent is in having Arguments *in promptu pro* and *contra*

for everything he meets with.[1]   In short I lett nature
work with them all, and plant no clove nor Cinamon
trees uppon them, but am content with the roses,
Raspea and Violetts, and even with the Hemlock,
nettles and thistles that grow vigorously.   The one
please the smel and taste of their friends, and the other
sting, prick, and poyson their enemyes.

106. *Southwell to Petty*.

[Tyrconnel had just been appointed ' Lord General ' in
Ireland.   The post carried with it, in fact, the supreme
powers which were actually given him when he became
Viceroy in the following year.

As Colonel Richard Talbot, familiarly known by the
name of ' lying Dick ', Tyrconnel had long been in the
confidence of the Duke of York, who on succeeding to the
throne, created him a peer.   Thenceforward his appointed rôle
was to secure the repeal of the Act of Settlement and thereby
restore Catholic domination in Ireland, while making his
master independent in England by means of an Irish army.
Southwell seems to have thought it advisable to ' compliment ' the ' great man ', and Petty afterwards contrived
to keep on good terms with him, though both must have
been well aware that Tyrconnel's activities spelt disaster to
the Irish Settlement and all that this meant for them.]

Kingsweston, 28 April 1686

Dear Cousin
        It is strange I should be soe long in ac-
knowledging yours of the 8th, but there are things to
tell you of.   I was since then at Badminton to meete
my Lord of Ormonde—I was at Bathe to compliment
my Lord Tirconnell—and at Longleat to bid farewell
to my Lord Weymouth, who goes not soe soon as he
pretended.   I have had alsoe some ill trickes of my
sore throat : and even your letter was sick, for all of
that post fell into the River and yours was tatterd and
torne, and it was almost Algebra to find it out.

---

[1] Henry Petty, who was later to succeed as Baron Shelburne to all the Petty
estates, spent a large part of his long life in constant litigation.

After this sincere preamble, I will as sincerely answer you as I can, for what you write concerns your selfe and 3 cousins whom I have reason to esteeme. I say your selfe, because you mention the *Explanation of* 12 *Theologicall Words.* I am afraid you may herein *Quieta movere,* and so blister your fingers ; and if you shew them at all to any, I wish you would lett me have the first sight. You know I am your Sawcy friend, and adventer to chide while others choose to accuse.

As to Cousin Charles, I like extreamly the Scope of his Travell. You point at severall usefull enter-prises, but say all in saying he is to shift among the dangerous men.

For his mimicall faculty I am as much at a plung as if my son were a great dancer on the High Rope. If there were noe falling in the case, the vigour and activity would be pleasing enough ! You handle the matter soe as to disowne and applaud it at once. You think it is a good offensive weapon and yett such an one as may neede a sword to defend It. You think it will allure women, altho it terrify men. And so you passe to say that his sister hath a dash of the same. Now I should be sorry to pervert the Observa-tion ; and that any she-friend of mine should either terrify women or allure men—Nor can there be a sword in this case to defend it !

Can you not remember a certaine lady of the Land, who for acting others in her Chamber was brought uppon the publick Stage, and Sempronia [was] punished more at once than all the Secrett farces were worth.[1] Tis true, in meere Children any Simptome of Witt is welcome ; but as to my cousin Ann that is now taking her ply, roote this weed out I conjure you, as you would a peece of Witch Craft !

[1] This seems to refer to an incident mentioned in Pepys' *Diary* (viii. 200). A certain Mrs. Corey had been taking the part of " Sempronia " in Ben Jonson's play, *The Catiline Conspiracy,* but had incurred the displeasure of Lady Harvey, who apparently thought that she was being ' taken off '. Lady Harvey was able to persuade the Lord Chamberlain to arrest and imprison Mrs. Corey though she was subsequently released by the intervention of Lady Castlemaine. Pepys records that "the heat at Court came to be very great" over this incident

I have been told of a Marshall of France, Mon^sr Clerambaut,[1] who was wont to say " Qui est maistre du Ridicule est maistre du monde " ; and that the Duke of Buckingham [2] was soe in Love with this saying and that man's example, that he resolved to build uppon the same foundation.   Build he did (as you very well know), but the foundation being naught, the Stormes and tempests beat down his House and great was the fall thereof.

As to my Cousin Harry, I am extreamely in Love with his faculty of *Pro* and *Con*, for that will certainly bring in guinyes at Westminster Hall, tho he should never comprehend whether *Pro* or *Con* were most in the Right.   This I say because I knew a great man that fulfilled It.

I will advise our Neddy to strick in with [3] Cousin Harry betimes, and to Steale a Sight of all the little and great Instructions you give to become picklock of the Law.   We have noe other engine at present but the demonstrations of Euclide.

I pay all service to my lady and kindness to the little ones, being ever S^r, Y^rs

R-S.

107. *Petty to Southwell.*

[The letters which follow are much taken up with the subjects of Mimicks and Ridicule, and may be compared with Petty's essay on " Ridicule " (*Papers*, No. 136) which was no doubt written about this time.]

Pickadilly, 4° May 1686

Dr Cousen

I received yours of yesterday by Neddy who is every way a fine Lad, and pertinently inquisitive. As to the 12 words you shall have them as you say. I am glad wee agree that the main end of Travelling

---

[1] Philippe de Clérambault (1606–1665), *Maréchale de France*, who distinguished himself under Louis XIII. in the wars in Italy and Flanders.

[2] George Villiers, second Duke of Buckingham (1628–1687).   He was at this time living in retirement in Yorkshire, after being for many years high in Court favour.   [3] ? Strike in with, or go shares with.

is to learne frugality, Circumspection, discreet Jealousy, and generall Prudence, with such behaviour as will adapt us to conversaĉon with all mankind ; without laying much weight upon Languages, University Arts and Sciences, and Interest in the famous men of other nations.

I cannot undertake to root out the weeds which you Judge so hurtfull, but will take a Care to keep them low and even with the ground. As for Hary's Law documents, they will be like Cloaths too short for my Cos Neddy ; But if wee can find any Jewels of that kind, Neddy shall wear them.

As I did, Dear Cosen, venture to fall upon the great Pascall, so I shall now again venture to set downe some of my thoughts upon the faculty of Imitaĉon which you think so Ill of ; and I say vizt:

(1) That no man can be an excellent Painter without a perfect faculty of imitating all Colours, figures and propoĉtions of magnitude.

(2) No man can be said to sing well, or to learn the same happily, that cannot redily Imitate all the sounds, Tones, and Times hee heareth.

(3) No man can Dance well or Fence well, that cannot redily imitate all the moĉons which are taught in these exercises.

(4) No man can bee a good Orator, that cannot assume and put on all the miens, looks, Jestures and appearances which attend the Passions that he would excite in his hearers.

(5) Representation is the Art of making absent Persons and things present, as often as is requisit, and this is Imitaĉon, Monstration, and Demonstration of Persons and things.

These are the mimicks which I only like in my Children applyed to good uses, and not to hurt their neighbors. If this bee crooked timber, instead of making it straight, wee must dispose of it to shipping for Knees and Brest-hooks.[1] I suppose you do not

---

[1] Bent timber used for support in shipbuilding, 'Breast hooks' being employed in the bows of a vessel.

blame mimicks in this sense, but rather mean the
Art and practis of ridiculing any Person or thing, and
making the same vile and contemptable — which
faculty whoever is master of, Your author Clerambau
saith is master of the World.   I incline to his opinion,
notwithstanding what you say of the Duke of Buckingham, whose Case requires a speciall Essay.   For why
do you learn to ride the great Horse, but to trample
downe your enemys ?   Why to fence, but to disarme
or disable them ?   Why do you affect great offices,
but to make men subject to you, and to become low
and weak in Comparison of your self ?   Yet in all
these Cases you are not certain of victory, but onely
incouragd to fight upon occasion.   Nor doth it follow
that whoever can Ride and Fence, and shoote and
wrastle &c, is thereby made the more apt to offend
and wrong his friends ; but rather to defend himself
against wrongs by the Reputacõn that hee can reveng
them.   Now if the Art of Ridiculing itself bee usd
as aforesaid, where is the Evil, when it is onely
another more manlike sort of fighting ?   Whereas in
the other sort of fighting Beasts comonly excel men.

I have expounded the facultys of mimicking and
Ridiculing.   There is another between both, which
is not to make men laugh at, but to bee facetious ;
that is to make the generality of men laugh, without
offending any but the conscious of their owne faults—
of which more hereafter,

I am yours &c.

108. *Southwell to Petty.*

Kingsweston, 10 May 1686

Deare Cozin

I have yours of the 4ᵗʰ, and your good
Thoughts of Neddy is a Cordiall which I swallow
with delight.   I reckon also on those Jewells you
hint at, those Rules I meane which may fitt him for

the Barr. The same may likewise serve as Spells and Charmes for Cousin Harry, and help them both to find reall Jewells at the Last.

I will expect also the *12 words* you promise. And for my Godson's Travells, you have erected such Figures and Statues for him to draw by, that he must needs returne as from an East India voyage.

Your 5 Remarks uppon the faculty of Imitation are worthy of Mr Penn ; and you have much reason to like in your children such faculty, whilst it tends as you say to good uses, and not to the hurt of their neighbours. For It shews the Strong and various Ideas they are able to take in, and how with advantage to expose them. And while the Exercise is thus Harmless, I would call It rather ' Representation ' than ' Mimicks '. For this latter word borders more on that Act and practice of Ridiculing and Scorning, and making things vile and contemptible, which you take notice of ; and which Mon^{sr} Clerambaut thought was a way of mastering the World.

Now by what I can perceive, you yourselfe are not much averse to this opinion of the Monsieur ; since you urge for Example, why do we learne to ride the great Horse, or why aspire to be officers of State, unless it be to humble others ? Doth the skill of Fencing and wrestling provoke us to offend our Friends ? does it not rather deterr our enemyes and Exempt us from their assaults ? And therefore where is the Evill of Ridiculing, if it answers the Ends aforesaid ? Nay, if it enables us to Conquer, not by the way of fighting, which is common to Beasts, but by a prerogative that is peculiar to Man ?

This I confess is a very home Thrust, and which I had better lett alone than contend with ;—and soe I would, if it were the Argument only that was at Stake. But the young friends I am concerned for makes me shoot a bolt, whatever may be the consequence of Talking to little Effect :

I take then the Ridiculing or Scorning faculty to be soe Dangerous a Weapon, soe apt to runn into

the side of Him that leanes uppon it, that I think a
Naked man is more secure than the Scorner. Is not
a plaine good naturd man, who hath all the neighbourhood for his Life Guard, more Safe and more in
Protection, than an Armed man who stands on Warr
with All? Can this man eate without feare of
poysoning? Can he sleepe sound while his enemyes
are watching? Doth he not live where his neighbours
(packt in a Jury) are masters of his life and Fortune,
and where they (and the Judges too perhaps) will be
content that a Serpent bite the Charmer, and see it
without Pitty or Reprieve?

Tis true your Officer of State overtopps others,
but is that all? Is he not alsoe paid for his office
out of the Exchequer? To ride the great Horse,
To fence and wrestle, doe enable Men to deffend
their Country and to gett great Commands, and to be
putt uppon the Establishment. Alsoe they learne
these Improvements inoffensively, nor is it in the
nature of such Exercises to provoke Them to offend
their Friends. But what getts the Ridiculer out of
the Exchequer, or what cares a Rugged Invadour
for his Mimicks? How can he even learne this Skill
without being an offender? and how many broaken
pates does he incurr before he comes to perfection?
Now if a Doctor Kills many before he comes to be
perfect, tis not questioned, because this killing enables
Him to Cure and it tends to the good of others. But
tis a miracle if a scorner be not taken off in his Career,
for feare he should grow perfect. Men think that
Tallent is a sort of Thunder and lightning which is
not to be trusted with flesh and Blood. That tis a
sword never yett worne in the Scabbard; that tis
like Pride, whose life and being consists in shew and
appearance. That the delight of It cannot be con-
tayned, nor he that is master herein more forbeare
offending, than Narcissus could resist his own drowning.
Therefore the People, reputing him as a Common
Enemy, batter at Him, and think all foule Play Lawfull,
as against a Hornett or a Scorpion.

The Truth is Horace hath a little told Tales out of Schoole in saying of Himself and of this Faculty :

" Omne vafer vitium ridenti Flaccus Amico
   Tangit, et admissus Circum praecordia ludit." [1]

Here he ownes that when his frank and debonaire friend had lett Him into his very Bosome, he could not forbeare to Sting.   He calls it indeed the *Vices* of his Friend which he playd uppon, but wee know how the true Ridiculer affects the nicest Infirmityes— Nay he is most intent to shout for Laughter, there where the world admires.

Soe that upon the whole matter, who would desire to carry Pistolls about Him that must ever be cockt ? Is there any fair Lady, if she be wise, would chuse to be mistris to an Inconstant Tyrant ; or who would norish a Lyon in his Bedchamber who is only tame but by fitts?   Soe I am not for Mons[r] Clerambaut, nor for his Admirer the Duke, since all his grace's advantage and applause ended in this :—

" He had his Jest, and they had his Estate." [2] I rather incline to the Lord Bacon's advice, who is soe farr from Descanting on the faults of others, that he would not desire to know the Descant uppon his owne.   " Could there " says he " be procured some Enchanted Glass wherein wee might behold the hatred and whatsoever malice is any way raised against us, It were better for us that such a Glasse were taken away, and forthwith broaken.   For we often fix evills which of themselves would fligh away ; It being a dangerous matter to provoke men's consciences who if they think themselves undiscovered, are easily changed to the better ; but if they once perceive themselves dismaskt, they drive out one Mischief with another."   Tis somewhere among Solomon's sayings : " He that conceals a fault keepes friendship,[3] but a

---

[1] Southwell is confusing.   The lines quoted were not written by Horace but of Horace by Persius (*Satires*, i. 116).
[2] This was said of Zimri in Dryden's *Absalom and Achitophel* (l. 562).
[3] Proverbs xii. 23.

Scorner ensnares a Citty ".[1]   And tis his great Elogy
in speaking of a good wife " that the law of kindness
is in her Lipps ".

By this you see what motive I have to be rather
for the soft answer that breaketh the bone, than for
turning the point and standing alwayes in Arms.
This posture seemes to declare a Diffidence in that
Law that is made to protect us all, and wee should
alwayes be contented with that which contents others.
I believe Mons[r] Clerambaut was noe less hated
than he was feared, and that he had some sighing
scenes, as well as those of laughter.   For you remember how uppon the sowing the Dragon's Teeth,
armed Souldiers and fighting did presently ensue.

I will conclude with a memorable saying of my
friend the Conde de Castle Melhor [2] when he was
shaken from his Ministry in Portugall.   The agitation
lasted for some dayes, and I stood by him in it.   There
came a Grandee to speake with Him (one whose
Ancestour found out the Cape of Good Hope).[3]   Being
gone the Conde told me that to fix this man, he had
pretended all went well, and that he never would
leave the ministry.   " Why " said I " if all goes well,
will you forsake the ministry ? "   " Yes ", said he,
" for such is the Danger and envy of the Place, that
I will not only lay it downe ; but on my soule I would
give it, if it lay in my Power, to the greatest enemy
I now have in the World."

Your letter ends with a Medium which you are
thinking of, namely the facetious Temper, which lyes
betweene the Mimick and Ridiculing.   I wish you
would (in Major Thornehill's [4] phrase) burne a candle
uppon itt, for this would profitt and delight us all.

---

[1] Proverbs xxix. 8.
[2] Don Luis de Souza e Vasconcellos, Count of Castello Melhor, was at the
head of affairs in Portugal from 1662 to 1666.   His arrangement of a marriage
between the King and a French princess brought about a palace revolution,
through which Alphonso VI. was banished and Castello Melhor forced to leave
the country.
[3] Bartholomew Diaz, the Portuguese navigator, 1486.
[4] A Captain Thornhill had been one of the managers of the Duke of York's
estates in Ireland.

Tis not now time of day to tell you that our Girles advance in their Dancing, but to assure you very truly, after all respects are paid, that

I am Sir, Yours

R. SOUTHWELL

109. *Petty to Southwell.*

Pickadilly, 12⁰ May 1686

Dr Cosen

To yours of the 10ᵗʰ I will answer your self in Person, when you come up to the Parliament the 22ⁿᵈ of November next, unlesse I prorogue my Penn before that time by saying I cannot. In the meane time I onely ask you whether to be Strong, Nimble, Sharp sighted, and to have Courage and skill with a Stiff, Tuff, Sharp Sword, a screwd gun truely board, with a lock that never misses fier, bee a dangerous condicõn ?

But to leave our Mimicks and Ridicules—what do you say to our Lands in Ireland ? To the Army, the Judges, Privy Councills and Parliament which are like shortly to bee there ? [1] Pray write me a word in earnest concerning this Matter. How can wee talk of being facetious, till wee have burnt a Candle upon these funest and Lugubrious points ? Let the Pretty spinsters dance on, but do you write seriously upon this matter to

Yoʳˢ &c

110. *Southwell to Petty.*

Kingsweston, 19 May 1686

Deare Cousin

I have yours of the 12, and as I had writt what occurrd on your melancholy queryes, behold a

---

[1] The allusion is of course to the wholesale changes which James II. was effecting in the Irish administration.

more melancholy subject in the death of my deare
Nephew Sir John Percivale.[1]   I could say much of
Him were you altogether a Stranger, but there is a
very good man gone and his country susteynes in
him no meane losse.   What I loose you may easily
calculate, when he was the last of 3 Nephewes that I
had taken some care to educate to men's estate.   I still
thought in the course of nature that I should leave
young children of my owne to their protection, and
soe my care for them was but the patterne of what
I proposed for them.   But they are all gone before
me, and I must renew my care for Sir John's Children ;
and by the course of nature, when I am gone, those
must succeede unto it that I leave.

Thus we are often mistaken in our Measures as
to these worldly things, but surely God is best pleasd
when we doe most readily submitt unto his Will.

When my small officer attends you, you will see
I have burnt day light rather than a candle to obey
your com͂ands.   But whether I say well or ill, tis
onely to your selfe.

I wish my Lady and the Children all happinesse
and ever am, Sʳ, Yʳ most affecᵗ kinsman & humble
servant

ROBERT SOUTHWELL

111. *Petty to Southwell.*

Piccadilly, 22 May 1686

Dr Cousin

This is to condole with you for the Death
of that worthy Gentleman Sir John Percivale, and
I begin my letter thus : There is a way of Rhetoric
as well as of Ridiculing, by finding out some quality
or circumstance wherein noble objects agree with

---

[1] Sir John Perceval had just died, from gaol fever caught while acting as
foreman of the Grand Jury at Cork Assizes.

vile and contemptible — As if one should call an Excellent advocate ' Doctor Dish-clowt ', because as the one wipes away all blots and blemishes from his client's concernes, the other wipes of what is fowle from pans, pots, and platters. And some orators make a Man (whom the Scriptures say is superior to Angells) a vile thing, because he was borne in an Womb placd *inter stercus et urinam* ; and would make the Loveliest Ladyes out of Love with themselves, because sattin made of silk and the Excrement of a Worme, is softer and smoother than the finest skins of the finest Ladyes.

I will not lessen your sense of loosing Sir John Percivale by lesning him ; nor lessen him by the arts abovemenčoned, but had rather say :

" per funera multa tuorum
surgis ad Imperium."

That by the death of your Father, Mother and Sister, of Sir Edward Deering and your 3 nephews, you are the Head and Governor of Both Familyes.   That by the death of Rupe, Ingenious Neddy culminates ; and by that of your Excellent Lady you are entitled to that million I mention of unmarryed teeming Ladyes. Deare Cozen, nothing in all this is unnaturall or prodigious, nor, *quod vitio tibi verti potest*, I believe they are all better where they are than here, and that they are taken away from the wrath to come.   Wherefore Letts follow Sir Thomas Moore's method of mourning. The Young Crew will have the benefitt of your doubled Experience in the Art of their Education and I hope you will live to give It them—And here I abruptly end.

Yesterday I saw Neddy on horseback in Hidepark, and on Monday the great Tirconnell gets in our horizon towards making his Aurora in Ireland.

I ask againe, what do you thinke of the Ship,[1] and of your owne Long Boate.   If the ship founder in

---

[1] *I.e.* the Ship of State and Southwell's private concerns in Ireland.

the ocean, what will your Longboate do ? " When
Thou are converted, strengthen thy brethren.'' [1]
I am Yr^s &c

W. P.

112. *Southwell to Petty.*

Kingsweston, 29 May 1686

Deare Cousin

    I had your condoling Letter of the 22nd, and
pray allow me to tell you what my Little daughter
said, being a while agoe full of mirth and good humour
at the Discourse that was betweene us : " Truly
father '', said she, " If a dogg should come into the
Roome, you doe say such play things, that I believe
you would make him Laugh.''

    Cousin, you doe wipe off Teares at a very strange
rate, but why did nature furnish Them if there must
be no Sorrow ? Can you, by pointing at what is
contemptible in a noble object, Establish your maxime
in this alsoe : That nothing is Stronger than its
weakest part ? I should rather say it is unnaturall
to lessen any thing that is either anihilated, or must
rise glorious. For tho your friends in Eutopia
triumph and sing Hymns at a Funerall, tis but to
fortify those that must Dye, and by this disguise
fling sugar into the bitter Cupp. If you would know
nature's mind, see what is done even by the men of
Leest Humanity. The Cafras and Hattintoes [2] never
loose a Friend or Relation but they cutt off a Joynt
from one of their Fingers—soe much they scorne the
acquisition of Mourning Rings. The Indian women
burne with their dead Husbands, And the Husbands
of Angola appoint when they dye who shall for 8
dayes Console the afflicted Widdow, and it falls to
their next of kin thus to cohabite with Her if they dye
Intestate.

---

[1] Luke xxii. 32.
[2] *Sic* for *Kaffirs* and *Hottentots.*

Funus justa petit and *Sal liquefit ut condiat.*
Teares are the true and naturall balsome, and they
who refuse Them robb the Dead.

But what Art—I was going to say play-words—
does your kindnesse find out to stifle my recentments ?
You tell me of Empire, and how much I assend by
the desolations that are past.   If by loosing one wife
I have Title to the million that are unmarryed, by
the same right your million have Title to me ; which
would proove but a hard Chapter.   And how can you
magnify my Headship over Infants by the loose of
Sir John Percivale ?   Is not this to magnify the
Rouling of Sysiphus's stone—to beginn againe at
the Bottome when I was at the Mountain's topp, and
thought I had nursed up those who in reason should
turne nurses to myne ?

Thus you see, Cousin, I will not be comforted.
For while your good nature finds Arts to divert
Sorrow, It discovers there is some sorrow due ; and
it being as debt, the soonest payment will be the best.

As to the Shipp, you have already had my
wandring thoughts.   I doe for Consolation sometimes
read the Chapter, how there arose a tempestuous
wind called " Euroclidon " ; yett after all, how some
by swimming, others on Boards and broken planks,
gott all to Land, soe as not a soule was lost.[1]   In the
next place, when I am more shaken, and thinke where
Neddy (The Pinnace) may have surest anchorage
in omne eventum, I start up and shape his Course,
blow high, blow low, towards Westminster Hall ; for
whatever happens Crafty Knaves will Live.

I am Yrs

R. S.

113. *Petty to Southwell.*

[It seems that Charles Petty—the ' Ingenious youth '
here referred to—had shown his father a letter from Sir

---

[1] Cf. Acts xxvii. 44, St. Paul's shipwreck at Melita.

Robert Southwell, in which the latter spoke with less than his accustomed reserve about the state of affairs in Ireland. Petty was delighted, though Southwell betrays evident anxiety, when there is talk of a copy having been taken of so incriminating a document.

The 'case with Lord Dunsany' was another of Petty's perennial disputes and is frequently referred to in the later letters. It concerned lands in Meath, which had been forfeited by Patrick Plunkett, the ninth Lord Dunsany. Petty, or his nephew William Napper, purchased these lands from the soldiers to whom they were allotted, but their original owner was, like many others, subsequently cleared of complicity in the Rebellion and the lands were apparently recovered by his grandson Christopher, the tenth Lord. A full statement of the case is in the MS. of the *Treatise of Ireland*, though it is not included in Hull's print of that Essay (Hull, p. 602).

Another of Petty's land controversies was that with Fitzgerald of Ticroghan Castle in County Meath. Frequent references to this dispute will be found in the later letters, but I have been unable to discover any details relating thereto.]

[London May 29. 1686]

D^{re} Coz^n

Within these few dayes a very Ingenious Youth, Heyre to a good Estate in Ireland upon the New Title, shewed me a letter from one who advised Him to Study the Law uppon account of the uncertainty of Estates in that Country. The Letter was long, without an Impertinent word, and was the best Systeme of what things are to be considered in that affaire, that I think extant anywhere. I will endeavor to gett a Coppy of Itt, and in the meane time will give you one paragraph of It, as neare as I can remember it, viz :

" As to particular Cases of Complaints of the Catholiques, some seemed very strange, vizt, where they are kept out even of what the Court of Claymes decreed them for want of indifferent Juryes and Judges ; and that it hath been impossible to gett one indifferent Sheriffe in the County of Meath since his Majesty's Restoration."

If it did not argue some guilt in me, I would sweare this paragraph were the case between the Lord Dunsany and Myselfe, for he saith I gott as much of his Lands in Meath for 2s and 7 pence as is worth above £300 per annum; made his grandfather 'Nocent' by a meane trick; hindred him from prooving his Father's deed of settlement, though he attempted it in all Courts; kept him from having a sheriffe for his purpose, tho' he had the King's Letter for such an one; kept off the Court of Claymes from executing a Clause for his Restoration; and would now hinder the Court of Chancery from Relieving him against all those Wrongs and Stratagems &c.

Dear Cozen, I read with care and pleasure the French book wherein you are so bravely vindicated to the Learned world by Dr Arnaud[1] &c. So you must read and keep by you the enclosed paper to which I will add nothing on this occasion to what hath been long since written. The matter is neare 30 years old, and hath been answered to every power that would question it. Pray read it twice at least, for tis wonderful how I should ever come by 300£ per annum for a debenture of 2s 7d—which cost but 15 pence in money.

The paper I first mentioned hath made great tourbillions in my mind, but I retreat to the sayings following :

1. God is above all.
2. Few designes hitt thoroughly.
3. *Naturam expellas* &c.
4. The ballance of Knavery.
5. The follyes of our Enemyes.
6. *Res nolunt male administrari.*
7. Wee shall live till we dye.
8. Time and chance &c.
9. Another shuffling may cause a better dealing.

---

[1] The allusion is apparently to Antoine Arnauld (1612–1694), the French philosopher. He was a doctor of the Sorbonne and belonged to the Jansenist party. Amongst his many works *L'Art de penser*, a treatise on Logic (which is perhaps the volume here referred to), is the best known.

10. Fish in troubled waters.
11. Trees may grow the better for pruning.
12. Lets do what we can.
13. Twill bee all one 1000 yeares hence.
14. *Una salus miseris nullum sperare salutem.*[1]
15. Some other Bowle may drive the Jack from the Rest.
16. Playing at Tennis in a Wheelebarrow &c.

I am now past my Climactericall,[2]
                    Adieu

[Endorsed by Southwell " London : May 29 1686 ".]

114. *Southwell to Petty.*

[Kingsweston] 2 June 1686

Deare C
          I have read your Case[3] over and over and
doe say :

    " Atque utinam pro te possint mea vota valere
    Quae pro me duros non tetigere deos." [4]

Pray state alsoe as closely the Case of FitzGerald of
Tegrohan, touching a deed prooved counterfeit by the
distance of one Shee (as I remember) who signed it.
I doe fancy there may be Indignation treasured up
as to that in particular, and that you are farr from
being a favorite in the General. It will doe you noe
hurt however to supose soe, for you will scoure your
Kettles the Brighter, and that Vulture Kerry will
leave of knawing. For you are wont to say (as of
the Hick[5]) that one will cure another. These are
words perhaps fitter to bee heard than read, and soe

---

[1] Virgil, *Æneid*, ii. 354.
[2] Petty was born on May 26, 1623.
[3] *I.e.* Petty's paper on his quarrel with Dunsany.
[4] Ovid, *Tristia*, I. ix. 4.
[5] This was the old form of the modern ' hiccough '.

lett them goe to the fire, and if you have taken a
Coppy of what you are pleased to call ' a Systeme ',
burne it alsoe ; for the burnt child dreads the fire.
Our young Westminster Hall man will explaine this
unto you.

The Late new addition to the Councell is a new
light, that is very dazleing and will need all your
16 axiumes for consolation. It puts me almost in
mind of a 17th—" Little man, Little man, there is
land for you in the Moone "[1]—And tho yours be
past, yett some might think it better if their climacteric
were yett to come.

I wish it were as easy to find the cure as the
disease. A consultation of Doctours is scarce to be
thought of, for such advising might be called Com-
bination and soe pass for witchcraft. Wherefore all
I can att present think off, is to pray God that there
may bee from all good Protestants such demonstrations
of Loyalty, zeale and affection to his Majesty's person
and government, that their enemys may not have
credit in objecting that his authority is not safe in
their Hands, or that they are still the Race of those
who once murthered the Faith.[2]

Your kindnesse and contentment in my vindication
that you read is very obleging unto

Yors

115. *Petty to Southwell.*

[London] 5th June 1686

Dr C

Yours of the 2d is very dire and dismall, But
I will set all the Goblins, Furys, Demons and Devills
which stand stragling up and downe within that

---

[1] Cf. *History of the Down Survey*, p. 299, where (in Petty's dispute with
Sankey) he is accused of having met rival claimants at the time of the settlement with this tag.

[2] Southwell, as may be seen, was afraid that Petty would make some display
of hostility to the new regime in Ireland, and as usual was a counsellor for
moderation.

letter in Battle-array, in Rank and File, Incamped and Intrencht, vizt :

1. You do not say my case with Dunsany is just and strong, but onely wish that your prayers for my good luck may bee effectuall, and that what I have said may have any operaċon upon the *Duros Deos* you menċon.

2. You think that wrath is treasurd up against mee for wrong done to the Tecroghanists.

3. You say I am very far from being a generall Favorite—I suppose to those whose favour is now a flaming.

4. That Kerry is like still to bee a gnawing Vulture.

5. As for the Systeme ; I took no Coppy. I had it all in my head before, and was glad to find that some others had it also.

6. I expect from the New Councill more good than ever I had from the Old. Who do you mean by the ' little man ' for whom there is ' land in the moon ' onely, and not in this world ?

7. I am of your opinion that 'twere better for me also, that my Climaterick were not yet past of 9 times 7, but that I had two septenarys yet good, as you have.

8. That my disease is manifest and notorious, but the Cure thereof inscrutable ; The Consultaċon for my Cure, is a *Noli me tangere*—a crime and like the sin of Witchcraft.

To all which I say :—

Hulchy, Pulchy, Suckla mee
Hoblum, Doblum, Dominee.

I heartily joyne with your prayer, and you know that my studys are how his present Majesty may (even by and with his Religion), do glorious things for God, himself and his Subjects, and trust his affairs in no worse hands than the maligned persons you mention, who will serve him upon Demonstrable motifs, not base Assentation, and who saith with our friend Horace :

"si fractus illabatur orbis
Impavidum ferient ruinae."[1]

I have sent you my thoughts upon *Mourning for the Dead*,

And am Yours &c.

116. *Petty to Southwell.*

[London] 5 June 1686

Dr Coz[n]

You have made me dogmatize upon the nature of good parts, against Mons[r] Pascall, and of mimicks and Ridicule &c. You bring me next to the doctrine of *Mourning for the Dead*,[2] to which I say :

When anyone dyes who had promoted your honour, pleasure or profit, and still desired so to do, Tis manifest you mourn for yourself and your owne Losse ; and may expresse or suppresse the signes of it as you think fitt, to make the world understand what esteem you had of the Defunct, and to encourage the Living to serve you as the Defunct had done. And you shall mourn very properly in this Case, If you give to the Defunct's surviving friends, what you owed to the Defunct for the good hee had done you in his Life, more than you had requited by reciprocall kindnesse ; whether by black, called mourning garments, or by Rings with Deaths heads on them, by boxes of sweetmeats, burnt wine, or rosemary wett in Sweet water, or by gloves or Skarfs, or by any other effectuall way or signes of gratitude, which the world understands ; but without cuting of your Joynts as the Cafras and other Coxcombs you mençon. I say you need not punish your self

---

[1] Horace, Book III. Ode iii.   [2] Cf. *supra*, p. 201.

otherwise than by parting with what you can spare as aforesaid, and giving it to those of the Defunct's friends that most want it. As for Bells, Sermons, Coffins, and Coaches, you are to defend yourself from the reproaches grounded upon the customs and opinions (true or false) of the Country and age you Live in.

If you found such signes of God's grace in your friend, as perswardes you hee is in Abraham's bosome with poor Lazarus, or in Paradise with the penitent thiefe expecting a glorious resurrection and Consuma-tion of his bliss, I think you need not mourne at all, otherwise than as aforesaid. But if you suspect him to bee in Chains of darknesse, you must grieve that you did not by your precepts and example prevent his sad Condicon. And if you believe that any sort of men can releive him, you shall doe well to hier them at any rate to do so, and in the mean time have such a Compassion with the Defunct as unison harp-strings have one with another. And you must warne the Living (especially the Defunct's friends) to avoid those things, that causd your feares concerning him. For Dives desired that one might bee sent from the Dead to his Bretheren on earth for that purpose. Deare Cos, I believe you are alredy of near the same opinion with

Yrs &c

117. *Southwell to Petty.*

Kingsweston, 7 June 1686

Deare Cousin

I have the favour of 2 of yours of the 5th and the 'State of a Case'[1] Inclosed. One of your Letters is uppon *Death without Mourning*, and seeing it is hard to defend passion against Reason, I will acquiesce in your Arguments and read them uppon ill accidents, in hopes they will support me.

---

[1] Against Fitzgerald of Ticroghan (*supra*, p. 205).

As to the State of the Case you send now, and the State you sent before, I cannot think how any Cases can be more strong that are not of Mathematicall Demonstration.

Nor did I tell you what I hapned to over heare, but with most friendly Intention — that you might looke early out.   I have known you formerly to mind your Cylinders,[1] while your Acres were Tearing from you ; and you would not desist from Philosophy, as long as it was not in the power of a Decree to forbidd Rubarb and Cena from purging.

But since the discovery of my owne feares hath exceeded all due proportion and that you send "Hulchy Pulchy " to defy It ;   I will take heart alsoe, as did your Boy Thom, who was sorely afrighted at the roaring of the Sea and the trembling of the Vessell, till he heard the seamen sweare.

I am glad you expect better things from the new, than you felt from the old Councill, and I had noe meaning in that phrase of " Land in the Moone " but to excite you as aforesaid.   For marriners doe usually cry ' all hands Aboard ' when there is thoughts of any danger.

I hope, Cousin, in the meane time it will be noe false Latin to looke well after my Hay, or if I goe on with my new Invention of an Oxe-House, where the Cattle are both to eat and drink in the same Cribb, and not to stirr till they be fitted for the Slaughter. *Magister Artis Venter*[2]

I am ever yrs

R. S.

118. *Petty to Southwell.*

[The autobiographical notes which commence in this letter and are continued in those of July 14, 17 and 31 (*infra*) tell us practically all that is known of Petty's first steps up the ladder of fortune.   Most of them have already been printed in Fitzmaurice's *Life* (pp. 294-296).

[1] The double-bottom boat was sometimes called by Petty ' The Cylinders '.
[2] Persius, Prologue to *Satires* (l. 10), *Magister artis, ingenique largitor venter.*

The only other account of Petty's early life is to be found in a MS. entitled *Vita W.P.*, consisting of some three hundred Latin hexameters. As I have explained elsewhere (*Papers*, xxi.), the difficulty of deciphering Petty's peculiar handwriting and of translating his more peculiar Latin has deterred me from the attempt to explore the document in question.]

Piccadilly, 12 Junii 1686

Dre Cozn

  To yours of the 7th I returne this humble long answer. I beg your pardon (1°) for comparing your friendly warnings to Goblins and Devills, (2°) for seeming to defy them all with the spell of 'hulchi' &c, wherein I did not doe well. Pray doe not punish me by supposing the like hereafter, for I took all very kindly and thankfully.

  Nevertheless what shall a man say who hath been used like mee (*e.g.* in Kerry), but at some times and to an Intimate friend use some words of contempt and desperation when Right and Reason will doe noe good? What I said to you was but like that of Rhubarb &c. to the Court of Claymes.[1] And I am glad that my spell 'Hulchi' gave you the same comfort that the Seaman's swearing did to Tom.

  Among other weapons that I am scowring up, I have drawn out a paper shewing what money I had at Xmas 1636—which was 1s. How it rise to 4s 6d, then to 24s, then to 4£. Then to 70. Next how it fell to 26, then rise to £480 at my Landing in Ireland. Next to 13,060£ at finishing the Survey. And how after I gott my Land in Ireland and Estate in England &c, it was 3200£ at the King's Restoration &c. And so all along to this very day. Perhaps the like hath not been seene. This and the like gave me courage wherewith I fought Zanchy.[2] Whatever becomes of me I can leave such arguments of 50 yeares art and Industry as will be a credit to my children

---

[1] The 'Court of Claims' had been appointed in 1662 to decide between 'Innocents' and 'Nocents' in the late Irish Rebellion.

[2] Sir Jerome Sankey, vide *Reflections upon some Persons and Things in Ireland* (Hull, *Bibliography*, No. 5).

and friends. And now instead of *Hulchi Pulchi* I say 'God's Will be done—Naked came I into the World and naked must go out of it.'

I did, Dear Cozen, obtrude upon you the Case with Lord Dunsany and obeyd you in sending that of Tegrohan. I take my turne to obtrude againe uppon you that of Macgillicuddy[1] which I think must needs come uppon the Stage. And then you shall comand another, and so as long as you please, but no longer.

Enlarge a little uppon the Meate and Drink Cribs which you have for your Oxen. I envy you rurall contentments—give me an alms out of your abundance. Feare not Neddy; Ile warrant hee will live, your Godson is short of him in that faculty,

Adieu

119. *Southwell to Petty.*

Kingsweston, 10 July 1686

Deare Cousin

Here has been a great Irish wedding in our neighbourhood, and by the title I tooke share in it, and part of the dinn has even reached this poore place. And these are the causes why I come thus slow to acknowledge yours of the 12th past.

I am now returning to the care of Hay Harvest and of my Oxe-House. In this there is nothing new, but that a Streame of Water is to run under the Cribb, soe they drink where they stand and when they please; and this want of Liberty is to hasten them for the Slaughter. If Irish Rents come in noe better, I must invent something more—either the art of fasting or Monsr Payim's (?) Invention to soften beanes.

I perceive you are scouring old papers, and your short hint of Meliorations from the yeare 1636 is soe entertaining that I wish I had more of It.

---

[1] See p. 5, *supra.*

I thanke you for the State of McGillocuddy's businesse which I have now read againe, and I think your measure is very hard, but the time now to redresse it much harder. For who can mind right or wrong touching Hamocks and Cabins when the whole Shipp is in danger, or lyes at Hull? And yett I am told (tho you say nothing of It) that Sir William P[etty] had great accesse to the Great Man [1] before his going over; that he gave him in severall Schemes as to Adventurers and Soldiers, and urged so well the preference of Money to any disturbance of the present Settlement, that the Great Man himselfe seemes to have a Byas that way; that he has been heard to say how his owne Fortune was settled by the Acts, and that His Majesty has noe thought of parting with a foot of his estate in that Country. And this is all I can say as to the Mayne.

I am glad you fancy that Neddy will find out the way of shifting among dangerous men. It will import him both for his owne sake and his sisters too.

I hope my good lady and all yours are well. We have lost in Sir William Coventry [2] a great man of our nation.

I am ever yr

R. S.

120. *Petty to Southwell.*

[In this letter Petty claims that if he had stuck to medicine he would have made his fortune without meddling with forfeited land in Ireland. The assertion is probably true, for his papers show that he had a good practice before he first went to that country as Surveyor and Physician to the army. He would, of course, have lost nothing by his subsequent connection with the Protector's family, and had he been content to remain in private practice he would no doubt have gone as far as any of his contemporaries.

Of the rivals whom he mentions Thomas Willis (1621–1675) had started life at Oxford and had afterwards secured

---

[1] Lord Tyrconnel, and not, I think, King James, as suggested by Fitzmaurice. *Life*, p. 280.
[2] Sir William Coventry (1628–1686), sometime secretary to the Duke of York, a Commissioner of the Navy, M.P., etc.

a very large practice under Charles II. He was, like Petty, an original member of the Royal Society. By " The Cock Lowre " Richard Lower (1631–1691) is no doubt intended. He also was a noted physician and physiologist, and became the first medical man of his day when Willis fell out of favour at Court.]

Piccadilly, 13 July 1686

Dr Cozen
        I will now answer but a small part of yours of the 10th Instant, and divide even that small part into the 3 partites following (1) Concerning myselfe. (2) Neddy.   (3) The great man you mention.

Concerning Myself, I say that I had 13,060£ in cash anno 1656, which at 10 per cent (above 12 being then justly taken) would anno 1666 have beene 26,120£, and anno 1676 52,240£, and in this yeare 1686 104 thousand 480£.   I further say that, without meddling with forfeited lands, I could Anno 1656 have returned into England and been at the top of practice in Oliver's Court, when Dr Willis was casting waters at Abington Markett and the Cock Lowre but an Egge.   And what the superlucration thereof (besides the 104^m £) might have beene in 30 yeares, I leave to your judgment.   I say the profitt of these 2 funds, would have exceeded my present State by——.[1]

As to Neddy, I say that this present great and early acquaintance, with the easy access to great Men, will give him bread and cheese by the Law before he bee ripe ; whereas my Harry may be an able man 7 yeares before he getts bread only.

As to the Great man, I had indeed strange accesse and acceptance.   I spake unto him as one having authority and not as the Scribes and Pharisees.   I said severall sowre things which he took as Juice of Orange Squeezed into his Mince meat, and not as Vitrioll.   For some of the things he told me [2] were these :

---

[1] Blank in original.
[2] Petty must have meant to write " I told him " instead of " he told me ", for the arguments which follow are clearly Petty's and not Tyrconnel's.

1°. That all the Lands which the Irish lost as forfeited were not worth Anno 1653, when they left them, neare 300ᵐ pounds.

2°. That the 34,000 men which the heads of the Irish were permitted and assisted to carry to forraigne States, at 10£ per head, were worth more than the said Lands ; but 10£ is not $\frac{1}{2}$ the value of negroes nor $\frac{1}{8}$ of Algier slaves, nor $\frac{1}{4}$ of their real value in Ireland.

3°. I said that what the Irish gott restored Anno 1663, more then what belonged to them Anno 1641, is now worth much more than all they ever lost.

4°. That they gott 1100ᵐ Acres of Land by Innocence, making 7 of 8 Innocent. Whereas it appeares by the arrears allowd to the 49 officers,[1] that there was a Protestant Army of 20ᵐ men from 1641 to 1649, which army together with the $\frac{7}{8}$ of the Irish that were Innocent, could not beate $\frac{1}{8}$ nocent part of the Irish, but necessitated my Lord of Ormond to make the Peace of 1648—vide the Articles.

This (as Sir Jerome[2] said) " was not halfe ". He heard me with trouble and admiration. He pressd me to speake of the Settlement. I told him there were things in it against the light of Nature and the current Equity of the World, but wether it was worth the breaking I doubted ; but if It were broaken by Parliament I offerd things to be mix'd with those Acts as should mend the Condition of all men.[3]

Thus much for the present from him who is Yours
W-P.

The next shall be how I gott the shilling at Xmas 1636. How I came by 4s 6d when I went to sea and how I advanced the same to 24s when I went to the Jesuits Colledge. What the setting of my Broaken Legg cost to the farrier's wife, what for Crutches &c.

[1] *Vide* p. 4.
[2] Sir Jerome Sankey.
[3] Cf. Petty's proposals put before the King at this time (*Papers*, Nos. 71-80).

121. *Petty to Southwell.*

Piccadilly. 14 July 1686

Dᵣₑ Cozⁿ

The next part of my answer to yours of the 10ᵗʰ Instant is : 1°. How I gott the shilling I menc̃oned to have had at Xmas 1636—which was by 6ᵈ I got of a Country Squire for shewing him a pretty Trick on the Cards, which begot the other 6ᵈ fairly won at Cards. 2°. How this shilling came to bee 4ˢ 6ᵈ : When I went to sea, 6ᵈ was given (or rather paid) mee by Mother Dowling, who having been a sinner in her youth, was much releived by my reading to her in the *Crums of Comfort*, Mr Andrews' *Silver Watch Bell*, and *The plain man's pathway to Heaven*. The next 6ᵈ I got for an old Horace given (why do I say given ?) or delivered mee by Len Green for often construeing to him in Ovid's *Metamorphoses* till my throat was soare—though to so little purpose that hee, coming to say his Lessen began *Protinus* (signifying ' soon after ') ' King Protinus ' &c. My next Booty was 18ᵈ given mee by my Godfather, for making 20 verses to congratulate his having been made a Doctor in Divinity by some good Luck.[1] The other shilling was impressed by my Aunt, whom I repaid by a Bracelet bought in France for 4ᵈ, but juged to bee worth 16ᵈ.

This 4ˢ 6ᵈ was layd out in France upon pittifull brase Rings, with coold glasse in them instead of diamonds and Rubies. These I sold at home to the young fellowes whom I understood to have sweet-hearts, for treble what they cost. I also brought home 2 hair hatts (which within these 11 years might have been seen) by which I gayned little lesse. Having been ten months at sea, I broak my Leg, and was turnd a shoare, strangely visited by many, by the name of *Le Petit Matelot Anglais qui parle Latin et Grec*. Neer my recovery, and when I resolvd to quit

---

[1] I have not been able to discover who was the D.D. who stood godfather to Petty.

the sea,—as not being able to bear the envy of our Crew against Mee for being able to say my Compasse, shift my Tides, keep reckoning with my plain Scale, and for being better read in *The Seaman's Kalender*, the *safeguard of Saylers* &c, than Seamen of our Ship—I made verses to the Jesuits expressing my desires of returning to the Muses, and how I had been drawn from them by reading Legends of our Country-man Capt Drake, in these words :

Nostrates Dracos nimis admiratus, abivi
Nauta, schola fugiens, et dulcia carmina previ.[1]

I must not omitt that ' La Grande Jane ', the farrier's wife, had an escu for setting my broken Leg, the Potticary 10 sols, and 8 sols a payer of Critches of which I was afterwards cheated. Upon the re-mainder (my Ring trade being understood and lost) I set up with the remainder of 2 Cakes of Bees Wax, sent mee in reliefe of my Calamity, upon the trade of playing Cards, white starch and hayre hatts, which I exchangd for tobacco pipes, and the shreds of Lether and parchment wherewith to size paper. By all which I gott my expences, followed The Colledge, proceeded in Mathematicks and cleerd 4£. And so much of this stuff for this time.

As for Kerry and McGillicuddy, my aylments are not Hamocks and Cabbins, but Keels, Rudders, main masts, Anchors &c. In all which I onely say that men's resentments of this my Case are the Scale by which I measure their honor, Conscience, Justice, sincerity &c.

The remainder of my answer shall bee of higher matters

Adieu.

This is Charles his Birthday. My wife and your other 3 servants will all drink your and the 3 spinsters health &c.

---

[1] The Latin poem from which these lines are taken is entitled " *Palinodia. Ad Patres Soc. Jesu Cadomaeos. G. P. Anglus* " (*Papers*, No. 149).

122. *Petty to Southwell.*

[Petty here continues the biographical reminiscences which he had commenced in the two previous letters, and gives a catalogue of all the misfortunes which had befallen him since the Restoration.   Most of the incidents to which he refers in this connection are outside the scope of this Correspondence.   Some of them, however, as milestones on Petty's road to fortune, deserve a few words of explanation.

His purchase of Lothbury, of which the original deed still survives, was made in 1659 in conjunction with John Graunt (of the London Bills of Mortality) and John Martin, "citizen and statesman of London".   The ground bought was the site of the Earl of Arundel's house and garden, and was known as Tokenhouse Yard.   The houses on this land were entirely destroyed in the Great Fire of 1666, but subsequently rebuilt.   The area in question remained in the possession of Petty's descendants till 1799, when it was bought by the Bank of England for £12,000.

Sir Allen Brodrick was the uncle of the first Lord Midleton, and was made in 1660 "Surveyor, Estimator, and Extensor General of Ireland".   This appointment seems to have thrown him into opposition to Petty, who up to that time had been entrusted with the Survey and distribution of forfeited land in Ireland.   Their quarrel terminated in a challenge from Brodrick which Petty accepted on the condition that the fight should take place in a dark cellar and that the weapons should be carpenters' axes (Evelyn's *Memoirs*, ii. 96).

Sir John King, created in 1660 Earl of Kingston, was connected with Petty through his marriage.   Petty's wife, *née* Elizabeth Waller, being the relict of Sir Maurice Fenton, whose sister had married Lord Kingston.   Lady Petty had had a son, William, by her first marriage, and the "wars with Lord Kingston" seem to have originated in the fact that both uncle and son laid claim to the same lands.   Sir William Fenton died in 1670 and Lord Kingston in 1676, but the disappearance of his stepson did not deter Petty (who had succeeded to his estates) from prosecuting the dispute on his own account.

The "Iron Works and Fisheries" were established in the neighbourhood of Kenmare, County Kerry, about 1670.   The Protestant Colony which Petty had founded there flourished exceedingly for a time, but was temporarily annihilated at the beginning of the Revolution (see *Life*, pp. 289-291).

The remaining paragraphs refer to matters which have already been mentioned in these pages.]

Piccadilly, 17th July 1686

Dr Cozⁿ

To expresse my Malice I persecute you with the charge of post Letters, when you talk of learning to fast and eat bones &c.

I said in mine of the 13 instant that, after I had with 13,060£ and 4000£ bought my Irish Lands, built Lothbury, and maryed my sister, I had at the King's restoration 3200£ left. Thus you have had the Debtor, now for the Creditor side : vizt,

1. My troubles with Zanchy, the Rump, and Army, 1659.

2. The 49 men's Siege of my Lymryck concernment, and Sir Allen Brodryck, Anno 1661 and 1662.

3. The Court of Claymes and Innocents, Anno 1663.

4. The great Double Bottom 1664. The Plague 1665. The Lord Ranalagh and fire of London 1666.

5. Warrs with the Lord Kingston 1667–68–69. 70 and 1671, when William Fenton dyed.

6. The rebuilding of London, yeare's value. Ironworks and Fisherys defrayed with the said yeare and 1672.

7. Reducement of Quit rent and Sir George Cartarett 1673 and 1674.

8. Sir James Shaen and Partners, and Kerry 1675, 76 and 1677.

9. Kerry *Custodium* &c in ferment (?) from 1678 to 1682.

10. More Mischief about the same in England and stopping the Law to 1685.

11. The Frights of 1685 and 1686, with the fayler of rents.

12. Strange wrongs from Paupers sett up on purpose to plague mee.

Now to what my said 3200£, Anno 1660, is shrunk to by this year 1686, I leave to consideration. Think alsoe of my 53 chests of Papers containing the Epitomy of my services and sufferings. My Fayr Books of Survey, and Copper Plates,[1] with the accurate and authentic History thereof and the first Distributions.

What I might have gotten without the least medling with Irish Estates, as per first letter. How little I have gotten by Religion and Factions. How I have been industriously opprest and supprest 27 yeares. Was never the Toole or Turn-Shovell of any Person or Party. Never convicted to have wrongd either private persons or public Interest, but have gotten all as I did the first shilling, 4s 6d, 24s, and 4£.

Dr Coz, Adieu.

When I am dead, pick mee out an Epitaph out of these 3 Letters, and let my children be asshamed of It, if they dare but outdoe It.

What Anatomy I have made of my selfe I am able to make of my Enemyes. I have herein followed the Advice which Sir Peter Pett heretofore gave, vizt : That at the Country Feasts, every man (when he was neare Drunk, but not quite Drunk) should declare to the Company the true cause of his coming for Ireland. Soe lett (I say) a dozen others, whom I can name, tell to the next Powers the cause of their coming to their Estates. I say ' to the next Powers ', for the last Powers that gave them were but the sumer, This next may be the winter, and frost nip them.[2] I have already past the sumer and winter both, as I gently told Sir George Lane[3] upon occasion given.

Again Adieu.

---

[1] The copper plates of Petty's general and county maps of Ireland (published under the title *Hiberniæ Delineatio* about 1683) remained in the possession of his descendants till 1875, when after a fresh set of impressions had been taken from them, they were unfortunately lost or mislaid. (See " The Lansdowne Maps of the Down Survey ", *Proceedings of the Royal Irish Academy*, xxxv. c. No. 12, 1920.)

[2] Petty's prognostication was correct, for the New Powers, as instituted in Ireland by James II., were not destined to survive for long.

[3] Sir George Lane of Tulske, County Roscommon (1620–1683), sometime Secretary of War and Secretary of State in Ireland. He had, however, been created Lord Lanesborough in 1676.

123. *Southwell to Petty.*

Deare Cousin   Kingsweston, 24 July 1686
    I am a deeper debtour for yours of the 13th
14th and 17th which I have read 3 times over, and
yett not perfect in some of your hyrogliphicks ! I
found the 2 last at my returne from Gloucester, where
I was foreman of the Grand Jury. Soe you see
how the scene is alterd. From haunting kings and
princes I am fallen to the care of Order ; and from
Crendentialls and Powers under the Broade Seale for
Peace or Warr, to *Billa Vera* or *Ignoramus* ! [1]
    Your 3 letters (in addition to the former) gave me
boundless scope of entertainement and reflexion, but
I have not time as yett to traine my selfe to the latter.
Onely as you touch on our Neddyes early acquaintance
in the world, and the bread and cheese advantages it
may bring him, I will tell you the doctrines I have
gone uppon in this matter.
    My good Father long since told me that my
portion must consist of 3 cards which were of equall
Strength—Land, Ability, and Friends. I have been
very Suspicious of dying early, and thought it better
to assigne over my friends to Neddy and to loade
him with good ones, than to leave him to a blind
choice. He has 3 sisters which are Incumbrances on
him, and by his early acquaintance in the world he
may the more early find Husbands for them.
    And lastly as to himselfe. There is lesse danger
of that Eruption which they call the ' Wild Oates '
and being seduced by young Trouncers, when he
is already familiar with those of an other Orb, and
has liberty as much within reach as the Grocers
apprentices have their Plumbs.
    Thus you have the philosophy of that Point, and
I congratulate my Godson's being 14 on the 13th of
this month. Neddy on the 4th of September will be 15.
Happinesse to them all, and   I am ever Y^{rs}   R. S.

---

[1] Southwell is here alluding to the important diplomatic missions in which
he had been engaged during the preceding reign.

124. *Petty to Southwell.*

[Fired perhaps by the successful achievement of his great survey of Ireland, Petty seems to have contemplated in 1656 the assumption of a coat of arms. There is at all events in the Office of Arms at Dublin Castle the record of a ' grant of arms ' made to him in that year. But the Restoration looked askance at grants of the ' Interregnum ', and twenty years later he obtained another, duly emblazoned and signed by Ulster King-at-Arms under the authority of the Great Seal of England. My illustration and the text (*infra*) are taken from this document which is now at Bowood.

The *Deca-stichon*, or poem of ten lines upon his coat of arms, which Petty now produces for the first time, had probably therefore been written some years before. Both the verses and the *jeux d'esprit* which he extracts from his motto, *ut apes geometriam*, are thoroughly characteristic of Petty in his lighter vein.]

Pickadilly, 31º July 1686

Dr Cosen

Neddy would needs send you my Decastichon in explanacõn of my Coat of Armes, where I should have told you that my Crest is a Beehive &c.

I like well your and your Father's Philosophy concerning the Sal, Sulphur and Mercury of a good being in this world ; vizt, Lands, Ability, and Friends. The Spinsters whom you say are an Incumbrance, do carry Defeasances to the same in their Faces and Manners ; wherefore you must give me leave to talk to you a little more of my self, vizt, to recapitulate the substance of my last 4 Letters, written to enable you, who are *Vir bonus discendi peritus*, to shew the world that your friend W. P. was no such horrible knave, no such Fox or Wolfe, as some would make him, vizt :

1º. I told you that in September 1652 when I first landed in Ireland, I had 480£ in Cash, and 120£ per annum out of Brazen-Nose, the Anatomy Lecture of Oxford and Gresham Colledge ; and that I had 365£ per annum sallary, and the vallue of 35£ per annum more out of the States Apotheca. In all

520£ per annum, besides my practis which, tho it were not in those hard times like Willis, Lower or Short's,[1] made my superlucration full 800£ per annum; which for 4½ years to Christmas 1656 was 3456£. Which made my aforemenc̃ond 480£ to bee 13,060£,[2] as in my Letter; which is about 2103£ per annum, a sume which Boys have gotten in the late Offices and which I onely had for measuring the whole world with the Chain and Instrument for neer 6 times about. The monuments whereof are to bee seen in the Surveyor Generell's Office, and in my Own Books, and in 2 Acts of Parliament, and by the Gayne which the King and his Officers have made by my said worke for these last 26 years; far exceeding the said 12,580£ for Sallarys and Survey, whereof the greatest part was paid by the Soldiers, not the State, by my procurement and Interest with them.

2°. I also told you that 13,060£ in 30 years (between the years 1656 and 1686) would have made by ordinary intrest 104,000£ without ever medling with Irish Lands.

3°. I left to your considerac̃on what I might have gott by my Practis in Physick for the said 30 years, whom Dr Fenitt did not think (nor do I myself) short of any of the 3 wee named.

4°. I told you that out of 13,060£ which I had Anno 1656, and 4000£ superlucration to the yeare 1660 (which is but the Interest of the 13,000£), I bought all my debentures,[3] estate in England, and maryed my sister, with an overplus of 3200£ at the King's Restorac̃on; which was the Bush I stood under till I saw many of my enemys defeated and some of them hangd.

5°. In my last of the 17th I gave you a Scetch of my Crosses and Losses between the yeares 1660 and

---

[1] ? Thomas Short (1635–1685), physician.

[2] The way in which this figure is arrived at becomes clearer by reference to Petty's will (*Life*, p. 319), where he gives another account of the foundation of his fortunes. He received about £9000 for the Survey besides some 'extras'.

[3] *I.e.* land 'debentures' in Ireland. There was a brisk trade in these on the part of the Cromwellian soldiers who desired to part with the land which had been allotted to them in payment for their services.

1686. I should have added the contents of my printed papers concerning Kerry, and the Auditor's Report of above 32,000£ due to me in Aprill 1682, with a third part of the said Case ready to be printed.

6°. I gave you an account of the 3 most egregious pieces of Knavery laid to my Charge, vizt: Concerning the Lord Dunsany, Fitzgerald of Tecroghan, and McGillicuddy.

7°. I have Indices and Catalogues of the grosse wrongs I sufferd between the years 1656 and 1686 by the Annabaptists, Presbiterians and 49 men, with the rest of the drinking Interest, till this present time, which I conceive the new expected Powers cannot well outdoe.

Notwithstanding all I have said I apprehend that it will be said to mee :

" Pro te non plurima Panthu
Labenti Pietas nec pro te vota valebunt."[1]

Nevertheless I will endeavor to leave in some good hand wherewith to shew I have deservd a better fate, and That the merrits of some men I could name and their pretences to 10,000£ a yeare, is but dung and drosse to what I can produce. That I am no musheroome nor upstart, but that my Estate is the Oyle of Flint, and that *Ut apes feci Geometriam.*

Dr Cos, I am above 63 years old when, as you are scarce 50, I hope you'l bee on my behalf the Depositary of these things, for which I shall bee ever

Yo^{rs}

GRANT OF ARMS TO SIR WILLIAM PETTY (1676).

To all & singular as well noblemen, as gentlemen and others to whom these presents shall come, Richard St George Esq, Ulster King of Arms of all Ireland, sendeth greeting.

Know ye that whereas antiently the vertuous acts of

---

[1] Cf. Virgil, *Æneid*, ii. 429:

. . . nec te tua plurima, Panthu,
Labentem pietas nec Apollinis infula texit.

worthy persons have been still recomended to the world by sundry monuments of their good desert, amongst which the chiefest and most usuall has been the bearing of signes & tokens in shields, commonly called armes, as evident demonstrations of their valour or vertue ; to the end that such as were faithfull and valiant in warr, and prudent and dilligent in peace, might have hereditarie signes of honour to distinguish them & theirs from the vulgar and ignoble multitude ; and alsoe to serve as incitement to those to whome by inheritance they are convayed, to imitate the vertues of their so well deserving progenitors, and inflame others to endeavour after valiant and vertuous atchievements ; and to make a difference betweene the legitimate and illegitimate, and to debarre them or any others from illegal intrusion into their inheritances.

Wheras therefore *William Petty*, son of Anthony, native of *Rumsey* in the county of Southampton in England, after many yeares foraigne travaile, was worthily approved Doctor in Physick, as by his Diploma from the university of Oxford may appeare ; therein attesting the abilities of him, the said Doctor in severall kinds of curious learneing, and more especially in what is Mathematicall or Physicall. And soon after made choice of him for Professor of Anatomy in the said Universitie, and was likewise made one of the Readers of Gresham Colledge in London, and admitted fellow of the most learned Societie of the Colledge of Physitians there. And, after many demonstrations of his skill in the faculties aforesaid, did come into Ireland in the yeare 1652, and was imployed to survey and admeasure all the Forfeited Land assigned for the satisfaction of the soldiery that suppressed the Rebellion, begun in this Kingdome on the 21st October 1643, and distributed the said Lands to many thousand officers and soldiers. Of which worthy action many publick monuments doe & will remaine to after ages, the same having been approved & confirmed by severall Acts of His Majesty & Councill in England & Ireland, and by two Acts of Parliament in this Kingdome, and likewise by the great body of surveys now in the Surveyor Generall's office. That His Majestie since his Restauration, as a marke of his merit, was pleased to conferr the honour of Knighthood upon him, the 11th of Aprill 1661, and to confirme unto him his estate in Ireland, as appeares by the Generall as well as particular clauses in the aforesaid acts of Parliament. And is now Judge and President of the High Court of Admiralty, under his Royall Highnesse the Duke of Yorke, in this Kingdome.

In consideration of all which, and being requested by the said *Sr William Petty* to assigne to him such marks of honour, as may not only preserve the memory of his merit to himselfe, but that the same may remaine to his Posterity, and distinguish him from any other of the same name and family for ever. I have therefore thought fitt to graunt, ratifie, and confirme unto him these armes hereafter mentioned : Vizt, *Ermin on a bend azure, a magnetick needle proper, pointing at the Pole star, or*. And for his creast, on a Helme and a wreath of his colours, *a Bee Hive or, fretted azure, Bees Proper*, mantelled gules, doubled argent, with this motto UT APES GEOMETRIAM, as in the margent above more lively depicted will appeare. Which Armes and Creast and every part and parcel, I the said Ulster King of Armes doe, by the Power and authority annexed to my office under the great Seale of England, give, graunt, ratifie, and affirme by these presents, unto the said *Sir William Petty* and his posterity for ever ; the same to use, beare, & injoy (useing their due differences according to the Law of Armes) without the lett, impediment, or interruption of any person or person whatever.

Whereof I have hereunto subscribed my name and affixed the seale of my office, this second day of January in the Twenty eighth yeare of the raigne of our Soveraigne Lord *Charles* the second, by the grace of God, King of Great Britaine, France & Ireland, Defender of the Faith &c. Anno Domini one thousand six hundred seventy and six.

RICHARD ST GEORGE
Ulster King of Arms of all Ireland

THE DECASTICHON.

Upon Sr Wm Petty's Coat of Arms, being upon a field Argent, an azure Bend, charged with a magnetic needle pointing at the Polar Star, and having for motto

Ut Apes Geometriam

Ceruleus candore color mea scuta decoret,
   Non Atrum, aut fulvum nec cruor horrificet.
Stellam ut spectat acus, positogue tremore quiescit,
   Sic mens quae spectat, sola quieta Deum.
Mella ut apes condunt, sic scire Geometer quaerit.
   Utile quaerere apum est ; scire Geometriae.

PETTY'S COAT OF ARMS

FROM THE ORIGINAL GRANT OF ARMS (1676) AT BOWOOD

Sedulus ergo ut apes feci Geometriam, ut inde
  Utile cum dulci scire, et habere, queam.
At si perdam ut apes, quae per Geometriam habebam
  Heu ! Vos non vobis mellificatis apes.

125. *Southwell to Petty.*

Deare Cousin   Kingsweston, 2 Augt 1686

Tho I am already deepely in your debt and
have severall Scores to Cancell, yett I am this day
honoured with yours of the 31st past, and had the
post before your verses from our Neddy. All these
things are matter, not of bare lecture, but of consideration ; and I wish 2 or 3 of the preceeding letters
had beene writt alsoe by Maurice[1] for I am sometimes
at a deadly plung.

When I tell you that my lady Percivale and her
eldest son came to us last Fryday, and that we expect
2 children more, and are fitting nurseryes and all that
is convenyent, you will be soe kind as to forgive the
Pawse I make. I will onely note that since you are
soe Indulgent as to think me worthy of being your
Depositary in this great Audit, and expect by the
Cource of Nature that I should speake when you are
Silent, you must allow me liberty without blame to
aske questions when you seeme defitient or Redundant.

That you are defitient may be suggested when,
on the fortunate syde, I find noe Item for my Lady
or of the hopefull stock she has brought you. But
I must take time before I can wrangle in other points.

My lady Percivale, who is very good and very
prudent, gives my lady her most humble service,
and the 3 spinsters make you very low Curtesyes,
—tho they smile and cannot but think that you
compliment.

I am ever Sr Your most affect & most humble serv^t
                    ROBERT SOUTHWELL

[1] Apparently an amanuensis employed by Petty, whose writing was easier
to decipher than that of his master.

126. *Petty to Southwell.*

Pickadilly, 7º Augt 1686

Dr Cousen

I and my wife do in the first place present our most humble services to my Lady Percivall, and congratulate hers and her childrens coming to bee with you.

Sedes ubi fata quietas &c.

And even according to my Doctrin about mourning for the Dead, I allow her to mourn for Sir John, and condole with her and the whole Country for their respective Losses. I hope the Spinsters, whom I made but to smile, will ere long laugh aloud. My spinster[1] hath had some Carded Wooll alredy offerd to spin, but wee do not like the Sheep it grew upon.

As for what hath past between us for this 6 or 7 last weeks, I reduce them to these periods :

1. To your excellent Prospect into the futuritys of Ireland, and your *retraxit* thereof.

2. To my being like Moses upon the Mount and your silence to my account thereof.

3. To your 3 pauses upon my 5 last letters and 3 Cases, none of which do happen by Chance.

Wherefore quitting this matter and instead of saying *Hulchy Pulchy* &c, I do rather, in the Language of the rising Church, say *Judica me Deus, et discerne causam meam de gente non Sancta ab homine iniquo et doloso erue me.*[2]

Nor did you pick any hole in my Coate of Armes, which that Hunny Seeking Boy Neddy did in a manner force from mee. Wherefore, to vindicate myself from wildnesse of Imaginaĉon in the Scutchin and Verses which were sent you, I further add by way of explanation, vizt, That I would have those emblems and symboles rather called my Coat *and*

---

[1] *I.e.* Anne Petty. But the allusion is not clear, for she was only born in September 1673, and therefore could hardly have yet received a proposal of marriage—as this passage might seem to imply.   [2] Psalm xliii.

Armes than my Coat *of* Armes ; for what is signified are indeed my Coat, Covering, Shelter and Defence, vizt,

1. Caeruleo candore agere.
2. Polum centra et principia motuum spectare.
3. Postremores et vibrationes quiesse.
4. Magnetismum habere in tenebris et procellis.
5. Ut apes opes quaerere.
6. Ut apes Domos Struere.
7. Ut apes geometrisare.
8. Ut apes Arithmeticem politicam facere.
9. Ut apes Damna et Injurias ferre.
10. Ut apes utrices Animas in vulnere ponere.
11. Ut apes rem quasi acre tangere.
12. Ut apes aliis mellificare.

And thus you have my field of Argent, my azure, my Magnet, my Star, my Pole and my Beehive expounded, and am for ever

Yo^{rs} &c.

127. *Southwell to Petty*.

Deare Cousin   Kingsweston, 11 Augt 1686

I have yours of the 7th and am soe conscious of my late silence, that you deale hardly with me to reproach it. You have sung soe many new and surprising Tunes that I am just like the Cobbler's Daw [1]—struck mute on the Caesurean Tryumph. But, as in a month he burst out with all the musick he had heard, soe I wish I may proove like that Daw in this part.

We have beene of late wholly Intent on our friends from Ireland, and on Sunday the last parcell arrived. And I have frequent returnes of a Scurvey Soare Throat, soe that, unlesse I would onely *admire*, I am not in a condition to speake to you at large.

Tis almost 20 yeares past that I have desired the

[1] The allusion appears to be to some Latin verses (Petty MSS.) written by Petty in 1679 on " A Cobbler and his Clock Bird "

explanation of *Ut Apes Geometriam*, and you may judge if I am not exalted now to see soe many master stroakes thereon, and more perhaps than ever you thought at First.   But tis now a cloudy and a rayny day, and I will not risk or execute what Tully sayes on such occasions—*periclitandae sunt vires ingenii, et ista mentis interna comentatio proferenda est*[1]—for I cannot yett think as I ought or utter what I think. Soe this is onely to bespeake your patience and to advise you to looke well after your flock, since already your spinster is called uppon.   I expect noe such humours till Irish Rents are better payd, or to pay Goates Hayre instead of wooll.

My Lady Percivale does most thankefully acknowledge yours and my ladyes kind remembrances.   She has here 2 brave brawny boyes as loud as bedlams and the Girle is of the same Tribe ; and in November we expect an other of the same Scantling.

I am ever Yrs

R. S.

128. *Petty to Southwell.*

[Petty had apparently conceived the idea that if he could prove to King James that he was all powerful, that monarch might shake off the trammels of France, and act more equitably towards his Protestant subjects.

The Essay which he was to read to the King at Windsor was the first of the *Two Essays in Political Arithmetic, concerning the people, housing, hospitals &c of London & Paris* (Hull, *Bibliography*, No. 18, p. 642, and *Philosophical Transactions*, No. 183).   It was the second of these Essays which had " stunned the French Ambassador ", subsequently referred to by Petty as " Monsieur Toby ".   This was Paul Barillon, Marquis de Branges—who had been instrumental in all the secret negotiations which had taken place between the two courts.   Both Essays were formally ' approved ' by the King a few days after this letter was written.   Curiously enough, they were first published in French (*infra*, p. 232), though an English version appeared in the following year (Hull, pp. 500-513).]

---

[1] The correct quotation is " Subeundus usus hominum et periclitandae vires ingenii ; et illa commentatio inclusa in veritatis lucem proferenda est " (Cicero, *de Oratore*, i. 34).

London, 14⁰ Augt 1686

Dr Cosen

To yours of the 11th. Without metaphor or allusion, I am really troubled by the often returns of your soar throat, and with allusion Ile say that a soar throat is a full excuse for silence.

Your saying that severall of my meanings of *Ut Apes Geometriam* were not thought of 20 years agoe, is no fault in a motto, wherein if there be two substanciall words (as I take *Apes* and *Geometriam* to bee) the hidden words may be supplyed with great Liberty. For if you ask me 10 yeares hence my Bees may give an other kind of buz.

The Character you give of my Lady Percivall's Children (to whom pray again present all our services) was very significant ; vizt, to bee loud and brawny. For the men of this world must *cum clamore et multi loquio arrogare*, and then with Brawny *brachiis et unguibus rapere aripere* : For tis a pittifull way to proceed by mine of. (1) *Caeruleo candore agere.* (2) *Polos et principia motuum spectare.* (3) *Ut Apes paulatim querere.* (4) *Cum ratione veritate et labore petere,* &c.

I am just now going to Winsor, to see what will be done upon the Festival of our Lady's Asumption, and to get an Essay read to the King, that London hath more people and Howses than Paris and Rouen put together and for ought appears the most considerable of the whole World ; and Mr Blathwight is to read it.

I have already stun'd the French Ambassador with an other Essay, shewing that there dye at L'Hotel Dieu at Paris 3000 per annum by misusage and without necessity ; the remedy whereof will do the King of France's Soul as much good as what hath been done against the Hugonots.[1]

No more at present from Yo^{rs}

---

[1] The Edict of Nantes, under which the Huguenots had for nearly a century enjoyed liberty of worship, had been revoked by Louis XIV. in October 1685.

129. *Southwell to Petty.*

Kingsweston, 6 Sept. 1686

Deare Cousin

I am at least a volume in your debt, but the King has been here among us, and some of his Trayne have clung closer to us. Then there is a Sore Throate, and my good lady Percivale's affaires have all kept me from the acknowledgements which for truth I am impatient to pay.

I hope you will be kind and forgett the time that slides by, knowing that I can never faile to be with all true regard, S^r

Yr most faithfull & humble serv^t

ROBERT SOUTHWELL

130. *Petty to Southwell.*

Piccadilly. 9 Septemb 1686

D^re Coz^n

I received yours of the 6 instant just as the french Printer brought in the enclosd; which makes mee think you have a familiar spirit, for that you, who had not written in a month upon so much matter as I had given you, should write just then. I think I have tickled Monsiers Toby in this paper.

Wee are all pretty well, and your servants. Adieu.

W. P.

131. *Southwell to Petty.*

[We have here to do with another of Petty's published Essays—the *Observations upon the Cities of London & Rome*, which, as the original title-page shows, was 'licensed' on September 21, 1686, and published in 1687 (Hull, *Bibliography*, No. 21, p. 644). This was no doubt also read to and approved by the King during the 'visit' which Petty mentions in his letter of September 30.   It is, however, evident that the monarch at this ' ample conference ' sadly deceived Petty as to his real intentions with regard to Ireland.]

Kingsweston, 13 Sept 1686

Deare Cousin

I have yours of the 9ᵗʰ and the Essay Inclosd therein.   If admiration could please you I can afford very good measure, but if you love Victory more than submission, I must displease you for I am not able to contend.   I have read the paper with strange delight, and doubtlesse soe will the Pope,[1] for my thinks that King should hould none of his Councills secrett while a blind man in London can discribe more of his Condition that he knew himselfe.   In the meane time you have done our King great Honour to shew the world that he Governes the greatest Citty that is in it.

When I consider this discourse and your others of like Nature, lett me putt you in mind how you have formerly promised a Sort of Grañar or In-struction whereby this Age may be enabled to calculate as you have done, and which assuredly was never done before.   Our Neddyes head might in time take this Byas, for he is Inclined to Numbers.

What shall I add more at present save my thanks for your great favour in this precious Token, and to one who is already soe much in arreare to you uppon other Accounts.   I still beg for time.   And if in the meane time you know what the great Lord [2] is doing, and to what end Mr Nagle,[3] the great Surveyor of Ireland, is come over with him, you will be soe kind as to impart a word unto

Yrs

R. S.

All services from herein to the Lady and the little ones.

---

[1] Innocent XI.   [2] Tyrconnel.
[3] Richard Nagle (*fl.* 1689–1691) was from this time forward prominent as the representative of the Roman Catholic interest in Ireland.   He was instrumental in repealing the Act of Settlement and passing the Act of Attainder and was knighted by James II., whom he eventually followed into exile.

132. *Petty to Southwell.*

Piccadilly, ult° Sepbr. 1686

Dear Cosen

I defered answering your last till I could send you the enclosed vast volumne of London, and the seats of the vast Spirituall and Temporall Monarchys.[1]

I have been at Windsor where I had private and ample Conference with the King, who told mee expressly and voluntarily that Hee would neither break the Act of Navigation [2] in England, nor the Settlement of Ireland ; that hee would never persecute for Conscience, nor raise his Revenue but as the Wealth of his subjects encreased. I also converst with some Grandees, who do seem to go close hald and not Quartering according to the best advantage of that wind which so blew from the King's gracious mouth. For my part I find the storme great, that I cannot lay my side to it, but am forct to spoon away before it without carying a knot of saile, and yet believe that all things may do pritty well if God bee not very angry with Us. In the mean time I must tell you that Rents being fallen $\frac{1}{3}$ and the number of years purchase $\frac{1}{3}$ also, that the Lands of Ireland are fallen from 9 to 4, and consequently seem not to bee worth this day so much as they were worth 3 years agoe by about 8 millions of mony, which is a Melancholy Consideraĉon to

Yo[r] humbled serv[t].

133. *Southwell to Petty.*

[Kingsweston] 4 Oct[r] 1686

Dear Cosin

Tis with all Gratitude that I receive your mighty Prospect of London, and with equall sorrow

---

[1] *A further Assertion of the Propositions concerning the Magnitude of London &c*, printed in the *Philosophical Transactions* of November and December 1686 and published in 1681.

[2] The Navigation Act of 1663 practically limited trade with England to goods carried in English bottoms.

that I see the diminution of Ireland.   If the Augmenta-
tion of the first were put to reprise the latter, London
and Rome would not differ soe much as now They
doe ; for you will allow me to remember how little
it Imports to have the soles of Iron if the upper
Leather be of Brown Paper, and that nothing can be
stronger than its weakest Part.

But you have done wisely to Point the Naile that
will drive, and onely to write that defect which ought
not to be, or be Felt not to be Spoken.   Yet I am
consoled at the Graciouse Declaration that you heard
—that the Settlement shall stand, thoe I see it is not
by the goodwill of others that it should be soe.   The
glimpse of Light you see through much darkness is
welcome to me, and you know we have now lived
23 years since the 4th of December,[1] when we lay at
hull and were goeing to the bottom together.   I take
it alsoe for a good omen that you are Privately and
patiently Heard, thoe I know no more than what in
your great Totalls are sumd up unto me.

Now as to the Grandour of London, Would not
England be easier and perhaps stronger if these
vitalls were more equally dispersed ?   Is there not a
Tumour in that place, and too much matter for mutiny
and Terrour to the Government if it should Burst?
Is there not too much of our Capital in one stake,
liable to the Ravage of Plague and fire ?   Does not
the Assembly too much increase Mortality and lessen
Births, and the Churchyards become Infectioux?
Will not the Resort of the Wealthy and emulation
to Luxury, melt down the order of Superiors among us
and bring all towards Levelling and Republican ?

I know these things do not concern your matters
of Fact which are so strangely ascertaind, but (they)
are my Politiks upon your Arithmetick.

Mr Haley [2] does most finely assigne the deluge

---

[1] *I.e.* December 1663, when the Court of Claims was set up to adjudicate
on those who claimed the restitution of their lands on the plea of innocence of
complicity in the Rebellion.

[2] Edmund Halley. He became a member of the Royal Society in 1678
and was afterwards Astronomer Royal.

to a withdrawing of the Center from the middle of
the Earth, by which all the waters Ran to the Habitable
part and overcame the mountains ; at which time
doubtless all other parts were left destitute and drye.

You will say I talk like a man wedded to his one
house and to the Rurall life ; and to deal truely with
you Tis noe more than needs, as our Rents (or Noe
Rents) come over. Tis for 2 years past that I have
been feeling the smart, and even now am eating the
Calfe in the Cowe's Belly, but *dabit Deus finem*, and
I think of Mr Cowley : [1]

> " Hope of all Ills which men endure
>   The only cheap and universall Cure."

My Throat is now somewhat Better since I parted
with the upper Tooth I had,

I am ever Yo[rs]

R. S.

134. *Southwell to Petty.*

[Kingsweston] 23 Oct 1686

Deare Cousin

We stand in neede of your Judgment in a
materiall point. A certaine wayfaring man calld the
other day, and taking notice that one of the 3 spinsters
had a very browne neck, " Child " sayd he " you will
not gett a Husband unlesse your neck looke whiter "—
" Sir " said she " by the time I neede a Husband,
Browne Necks may come into fashion "—" Noe "
sayd he " I will here present you with an Amber
Neck-lace which will gaine you favour imediately ;
but once that it is on, you must never take it off "—
" Noe Sir " sayd she " perhaps I may live soe long
as that such a neck lace may come to throttle me at
last." Now what think you of the Girle's Answer ?

I read lately a melancholly prophesy, and the

---

[1] Abraham Cowley (1618–1667), poet. His collected works were published
in 1688. The quotation is from the poem " For Hope ", one of the series entitled
The Mistress or Several Copies of Love Verses.

contents were much to my owne sence, and the
prophet was a Great Caldean, and had long conversed
with Men and Starrs ; soe as I was much disquieted
thereat.[1]   But when I considered that these things
were not writt either in Serious Prose or in broaken
ejaculations or distracted words, but in smooth and
flowing numbers—then sayd I, " the bitternesse is
over past, for who can utter Melody in his sadnesse,
or sing tunably when he is in a Strange land ? "
Since therefore the matter and the manner doe not
agree, I also will sing :

" As men by stormes may to their Haven Sayle,
   Soe lett your Numbers, not your Sence prevayle."

135. *Petty to Southwell.*

Piccadilly 26⁰ Octob*r* 1686

Dear Cosen
        To yours of the 20th[2] and 23rd Instant.   I
thank my Lady Deering and your self for the friendly
advertisment, and hope by your assistances to make
good use of it, altho' it bee a worke which requires
Tools hard to bee got.
        The Spinster you mencͦon was, Ile warrant her,
a right cunning Jepsy, no lesse than our Neddy is a
subtile soothsayer.   Let us have patience till our
browne necks returne into fashion, nor venture upon
any necklaces that will strangle us and that we cannot
unty when we please.   Nothing more need bee said
upon this point, nor nothing better could bee.   Wherefore you may suspend the latter part of your Chaldean's
Vaticinium from *De Cruce* &c downwards, and rather
take up your *Huc ades ergo celer* &c, for I protest
here is not a Man that dares affirme that 2 and 3 is 5.

---

[1] Southwell (as some subsequent allusions show) is here referring to some
jocular Latin lines which Petty had sent him from Ireland a few years earlier.
They are headed " Ad Sodaelum Vaticinia ".
[2] This letter has been omitted.   It contains an ' advertisement' of " Otterden ", an estate in Kent which Southwell wished his friend to purchase.

For myself I am seriously warnd against speaking truth, nay against letting the Grandees know I can doe it : *Ita odit*[1] &c.   Things are not so well as you imagine, for as

" Some weep for Joy, so some for sorrow sing ;
Thus circumstance interprets every thing "

Salute the Ladys and Spinsters on my behalf,
Who am, Yo^rs as ever,

136. *Southwell to Petty.*

[Kingsweston] 3 Novr 1686

Deare Cousin
By yours of the 26th past I see how dangerous it is where you are to tell the compound of 3 and 2, and therefore notwithstanding *Huc ades ergo celer*, I will stay were I am, remembring the Spanish proverb ' Be not a Baker if thy Head be made of Butter '.

Now tho you complaine that you may not safely speake, yett I hope you have secured some reward for holding your Tongue.   Lett me know as a friend if you are promised any roome in the Cockboat ?   I confesse you were hardly used in the former Shipp, and cast over to the whaler, and dasht uppon the Rocks of Kerry ; and therefore tell me truly are you not providing for one ?[2]

You cannot imagine but that, as I am already bemused for want of my Rents, soe I am sheard in future prospect ; and comonly after a revolution of sorrowfull thoughts I fall fowle uppon Neddy. I admonish, I whipp, I spurr and drive him all that is possible to his Booke. Soe that while misfortunes prevayle, this boy will live no better than Robin Marshall's Catt. Tis true the Catt was not told

---

[1] These are all quotations from Petty's *Vaticinium*, mentioned above, which appears to be a veiled lament at the Catholic party getting the upper hand in Ireland.

[2] The above somewhat cryptic paragraph refers to the Irish Settlement, which both Petty and Southwell often spoke of metaphorically as a ' ship '.

why nor wherefore; nor could she Studdy by way of future Redresse, as I hope our Neddy will doe. He is now uppon Aristotle's Rethorick as a Stepp towards the Great Hall. I wish Mr Waller,[1] when he comes to drink his Tea, were by you provoked to utter his advice or directions for the more profitable reading of the peece. He has dugg deepe in that mine in his younger yeares, and it has afforded him ready money ever since.

You have all our services to the lady and the little ones.

Is the Revenue of Ireland to be Farmed out?

137. *Petty to Southwell.*

London, 6° Novb^r 1686

Dear Cosin

You mistook mine of the 26 past, for I did not there-in expresse my shynesse of telling you my thoughts, But complayned of the Cowardice which concerned Persons had in telling the King that 2 and 3 was 5. Notwithstanding which you say that you will not hearken to my *Huc ades*, because you do not think fitt to make a Baker of him whose head is made of Butter. Do you mean that your head is apt to melt it self into sauce for all sorts of Meats?

Nothing hath prevaild with mee to hold my Peace where I have thought fitt to speak. I will not tell you of any Roome I have in the Cockboate, for fear of being laught at for having none. I will secure one; for having been dasht in peeces on the former ship, I am sorry the Rocks whereupon I have formerly split must bee shaken downe by a generall Earthquake. The Posts which supported us were rotten and painted; you must not wonder that they should moulder away.

Blame not Neddy, for hee is as forward a youth in practicall matters as any I know and not backward

---

[1] A relative of Petty's who would seem to have been of a loquacious disposition.

in other respects.   Hee will be a subtile sooth-sayer.
As for my owne Children, I leave them too much to
the spontaneous operations of nature.   I make them
not Cats, nor my self a Robbin Marshall unto them.
I do not understand how my Cosen Waller's having
digd in the mines of Rethorick in his younger yeares
hath yielded him ' ready money '.   In briefe I am
beginning the world again, and endeavor instead of
quarelling with the King's Power, to make him exert
all hee hath for the (use) of his subjects.

As for farming the Revenue of Ireland, the Irish
Merchants of London are every day with My Lord
Tirconnell, and the Revenue upon beer and Ale was
by a tenth part greater the half yeare after King
Charles the 2ᵈ his death than before or since.

Mine and my wives humble service is presented to
you and yours.

138. *Southwell to Petty.*

[Kingsweston] 12 Noᵇʳ 1686

Deare Cousin
       Tis noe wonder if yours of the 6ᵗʰ be as an
earthquake to me, when I see that even rocks are in
danger.   I did not think to heare soe soone that our
posts were rotten and painted over, when you told
me (and had it from soe good hands) that our Settlement should stand.   But as it is in the Great Stoick—
O Crito si ita deis visum fuerit Ita fiat.[1]

I see you meane to begin the world anew and are
for extending and exalting authority.   I hope you
take care not to appeare wiser than the great ministers,
for they will (right or wrong) rapp you on the fingers.
Twere better be conscious of a soft head, even as soft
as butter, than to run a tilt at them who can putt
even the hardest Head under the File or Anvill.
However if your dice be cast, lett me know the throw
when you think it seasonable to comunicate.

---

[1] Plato's *Crito*, Socrates *loq.*: εἰ ταύτῃ τοῖς θεοῖς ᾿φίλον, ταύτῃ ἔστω.   Only
Latin translations of the Greek classics were at this date generally available.

By Mr Waller's ' ready money ', I meant his ready discourse, flowing as from a fountaine uppon every subject. And if this came to him by his having dugg Industriously in the mines of Rethorick, twere worth consulting him for a few Rules which perhaps noe man else can give soe well.

I am glad to heare all yours are well, and proud that you prayse Neddy, tho I always bate you one halfe.

As they proceede in the Farme, pray lett me heare it. And for the remarke you make in the State of the excise, I think it were not hard for you and I over one dish of coffee to adjoust the reason of it.

13th

This morning the good lady [1] here with us is happily deliverd of a brave Boy, and all very well.

139. *Petty to Southwell.*

London, 20 Novb^r 1686

Dear Cousin

To yours of the 12th, wee are all here your servants, and very glad of the ' Multiplication of Mankind ', which has happend at your House.

As for the Metaphors of Earthquakes, Rocks, painted Posts, Heads of Butter, raping of fingers, the files, anviles and great hamers, casting of Dice, telling of throwes &c, I think it best to lett them all alone. For each of them may bee interprited a thousand wayes, and by 999 of those wayes to my prejudice.

Wherefore in plain English I tell you againe that I have heard nothing from the King contrary to what he was formerly pleasd to tell mee concerning the Settlement ; but say, as I formerly said, that others goe very close hald upon that wind.

[1] Lady Perceval. The child was posthumous, Sir John Perceval having died (*vide supra*) six months previously.

When I told you I would begin the World anew, I meant that I would take a new flight, and not any more from Irish Grounds.

I behave myself towards Great Men as cautiously as I can, and repent of my former Methods ; But being now become a ' Catt in Cubard ' must leap out &c, and must run my Spit into such Rotten post as I find to bee but painted.

I have Matters under my hands which I cannot but beleive do excell all I have ever knowne of that kind, and do studdy how to proceed humbly with them.

The King told mee last week that my Essays were answering in France, and (I) am told by severall others that the mightiest Hamers there are battering my poore Anvill.[1] And all those who profess themselves my friends here, do but laugh to think of the sport they shall have, But promise me no help. In all these Cases I hear an old voyce : *Tu ne cede malis sed contra audentior ito.*[2]

What favour or good fortune did you find in the Accompt (which you have forgot) of my 50 yeares adventures from the year 1636 to 1686 ? God is the same still and let his Will be done.

I long for the 15 February because I hope you will bee here the 16ᵗʰ.[3] Adieu.

W. P.

140. *Southwell to Petty.*

[Kingsweston, 24 November 1686]

In yours of the 20ᵗʰ there are 7 Capitoll points. The first contains certaine metaphoricall words lately in use, now Rejected by you as of dangerous interpretation—soe very dangerous as [that] 999 is the greatest part of a 1000. You fall to new ones as ' Catt in Cubbard ', ' Spitt into Rotten Posts ', ' new flight '

---

[1] *Infra*, p. 247.
[2] Virgil, *Æneid*, vi. 95.
[3] Presumably for the meeting of Parliament.

and 'the world anew'; 'somewhat in hand'; that is all "Taminaple deepe" &c. Now are not all these no Metaphors, and you (Cousin) still in the darke? Soe that if for writing's sake I should be grooping after sence and ask a few questions, I know you will not take it amisse. Is this catt of yours any way related to the Catt of Sir Pantophilus? or to Cardinall Mazarin's Italian Catt,[1] where the confessour declard " el peccato e grande ma l'inventione e bellissima "? Is she a plain English mouser? For my part I would wish the latter, because then something would be gott as well when out the Cubbard as when in, besydes the being delivered from vermin. Pray in your next afford me one chip or a little powder of the Rotten Posts, that by sight or smelling I may know of what wood it is. Tis I know of the groaning kind, but I know not if the Spitt you will run into it be hott or cold. If hott then beware fingers and the smoake, but if cold there is no danger at all.

Thus cousin you see how I write coments uppon your Apocalips, and you had better speake to me in plainer English.

As for our Settlement (as painted as it is) I yett am glad we have one strong vote for it—I see there be sons of Zeruiah [2] but I hope they will not prevayle.

I perceive the French have vowed to be revenged of you, and you already censure your friends as prepared to laugh and not to help you. If it were a warr of Crabb Tree cudgells, I know one would not stick out, but think you ought rather to glory, that in this none are able to help you. For your skill in calculations is as much a Peculiar as if you could fligh in the Ayre or Swim under the water.

As to your 50 years Adventures, I have them and keepe them more preciously than Caesar's Comentaryes and I could easily allow you the same starrs you have

[1] This is perhaps an allusion to Mazarin's part in the negotiation for the Treaty of the Pyrenees. There is a paper on this subject by Southwell in the British Museum (Ad. MS. 20722).

[2] Joab, Asahel and Abishai, the sons of Zeruiah (1 Samuel xxvi. 6).

formerly had, if nature would but consent to a Renovation of 50 yeares more, but *hic labor hoc opus.*

You conclude with an important hint of our meeting in February which I have from noe other hand, and fancy you may have learnt it in the Cubbard.

All here acknowledge your favour and pay you their respects.

[Endorsed by Southwell: " Copy to Sir Wm Petty ; 24 Nov. 1686 ".]

141. *Petty to Southwell.*

[The King had told Petty in November (*supra*, p. 242) that his essays were " answering " in France. Pierre Bayle had in fact reviewed the *Two Essays* in October in the sense indicated below (cf. Hull, p. 525 *n.*). Petty's threatened reply to Bayle appears in the first of the *Five Essays in Political Arithmetic*, which were printed a few months later. It must be added that his argument (as Hull points out) rests entirely on a chronological blunder or misprint on the part of Bayle, in stating that Rey in Persia had boasted of 44,000 mosques in the sixth, when he evidently meant to have said in the ninth century.]

London, 4° Xbr 1686

Dr Cosen

To yours of the 24th past. As I renounce all former Metaphors, so I do these new ones of Catt in Cubard, Spits and Posts &c.

I told you I must begin in the World again, without further building upon Irish ground ; to which purpose I beg My Lady Deering to continue her favour in telling mee what she knowes concerning Sir George Curtis his Otterden, vizt (1°) what hee gave for it ? (2°) Why hee leaves it ? (3°) What Inconveniencys shee knows in it &c ? I have had a particular of it from two strangers this weeke, who both say my Lady Deering understands this matter very well. The other things I have in hand are such as you should know if you were here, because they may prove a good exercise for Neddy.

The French Bombs are not yet fierd, but the Author of the Republiq of Letters saith that " Le Chevalier Petty se verra Critiqué bien tot par quelque scavants de Paris ", and begins to do it himself by objecting Rheis, an old Citty of Persia, to be far bigger than London. But your Cosen intends to answer him by shewing that from his Arguments Rheis had above 40 thousand Moschees in it, probably before Mahomet was borne. There is a Rap of a Crab tree Cudgell for you now ! I believe you[1] are meeting in February next.

Adieu.

142. Southwell to Petty.

[Kingsweston] 8 Decr. 1686

Deare Cousin
		I have yours of the 4ᵗʰ conteyning 3 questions, in all which I have consulted the lady whose knowledge is but superficiall. But first she says that Sir George hath much spared and cherished the woods, and improved the land, soe as he may aske much more than he gave ; tho she know not the price he bought at, or certainly for what he will sell.

Next, for his leaving it. Tis as she thinks, first to humour his lady, who can hardly be comforted for the losse of some fine daughters who there dyed. Then that his son is very lewd, and is fallen into base and meane company thereabouts, and is puft up and obstinate uppon the expectation of this seat. Soe Sir George thinks of going to a Farme he has of 300£ per annum neere Canterbury.

As to the Inconvenyencyes—The wayes for 4 or 5 miles about it are but narrow and stony, and she thinks the well is somewhat deep from whence all the water is drawne. I here inclose you a letter if you think it may be of any use.[2]

---

[1] *I.e.* the House of Commons.
[2] The enclosure was a letter to Sir Edward Dering in which Southwell requested his good offices with Sir George Curtis in the matter of this transaction.

But my opinion is that first, for the beauty and convenyency of the Place, You send downe the same Surveyour that once you sent into Kerry.[1] She has good eyes and a good Relish. She will know if all be true that my Lady sayes of the Inviting part; and if 2 or 300£ added to some alterations in the House would—as old Sir Edward was wont to say— make it the finest seat of Kent; and what she thinks of the numerous good neighbourhoods thereabout &c.

Next I call to mind that when Old Roger[2] stood Candidate for Secretary of State, he sent to whisper with Sir S. Morland[3] how to mannage forraigne Intelligence. And Sir Samuel told him that in all great places he should have 2 Secret Correspondents, the one a Jesuite, and the other a Jew. Now your businesse being to know the Intrinsique value; to know wheather it be uppon the rack, or yet capable of further Improvement; to take some estimate of the value from the booke of payments to Church and poore, and to goe among the Tenants and by ale and Tobacco to find how the matter stands—I would propose that you consulted Mr Parry if there be any Chimney or excise men in that district who may be fitt for this prospection, and equalise the Jesuite and the Jew, and that he enjoyne them to labour for you. This is all I can say or doe, till you make the purchase, and tell me you want help for an Oxe House.

I see I am not to know the other things you have in hand, and soe am not able to sitt cross-leggd for you. Neddy is soone to take his leave of you, and to make acknowledgment of all favours from your selfe and my lady and his kind cousins. If by him you drop a word, it shall be in your owne phrase ' like the bullet against a mudd wall '.

As to the Frenchmen's bombs against your Essay;

---

[1] *I.e.* Lady Petty, who had sometimes gone over to County Kerry to look after her husband's interests there.

[2] ? Roger Boyle, Lord Broghill and Earl of Orrery (1621–1679), third son of the great Earl of Cork. He was highly thought of by Charles II., but I cannot find that he was ever ' candidate for Secretary of State '.

[3] Sir Samuel Morland (1625–1695), diplomatist, mathematician and in - ventor, prominent during and after the Restoration.

I see you have prepard a reply, before they can make their Answer.   If Mr Frazer be returnd from thence he will tell you much of these matters.

All speake of a new Lord Lieutenant,[1] tho you say nothing—

" What makes the Bell stand mute within the Towre
   Knowes it not that 4 quarters make an houre ? "

(This was sayd by d^r Corbett,[2] then Vice Chancellour of Oxon, going with his Bedles by St Maryes at one of the Clock, and when the quarters onely struck, but the Bell not.)   Now the preparation of Plate, Coaches and liveryes speake aloud, but what then is the mistery of noe declaration ?   Pray Cousin—for this once—lett your Catt out of the Cubbard.

Yrs.

143. *Petty to Southwell.*

[The ' French Bombs ' continued to excite Petty. Adrien Auzout, astronomer, mathematician and writer, who had lost his seat in the French *Academie des Sciences* owing to an intrigue against him and had transferred himself from Paris to Rome, was one of those who hurled them.   He was answered in the first of the *Five Essays in Political Arithmetic*, published both in French and in English in 1687 (Hull, p. 526).

I have been unable to identify the ' famous Abbot Bernou ', though (with due allowance for Petty's script) the name might perhaps be equated with that of Jacques Bernoulli, the French mathematician, who had started life in holy orders.   Neither Bernou nor Bernoulli, however, seem to have been among those who disputed Petty's arguments in the case in question.   The ' other essays ' referred to by Petty will be likewise found in the volume mentioned above (Hull, pp. 522 and 537).]

---

[1] Lord.Tyrconnel was shortly to replace Lord Clarendon as Lord-Lieutenant of Ireland.
[2] Richard Corbet (1582–1635), Dean of Christ Church, Bishop of Oxford and of Norwich, a famous wit.   He wrote a poem on the Christ Church Bell (*Notes and Queries*, third series, ii. 494-495).

London, 25th X br 1686.

Deare Cosen

Wee have not seen Neddy these 3 weeks and therefore suppose him to bee with you. If hee had cald here, I would have given him the hints you desired ; altho in truth it is not necessary, for I do not know what is what, and my owne cake, whereof I thought to have given you a Bitt, may prove dough. I have had a letter from Sir George Curtis, but can say to you little about it as yet. My observing the wind too much, makes mee not sow.

But Cousen, the Bombes against my Essays are fierd, one by *La Republiq de Letters*, and the other from the great Monsr Auzout from Rome. More are daily expected from Paris and particularly from the famous Abbot Bernou. I received Monsr Auzout's on Wensday last between 9 and 10, and caryed the King an Answer before 12, made before all the White Staves in the Bed Chamber. The chief objection was, that the out-Parishes which have stood these 50 yeares in the Bills of Mortality, should not be accounted London. His paper did fall most upon what Captain Graunt and myself had ever writ upon these matters.

I promised the King my speedy remarques upon all hee said, which I have since done and I hope pretty well. And afterwards I made 2 new Essays in one, where I proved over again all that I had said before of London, Rome, Rouen and Dublin, even allowing Monsr Auzout all his Demands ; even those for which hee had offered no manner of proof.

In the other Essays, wherein I deale with lesse favour and more Justice towards the Interest of Paris and Monsr Auzout, I shew London to bee equall to Paris, Rome, and Rouen, from their owne sayings, altho' I do not beleive it myself; which things I intend to shew the King tomorrow if I can. I also, in answer to their objecting a Citty in Persia[1] to bee

---

[1] *E.g.* Rey (*supra*, p. 244).

greater than London, [show] that (by their owne sayings) the, said Persian Citty had 44000 Moschees in it
before Mahomet was come.

This do they get who wrong your poor Cousen,
who wisheth you a Merry Christmas, and that the
next yeare may bee no worse than the past, and who
is your good Company's and Kings-Weston and your
owne

honest servant.

144. *Southwell to Petty.*

[Kingsweston] 6 Jan 1686/7

Deare Cousin

Yours of the 25th past made our Christmas
here looke like it selfe, and we were all rejoycd to
heare how you repelld the Roman Gyant[1] and gott
his Majesty of your syde. When all is setled that
relates to this predicament, I hope I shall not be the
last to solemnize your fame, if you will but give me
the meanes.

Neddy is with us and preparing his mind to passe
a little time in Oxford. My Lady Percivale lately
lost her onely daughter by convultion fitts, but the
3 boyes doe bravely.

I see how cautious you are in Joyning issue with
Sir G. Curtis, and who can blame you? We are
stund on account of the same motives. What you
think fitt to spare as newes or Information shall be
lookt on as from the hand it comes.

Doe you still think that the Parlyament will here
meete? I suppose their will soone be one in Ireland.[2]

My Lady Dering prepares to be going up on
Monday, and my Lady Percivale goes after, and they
needes will have two of my girles of the party. I wish
a happy yeare to my lady and to all yours, and am ever,

Yrs

---

[1] *I.e.* Auzout.
[2] No Parliament had met in Ireland since 1666. James called one together
in May 1689, after he had fled from England.

145. *Southwell to Petty.*

[Kingsweston] 15 Jan. 1686/7

Deare Cousin

I would now give a great deale for a Sheete of your free thoughts, how melancholy soever they would make me. The evills of this life that cannot be prevénted are chiefly sharp by their surprise. When the mind can converse with them before they happen, and know something of their bounds and extent, they loose much of their force and tyranny.

Two of my spinsters are gone to London with their good Aunt. They will not faile I hope to wayt on my good lady ; tho they want confidence and good manners to doe their duty, tis not want of sence, but want of vigour, and a too great feare of doing what is amisse.

Neddy is preparing for Oxford,[1] where in lesse than a yeare he may gett Logick and soe knock off.

With a happy yeare to my lady and all yours— I am ever,

Yrs

I can onely thank you for your long one of the 25th past, and glory in your successe.

146. *Petty to Southwell.*

[In the following letter Petty reverts again to Irish affairs, which were proceeding in a manner not at all to his liking. Clarendon, the Viceroy, had now been recalled, and Tyr-connel was to take his place. Protestant functionaries were being everywhere removed to make room for Roman Catho-lics, while the Corporations were being subjected to writs of *Quo warranto* in order that their Charters might be con-demned and new Corporations, consisting only of Catholics, substituted.

Poyning's law, which acted as a check on the Irish govern-

---

[1] Edward Southwell was this year entered as a gentleman commoner under Dr. Thomas Lane at Merton College, Oxford.

ment by making it obligatory that its legislation should originate in the English Parliament, was also threatened, though it was not actually repealed until two years later.]

London, 18th Janry 1686/7

Deare Cousen

To yours of the 15. I do not wonder at your apprehensions because I take them to bee very like my owne. I cannot tell what to say that may sweeten them, nor do I beleive I can write you any news in matter of fact but what you may know better from other hands ; but do wish with all my heart I could bee one hower with you &c.

I find no man doubts but that the Chief Government of Ireland, the Privy Councill, the Benches, the officers and soldiers also of the Army, the Commissioners and Collectors of the revenue, The Sheriffs and Justices of Peace, the Magistrates of Corporaçons and the Officers of Courts and Christ Church Itself, to say nothing of the Colledge of Dublin, will shortly bee all in one way. Whether tolleraçon bee intended to Dissenters I know not, but find some bitterly against it ; altho the King hath most expressly told myself the contrary, with as good arguments as could bee used for that purpose.

It is manifest that a Parliament will bee called there. It is said that a *Quo Warranto* will bee forthwith brought against the Charter of Dublin, and consequently against many more, to make all things fitt for the great worke. Some also say that Poyning's Laws shall bee dispenced with, and bills directly past as here.

I heare credibly that 2 or 3 of the new formd Irish Regiments shall bee brought from thence hither, and that 3 English Regiments shall in lieu of them bee caryed from hence thither. Wee heare that many of the most considerable persons of Ireland will come away with my Ld Clarendon, and that there are thousands coming away alredy, the violences in Ireland of severall sorts being so many and unpunisht.

The consideration whereof dos make poore people (even of London) weep.

Dear Cousen, when I first treated with a great man, things were not neer this rapidity, but I saw an Eddy in that Tide (tho indeed strong enough) wherein with pains one might rowe, and I had prepared oares for that purpose—that is to say Innocent and beneficiall Designes for the good of mankind, which I had contrivd should have been driven on by the same Current that was like to drive on worser things. For myself I yet stand faire with many, but feare as I told you in my last that my Cakes will never bee baked.

My wife and I were last night to see the Spinsters &c, but mist them. Neddy's going to Oxford is according to fashion, but I feare the old fashion. As for Logick, Charles learnes it without the Schoole Rules, as hee did french without Grāmer, that is to say by reading peeces of the purest reason without the *Quid* and *quotuplex* of Oxford. Hee is now deep in Justinian, and the Institutions of the Civill Law, which dos strangely agree and incorporate with him. I presume that besides the Law, hee learneth as much reasoning as hee could do out of any Logick book of that bignesse.

I send you herewith the Coppy of what Mr Blatwight read last Thursday to the King at his Levy,[1] but have a world more, part whereof you'l see in the next transactions of the Royall Society. I have also 9 or 10 such uses of my doctrine concerning London which one would think should keep me from starving;[2] One whereof is that whereas the next London plague will probably sweep away 140 thousand people, I hope to compound with it for the od 40ᵐ· Adieu.

---

[1] This again must have been some part of the *Five Essays*, which were licensed to be printed on Feb. 18, 1687.

[2] Cf. "An Essay for the Improvement of London", 1687; "Concerning the Plagues of London", 1687; "The Uses of London" 1687, etc. (*Papers* Nos. 12, 16, 17).

147. *Southwell to Petty.*

[Kingsweston] 22 Jan. 1686/7

Deare Cousin

Yours of the 18th was full of Hurracanes. We shall soon see the beginning, but God knowes who may live to see the end! I perceive you had once better Hopes, and thought you had good warrant for It, but as the Italian sayes *El credere, é cursesia.* As anything newer than your last appeares, pray lett me have share. I hope there will be some moderation as to the taxing of the Meane profitts and making it payable out of other lands, if such fall in their way.

You are happy in two respects : one that you are Involved in such calculations as noe man ever heard of before—Why, you whipp Monsieur Azout over your knee or rather make him to whipp himselfe! Surely these things must fill your mind soe as to exclude the torture of the Politicks, or else it were better to be a foole.

I will impatiently attend the next Transaction[1] to see what you afford. And for your Project to save 100^m the next plague, you ought to have a statue before you dye.

Your next good point is the good reception of Justinian by my God-son. Tis a high point, for *multum profecit in eloquentia cui placuit Cicero*, and it is witt to know witt. I congratulate it most heartily unto you, and wish I may say soe much hereafter between Littleton[2] and my son. He is preparing for Oxford, rather to understand the gibberish or *lingua franca* of the world than to grow wise. I am taking all the care I can to season this dish that it may not be too fulsome, and I tell him very much of what he is not to doe.

One of the spinsters now tells me that you and my lady had the goodnesse to returne theither againe

---

[1] Of the Royal Society.
[2] Chief Justice Sir Edward Littleton (1589–1645).

and to grace them by your smiles and favour, which they will lay up in Store against they returne to a country life.

I am going to read over the two Peaces of 46 and 48,[1] that I may by that which once past compute on what may come.

Y^{rs} ever

148. Petty to Southwell.

London, ye 8 feb 1686

Dear Cousen

I enclosd send you a peece of the Philosophicall Transactions. I have 3 Essays more which are new and real additions to the Matter.[2]

Fitzgerald of Tecroghan hath brought his ejectments. We have allready had 6 verdicts in severall Countys against him.

We must now thro feathers against the Wind. Dunsany is allso at me, quits the Chancery and returns to Jurys. When we are thus Weeded, We shall be afterwards Mowed, and what then I know not. Bad fortune is as unconstant as good. I have had 28 years of the former, if the same Continue 8 more twill have done its worst. This is all and too much from

Yrs &c.

---

[1] The Peaces, concluded by the Duke of Ormond as Lord-Lieutenant of Ireland, in 1646 and 1648. By the first the Irish who were in rebellion against Charles I. were forgiven in order that their services might be enlisted for the King against the English Parliament. Two years later, after this plan had failed, he threw up the sponge, and by making peace with the Parliamentarians left a clear field between them and the rebels. Southwell was correct in expecting that history would repeat itself.

[2] These three papers (in answer to the objection of M. Auzout against Petty's conclusion that London was greater than Paris and Rouen taken together) were produced at the meeting of the Royal Society on Jan. 5, 1687 (Birch, iv. 517). The 'piece of the Philosophical Transactions' was no doubt that containing Petty's notes on the same subject which were given into the Royal Society in December 1686 and had just been printed (vol. xvi., No. 184, pp. 237-240. Cf. also Hull, p. 522).

149. *Southwell to Petty.*

Deare Cousin   [Kingsweston] 14 Feb 1686/7
    I am in the first place to pay great acknow-
ledgements for my ladyes great favour to my girles.
And next for what you Inclosed in yours of the 8th,
which has served me as opium and amusement against
what your letter conteyned of the weeding and the
mowing. As to this letter I know not well what to
say, or wheather I should be better if I did. Tis
your case today and myne tomorrow, which is all I
can think of.
    Your demonstration against M. Azout runs like a
mighty streame. He will denie to be friends with you,
and all the rest will come in by his example.
    When I consider this matchlesse Flayle that
nature and Art has given you, wherewith you make
all Cittyes of the World submitt to that you stand on
and that it should be in the power of a louzy jury to
wound you, It gives credit to the fable and how An
Elephant may be ill treated by a mouse. In the time
of 2 Warrs with Sir G. Carteret, then Juryes were anti-
dotes when he came armed with his court thunder-
bolts. But how many things else are also Invented!
It was formerly thought best to have exchanged breed-
ing women from syde to syde; but the designe being
alterd, tis now thought fitt to practice it with men.
    How did I hope that every west wind would have
filld my Nostrills with odours of Spices, when Kinsale
was to be made the Center of the East India Trade!
But, Alasse, those winds bring now nothing but
feares; sometimes an Insolvent Bill; the dropping
down of houses; and visions that already they see
the very land begins to creepe. How much happier
is it in the Leeward Islands where tho visited with
Hurrycanes, yett still the land is left behind.
    Our Neddy is hard at the Ireducibles.[1] To
Charles and the rest all service.

---

[1] Southwell is apparently alluding to his son's preparations for Oxford
University (*supra*, p. 250).

150. *Southwell to Petty.*

Cornebury, 28 Feb 1686/7

Deare Cousin

Heither I came on Saturday and doe purpose to stay for a weeke, and then to my house. Neddy alsoe is here for two or 3 dayes. But my concerne is to know the meaning of what I lately was told by Mrs Helena of my ladyes suddaine purpose to goe for Ireland. I am afraid the motive is some new allarum, if soe I can send onely wisshes after Her.

Pray favour me in your next with a few answers to these quaeryes :

(1) Was it not 5 millions of Irish Acres which were sequestred as formerly belonging to Irish Papists ?

(2) How many of these had decrees of Innocence, and how many Acres did they Recover thereby ?

(3) How many Acres were gotten by the Irish *Provisoe* men ?[1] And how many by the *Letterees*[2] or any other grant ?—Soe as to see how much they possesse of what they had in 1641.

(4) How many Acres are comprehended in the Duke of York's Provisoe ?

(5) How many were found *Nocents* ?

All these matters I have heard you speak of in familiar discourses, but the Computations are now out of my mind. You will oblige me with them, and P. Madox will convey your letter to me ; That is he will know when I go hence, tho as yett I am not very certaine.

All good wishes attend my Cousin Charles and the little ones.

Yrs ever

---

[1] The ' Proviso men ' or ' Papists per Proviso ' were those to whom land was specifically restored by the Act of Settlement.

[2] The ' Letterees ' were those restored by virtue of special letters of King Charles II., sometimes called ' mero motu ' men [*Political Anatomy* (Hull, p. 131)].

151. *Petty to Southwell.*

[Petty's answers to the ' quaeries ' propounded by South-well in the last letter are not without historical interest. The rights or wrongs of the Cromwellian Settlement have been the staple of Irish controversy from his day to ours, and the estimates of its scope have widely differed, often according to the political views of the historian.

Petty was in a better position than most to know the true facts, and though he was himself largely interested in the general result, it may be claimed for him that his outlook was less narrow and his partisanship less marked than was the case with most of his contemporaries.

The figures he gives below are substantially the same as those in his *Political Anatomy of Ireland* (Hull, p. 136), though this was written fourteen years before the letter which follows. There is in appearance a great discrepancy between Petty's account and that generally accepted as to the number of those who claimed ' Innocence ' of the Rebellion after the Restoration. It seems agreed that some 700 persons actually obtained decrees of Innocence from the Court of Claims, but, whereas Petty states that they constituted seven out of eight of the claimants, it has been asserted elsewhere that as many as 7000 were never heard at all, while even Lecky gives the number of those ruled out as 3000 (ii. 81). It seems that Petty takes no account of these unheard cases and bases his estimate on those only which actually came before the Court.]

London, 5th March 1686/7

Deare Cousin

To yours of the 28th past. My wife thought to go for Ireland upon the account of some domestik disorders, and of Actaeon's danger of being eaten up by his owne Dogs ; but whether shee will proceed is as yet some question. Pray sling your good wishes hither, so as they may stick upon her, whether she go or stay.

I am thinking again of sending Charles abroad but *quaerenda pecunia primum est.*

Tecroghan's Ejectments go on bravely against 7 verdicts in 2 Countrys. Dunsany also sueth with like fury for what did not belong to him in case there never had been any Rebellion ; and Mcgillicudy (is) the most glorious Sherriff of Kerry.

For these 3 or 4 dayes all the talk at Court and at Gresham Colledge, and of other Virtuosi, hath been about a speaking head which pretends to bee the equivolent to an Eccho, which repeateth many words, and such as is the reall eccho of Arnagragh in Kerry.[1] I have seen it 3 times, and at first disired to beleive it was such, because it had been a great Inlet into the Science of Sounds. The 2^d time I saw it I concluded that it was neither such an eccho, nor was the trick performd by the *Ventri loquium* of an Actor. The 3^d time I became satisfied that the whole was a Jugling contrivance (but dexterous and Ingenious enough), wherby a Cheat in one Roome spoak to his Corrisponded Cheat in another Roome by the mediation of a Sham head. I would have given 50£ for the sake of Science and Philosophy that it had provd an artificall eccho, which I think is possible ; and the King saith If I will undertake it hee will venture a wager on my side.

As to your quaeries I say : (1°) that 4800 thousand Irish Acres did belong to the Catholiques of Ireland Anno 1641, and were seisd and sequestred from them Anno 1653, but not one acre thereof upon Account of Religion, but about 800 thousand were given to neuters in Conaught and Clare. But not a penny worth of reall and personall Estate was taken from them who provd their Constant good affection to the State of England without any consideration of Religion.

2°. That 7 of 8 of all that Claym'd Innocence obtained Decrees for it, being about 700 in number, and caryed away about 1180 thousand acres, whereof above 300 thousand acres never belongd to them in 1641.

3°. Upon the whole matter, The Irish have at

---

[1] Ardnagragh, near Castle Island, in County Kerry. This was a Geraldine stronghold of which the ruins still remain. Close by is the burial place of James, fifteenth Earl of Desmond.

this day in their hands neer half of what they had in the yeare 1641.

4°. The Duke of Yorke had not an acre in his owne Right, but had about 120 thousand acres under the Title of Regicides, Adventurers and soldiers ; and all the obnoxious Democraticall and fanaticall Persons sheltered themselves under my Lord Anglesey,[1] My Lord Kingston, and 3 or 4 more.

And now Cousin answer my quaeries, vizt : Why you ask these Questions, and studdy the severall Peaces that have been made ?

What became of a paper dated the 6 of July 1665,[2] whereby It was agreed between the Grandees of both Parties, (1) that The Decrees after the 22° July, should bee confirmd. (2) That the English should retrench Thirds, and take Reprizalls in number of acres, not [in] equall value worth and purchase. (3) Should confirme *Letterees*, and admitt 54 *nominees* to be restord without tryall to their Chief Seats and 2000 acres about each (Kilmedan onely eccepted), and that in lieu thereof there should bee no more Tryall of Innocents ; So as whosoever was not adjudged *Innocent* should passe for *Nocent*. My Lord Tirconell and I have been at Daggers drawing concerning this paper ; I have traced it to the Commissioners of Inspection Anno 1672.[3]

O God, Cousin, how doth my foot slip when I consider what providence hath winked at in its Dispensations of Ireland ! I have given many notes to Thom Sheridan,[4] at my Lord Tirconell's Importunity, who pretends to write the History of Ireland. To what a good passe had I brought matters to with that great man, till Dick Nagle came over !

[1] Arthur Annesley, first Earl of Anglesey (1614–1686). He had been the negotiator between Charles II. and the Parliamentary party, and became in 1660 Vice-Treasurer and Receiver-General in Ireland.

[2] This was apparently the agreement preliminary to the Act of Explanation (see *infra*, p. 261).

[3] The Commissioners who had been appointed in 1671 when the Act of Settlement was reopened by Charles II. at the instance of Col. Talbot (Tyrconnel).

[4] Sheridan was now secretary to the Viceroy, Lord Tyrconnel.

My Lord of Anglesey's friends tell mee that his
Lordship desired I should perfect his History of
Ireland if he were snacht away. I have perused his
papers, but cannot put new wine into old Bottles.
Hee writes like my Lord Chancellor Clarendon
against Mr Hobbs and treats more of Persons than
Things.[1] In so much as I say ' Let the Dead bury
the Dead '. When I dye the World shall see a
Treatis *de Jure Belli, Jure Naturae* and *Jure Gentium,*
concerning the Lands and people of Ireland ; being
the History in fact, number, and measure of what
happened since my Landing in Ireland in September
1652 and a very few yeares before.[2] I do not envy
what Sir John Davis hath said of the Politiques of
Ireland ; much lesse of his celebrated Report concerning mixt money.[3] Hee was indeed an excellent
Person, but bescribled with Law and Learning. Hee
made excellent Patches, but set them beside the hole.

Adieu, Dr Cousin,

152. *Southwell to Petty.*

[Southwell, who was staying with the Duke of Ormond
at Cornbury in Oxfordshire, here indulges in some of his
rare reminiscences.

The incident in connection with Cromwell and Magna
Carta to which he alludes took place in 1655. One Cony
had been committed to the Tower for refusing to pay custom
duties, and certain judges intervened in the case by granting
the prisoner a writ of Habeas Corpus. The Protector thereupon summoned the parties to appear before him and told
them that " their *Magna F . . . a* should not control his
actions which he knew were for the safety of the Common-

---

[1] Sir Peter Pett published (in 1693) a volume of *Memoirs* by the Earl of
Anglesey. This no doubt contained the papers to which Petty here alludes.
[2] Amongst the Petty papers there is one entitled " Several Questions *in
Jure Gentium, Jure Belli et Pacis,* and in policy, concerning matters in Ireland
between the years 1642 and 1662 ", but the description of the Treatise would
fit Petty's *Political Anatomy of Ireland.*
[3] Sir John Davies (1569–1626), Attorney-General for Ireland, poet and
writer. He wrote *A discoverie of the true causes why Ireland was never entirely
subdued nor brought under Obedience to the Crowne of England untill the
Beginning of his Majesties happy Raigne* (1612), also a Treatise on Taxation.

wealth, and that they had not authority to sit but what he gave them ". (Isaac Kimber, *Life of Cromwell*, 1725, p. 328.)

As a young man Southwell travelled in Italy. It must have been at this time that he met Lord Carlingford, who was in the service of Charles, Duke of Lorraine, and afterwards became an Austrian Field-Marshal.

I can find no historical mention of the meeting which Southwell describes as having taken place at Lord Anglesey's house in Drury Lane in 1665. It would seem to have been one of those private conclaves between the leaders of the rival parties which led up to the final agreement embodied in the Act of Explanation. The Earl of Clancarty (Donough M'Carthy, so created by Charles II.) was brother-in-law to Ormond, while Nicholas Plunkett was prominent after the Restoration as the intermediary for the Irish Catholics.]

[Cornebury] 7 March. 1686/7

Deare Cousin

I have yours of the 5th and thanke you for the honour of It. All you write is to me a matter of Record. I could not conceale it from the Lord I am with, nor he forbeare to desire an extract of it, soe authentick it was in matter of moment and soe entertaining in all the Rest.

I deplore the ejectments you mention and it drives me to remember a dirty rime imputed to Cromwell when they told him of Magna Charta.

My lady has my best wishes wheather she goes or stays, and to make them stick I would fasten them with goulden pinns if I had them. My daughters bragg of her ladyships favour towards them, and if my God-son take a stride into the world to enable him (in your own phrase) to ' live among dangerous men ', may he prosper like his father's Bee Hive and returne home againe *Crura thymo plena.*

You have so anatomized the wooden head, that I shall never mind it more, but for an eccho, I wish you had heard one which the Lord Carlinford cairyed me to see within a mile of Milan. We stood in the gallery of a Gentleman's House, one story high, and in his garden (where were Trenches and I think some

standing water), the eccho repeated after me the word
" Home " 21 times distinctly.

I thanke you for all the proportions of Land you
mention. The reason of my enquiry herein was to
enable me to Answer those who rashly affirme (and
that in print) that the Irish had nothing by the Settlement ; that if by the Usurper they were whipt with
Iron, it has beene since the Restauration with
Scorpions.

What you add beyound what I requested, which
is the Compromise of the 6 July 1665, is what I have
long had in my Head, which you now diffinitly
explaine. I doe believe, and I think remember,
that this Agreement was signed at my Lord Anglesey's
House in Drury Lane, where the Lord Clancarty,
Sir Nicholas Plunkett and the Heads of the Party
did meete and agree thereto. I cannot say I saw the
Paper, but I remember it was reported in Councill
that all was Agreed. And when in 1672 the Comission
of Enquiry was on foot and Sir Henage Finch[1]
acted his part as a Champion for the Settlement, He
soe vigorously insisted on this Agreement that I
remember the good King sayd in Councill, " Nay I
doe well remember there was some kind of agreement
in this matter ".

It seemes this Paper is now lost or buryed with
these proceedings—which I once received from Sir
James Shaen all in a deale Box ; and for want of
other Roome, they were placed under the great Table
in the Councill Chamber and I beleive remayned there
till the Chamber was lately altered. And who knowes
but it may still be found in the same box—if it be
not a crime to looke for it. As to my having Studdyed
the severall Peaces, it was purely to find by those
Sibill's Bookes what might now ensue (at the least).
For that which was once contended for with sword
in hand, will now certainly be taken when it may be

---

[1] Sir Heneage Finch, later first Earl of Nottingham (1621–1682). As
Attorney-General in 1672, it fell to him to defend the compromise which had
been arrived at seven years before by the Act of Explanation.

had without contention. And what the moddell will be, is now I think the expectation of every Post.

I see how you have layd by the *mala stamina* of a History that was Intended, and what you say of Sir John Davys his Essayes, and the misfortune of his Law and learning, which onely enabled him to putt the Patch besyde the Hole. If I live to see you I hope to be happyer than the world, and see those treasures *De Jure Belli, Jure Naturae* and *Jure Gentium.*

I return home in 3 dayes.

153. *Petty to Southwell.*[1]

Piccadilly, ye 19 March 86/7

Deare Cousen

I thank you for what you said about the agreement of the 6th of July 65. Pray think again of it to effect, and of the Paper enclosd, for it is the Worke of the Day. I need write noe more at this time, but to give you the best services of the Family.

154. *Southwell to Petty.*

[It is interesting, if not material, to try and equate the documents which appeared in print about this time with those sent by Petty to Southwell. The ' Paper ' mentioned in the last letter, here acknowledged by Southwell as a ' book ', and subsequently referred to as an Essay ' which might have loaded a chariot ', seems to have been the *Five Essays in Political Arithmetic*, which were actually licensed on February 18, 1687, and may be presumed to have appeared in print about a month afterwards. The ' two points ' which Petty says (*infra*, p. 265) this book contained, namely, suggestions for dealing with the Plague and for a wall round London, are both to be found in the *Five Essays*, though he frequently recurred to them elsewhere (see *Papers*, ch. ii., London).

In an earlier letter (*supra*, p. 259) Petty had bewailed

---

[1] This letter is in Lady Petty's hand.

the evil influence of ' Dick ' (Sir Richard) Nagle over Tyrconnel. The so-called ' Coventry Letter', which was published broadcast at the time, was the handiwork of the former.
Though ostensibly written from Coventry by Nagle to
Tyrconnel while on his way to Ireland on October 26, 1686,
it seems to have been in fact concocted between the two
before Tyrconnel's departure from London, as a sort of
manifesto against the Act of Settlement and the Irish
Protestants.

Petty, as we shall see, afterwards wrote a formal answer
to the letter, though this was never published.]

[Kingsweston] 23 March 1686/7

Deare Cousin

I give you a thousand thankes for your booke.
The glory of England was never soe exalted, nor the
proud Cittyes of Europe out done, as by this new Art
of Comparison and your Doctrine uppon the living
and the dead.

I thank you alsoe for the Coventry letter. I have
read it more than once, and see how the Settlement,
like St Sebastian, is stuck full of Arrowes. But the
worst of this Saynt was his being tyed fast to a tree,
and not sufferd to evade or send back any darts of his
owne. Must this paper be taken for Gospell, and will
noe answer to it be admitted ? The foundation of it
all is the care and culture of Catholick Religion ; the
giving it such growth, vigour, and authority by wealth
and Acres, as may persuade a Successeur to be friends
with them uppon faire and equall termes. What may
be in the power of this great wheele to effect I know not,
unlesse his Majesty stand firme in the gapp.

I heare the Corke Merchants, who had forbid the
sending more goods from thence, have taken courage
from the late proclamation at Dublin to trade on.

When does Cousin Charles sett forth to his Travells
and whither does he goe ? If Monsr Mesnell[1] goes
with him, then I would advise you to putt Cousin
Harry to Monsr Renaudot who last taught my son.
I do not think there is a better Infuser of knowledge

---

[1] A French tutor.

into youth in the world, and his store is very rich and varyous.

I am, with all true service to my Lady and the little ones.
                                    Yrs

155. *Southwell to Petty.*

[Kingsweston] 31 March 1687

Deare Cousin

With your short one of the 19th, I had your Essay ; which, tho folded in a letter by the post, might have loaded a Chariot, had it beene done by all the surveyours of Europe. I did before thank you for it ; But reading it since againe with more attention, I cannot conceale to you my admiration of It. Tis soe new, soe daring, and yett soe conclusive ; that next to the removeing Mountaines, I know not any thing that ought more to be wondered at. If you leave to posterity the way of putting bounds to the plague, you will be Imortall.

While I was thus thinking of your power in Numbers, and that I could pay noe thankes but prayse, I lookt againe on the paper that you annext, and since you required my thoughts I would venture to obey. It will come to you by another hand, and if it savour too much of the Oxe-House, fling it in the fire. If not, yett lett not my name be mentioned for reasons, I conjure you.

With all true service to the Lady and the little ones, I am ever
                                    Yrs

156. *Petty to Southwell.*

Piccadilly, 7 Aprill 1687

D[r] Coz[n]

The book (which you say might have been a Cartload) had 2 points in it : the one about the

Plague, the other about the new Wall propounded for London. Nobody but yourselfe hath taken notice of the former, and nobody at all of the latter—So deafe are the Adders wee charme unto !

As for the Settlement, Let us fancy it to bee a Ship and to be repaired and made better.

1°. The 'Coventry letter' propounds to breake it up, burne most of the materialls, and build some other Thing (not another Ship) with the rest.

2°. I meet with another who advises the sawing of it in 2 and making it longer, as also taking downe her Upper-workes wherewith shee is top-heavy, " for so " sayth Hee " She will be a bigger and a better ship "— but Wee have not Carpenters to do it.

3°. The letter of the 15 November (which I praise and admire) thinks That calking it a-new, and phay-goodling (?) it almost, may serve turne.

4°. But I lately met with an old Carpenter sitting upon a Log of Timber, smoking his short pipe, to whom I said : " D'yee see that Ship yonder in the road ? "—" See her " sayd hee, " A pox on her ! I remember when she was built, and wrought myselfe for a while upon her, till I found knavery among the Chief owners and the workmen too, by Gad."—"Well" sayd I, "What d'y think of her ? "—" Shee's a rotten Toad " quoth hee, " There was a Couzen of the owner's that serv'd us in rotten Timber and plank, which as twas lay'd was tarred over and lookt like sufficient stuffe, and the Devil and all."—" But d'y think shee may bee mended ? "—" Never " says hee, " without bringing her into a dry dock and taking out these planks and some of her principall timbers. Nay, a peece of her keele, by Gad." I intended to talke on with this Waspish Nimps (?) but [we] were inter-rupted &c.

Within 2 dayes I mett with Mr Houblon of whom I inquired concerning this Choleric old Coxcomb. But Mr Houblon sayd : " Hee is not so choleric as one would think, but having been horribly abusd in and about that very ship. If you name 3 or 4 words

('Column' is one, the other 2 I can send you) Hee
will, like Dol Common in the 'Alchemist',[1] fall into
Extravagances. Otherwise he is sober enough." "May
be so", quoth I, "for though I gott into the 'Anchor'
I could not make him drink above a glasse or 2."—
Thus ends the parable &c.

To conclude. I find That if wee had a dry dock,
These few timbers might bee mended without prejudice even to the mold of the present Hull.

157. *Southwell to Petty.*

[Kingsweston] 20 aprill 1687

Deare Cousin

I had the honour of yours of the 7th and have
much considerd the Parable of the Shipp and your
wishes for a drye dock. If a new draft were made,
and every one certainly knew what would be done in
this dock, and that the majority saw hopes of a
Saving Voyage, the thoughts and votes and wishes
of the powerfull might run one way. But if a Chipp
be toucht without some such preamble, every planck
will groane and expect to be flung into the fire.

The 'Coventry letter' runns now about in every
hand on the other syde, and gives terrour as I am told ;
tho the Proclamation there, and the later declaration
here,[2] seeme (as to Property) to Speake better things.

I am glad I animadverted on that peece of
Angelick vertue in your Essay of *limiting the Plague.*
It was new to me, and a blessing to mankind which
I could not but admire. But for the other point of
the London Wall, I had heard you speake of it before,
soe it was not altogether new. Nor am I martiall
man enough to take all things in that appertaine
to such a proposall. But we have a Martial King,

---

[1] By Ben Jonson.
[2] The 'Declaration of Indulgence', which suspended the Penal Statutes
against Roman Catholics and Protestant Dissenters. It had been promulgated
on April 4, 1687.

who heares you patiently, and might putt you to It. And I wonder He or his Lieutenant Generalls doe not discusse this great point; as alsoe an other you have in store, touching a defence by wooll packs, applicable to land and sea.[1]

My friend Monsieur Renaudot is ambitious to wayt uppon you. He is, among other Ingredients of ability, a good Geometrician; therefore pray smile uppon him.

To my lady and the little ones all happinesse.

Yrs

158. *Petty to Southwell.*

Piccadilly, 26 Aprill 1687

Dr Coz[n]

I will observe your direction with Mons[r] Renodot.

Charles was to have travelled with My Lord Essex[2] to please his mother, but finding Sir Henry Capell governes the designe, I will not venture upon his conduct.

As to the ship, I have neither dry dock, carpenters, timber nor plank wherewith to mend her; but I heare They have brought her downe of one side and set severall Bohemian shipwrights upon her, who are taking out the good plank to come at the rotten timbers—God's will be done!

159. *Petty to Southwell.*

Piccadilly, 17 May 1687

D[r] Cozen

I had till now little to write, but now I have the Devill and all. Dunsany hath carryd his Cause

---

[1] Cf. "Of Wool Walls" (*Papers*, No. 103).

[2] Algernon Capel, second Earl of Essex (1670–1710), had succeeded the one time Viceroy, Arthur Capel, first Earl. Petty, who had disliked the latter, seems to have extended his disapprobation to his brother, Sir Henry Capel.

against William Naper upon a hearing of 9 howers Continuance. My relation (agreeing with many others) sayth, That Nothing was ever more learnedly urged, more Ingeniously Managd, nor the Objections against his deed more fully provd than in this case. Yett all signifyd not a rush! I expect the same for Tecroghan, and the old proprietors are all getting into Kerry, as lands in the King's hands.

And what shall wee now say of Neddy, Logick, Travell &c, or of the Duke of Buckingham his life or death, religion or manners? I am stund with this blow, And must have time to recover before you may expect long letters from

Y^{rs} &c.

This being the first and plainest case, hath begotten a stronge dread in the minds of the people.

160. Southwell to Petty.

Kingsweston—21 May 1687

Deare Cousin

The last post brought me, in yours of the 17th, a most unwelcome account of damage to your nephew and of approaching danger to your selfe. I see the Juryes are sett uppon it, and every man must looke about; since in this tryall there was noe defect in any circumstance or essential thing, but singly in the verdict. As for the scramble in Kerry, I see and admire your philosophy that you name it with patience. Before, you were lancd and scarifyd; but this is plaine fleaing off the whole skin. But have the philosophy, and the same patience must alsoe take place.

My present care is to save my stake at Kinsale by getting (if I can) a provisoe in the new Charter that must follow the destruction of the old, and in which tis expected that all old members may be layed by. I am herein sollicitous for the future, since at present I can gett noe rent from thence. The towne is become a poore skelliton, for all the trade is now centred in Corke—and tis high time that your friend Neddy doe hasten to the Law.

We are well in this place, as I hope it is with my lady and the little ones.

I have beene writing a close sheete to Peter Welch [1] in which you are often named. Tis on that part of his letter to the Bishop of Lincolne (p. 224) where he speakes of the Irish Rebellion and extenuates the first Massacre, and I think by the hedings of your calculations [2] I have the better of him.

Our Neddy is now gott into Ethicks. I am ever Yrs.

R. S.

I rejoyce however that your nephew Naper did behave himselfe soe like a man in the day of battle. I remember well since his Father [3] sweat for it in the Court of Claymes, till all his hand was wett.

161. *Petty to Southwell.*

[The ' Paper of Powder ' which Petty had just received can be explained by the date of this letter. It is among the MSS. in the form of an order dated June 2, from the Commissioners of the Treasury to the Viceroy, that proceedings against him in the matter of arrears of Quit-rent should be stayed "until his Majesty's determination thereon be signified to your Excellency in due form". Petty was, however, quite correct in thinking that this was only a respite, for his Quit-rent troubles were by no means at an end.]

Piccadilly, 4 Junii, 1687

Dr Coz

I told you in my last I was stund. I send you enclosd the paper of Powder, which of late has

---

[1] Peter Walsh (1618–1688), " Valesius ", the Irish Franciscan. Prominent in the religious controversies of the day. He had recently published in reply to Bishop Thomas Barlow's *Popery* some controversial letters against the claims of Pope Gregory VII., 1672–1684.   [2] P. 258, *supra*.
[3] James Napper, who had married Petty's only sister.

been given mee after my Irish torments to make mee
able to endure more ; for this very terme I expect
2 blowes more at Dublin.   In brief I suffer by fulsom(?)
perjury and forgery, managd with ridiculous Impud-
ence against me &c.

I was last Monday invited to see Mr Meyd with
[his] scholars make speeches, pronounce verses &c.
Many did very well—Sir John Lowther said Extraordinary (?)—as they were taught, but I say That
such exercises of pronouncing periods in a Tune, will
not make them better Orators than Colonel Birch.[1]
Your godson Charles, and even his sister too, outdoe
them all by instinct of nature, without any teaching
and little practise.

Charles is not yet gon, but going to the Academy
at the Hague.   Henry [is] alredy fixt with M^r de
Meurs.   1. Because his Mother will have it so.   2.
Because hee goes in for latine in the same method
he hath hitherto used.   3. Because he is as good company as can bee.   4. Because I like M de Meurs and
his wise moralls very well.

My 5 Essayes [2] are threatned hard out of Holland,
but It must be endured.   I have one with an A[ccount]
of 18 of their chiefe townes which confirmes [my]
ratiocinations to $\frac{1}{10}$ pt.

Here is an other answer of 10 sheets to the
' Coventry letter '—Wee must not say Mr Nagle's.

162. *Southwell to Petty*.

[Kingsweston] 11 June 1687

Deare Cousin

This being the longest day in the yeare, I
could wish it were Imployd from morning to night in
reading or writing like orders in your favour with

---

[1] John Birch (1616–1691), Presbyterian colonel.   He had taken a prominent
part in the Restoration, and was till his death a member of the House of
Commons.
[2] The *Five Essays in Political Arithmetic*.

what you had on the 2nd from the Treasury ;   And tis
most kindly done to send me the Copy of it.   If
my Lord Godolphin [1] would now take consideration
of what Sir Edward Dering Intended, I am able to
give a large Testimoniall of his being strangely convinct of your hard usage ;   and that he resolved to
intercede not onely for a full settlement in your affaires,
but to the abating one hundred pounds per annum of
the Quitt Rents which you submitted unto—which in
truth you did at his persuasion—I meane as regards
concernes in Kerry.

What you apprehend of Shocks and disorders in
other parts, I can but deplore, and imploy wisshes that
it were otherwise than you find.

I have a great share of disappointment in my owne
small concernes, scarce getting any Rent at all, and
I am menaced by the Courcys [2] with trouble and law
suites for having what their Ancestours, they say,
had noe right to dispose of.   And this is the gratitude
I find for respects to that poore family for neere 40,
or rather 50 yeares past, from my Father and my
selfe.   I suppose tis because they think witnesses and
Jurys can now doe any thing !

I see my Godson is going to the Academy, which
I very well approuve of, as alsoe the disposal of my
Cousin Harry.

If you can lend the answer of ten Sheetes [3] to
Phillip Madox, he will presently gett it copyed out
for me, and sent by a safe hand.   I see you expect
a broadsyde from Holland, but you have 18 Cittyes
already for you, and soe neede not tremble before the
Thunderbolt falls.   I am apt to think they will consider well before they shoote, or repent their shooting.

I perceive you have beene hearing of exercises at
a Schoole, which you think to be a sort of Musick
meeting, and that there may be Euphoniacall Non-

---

[1] Sidney, first Earl of Godolphin (1645–1712), was now a Commissioner of
the Treasury.
[2] The Courcies or Coursey is a barony in County Cork, near Kinsale. It
appears that this district was named from the family which once owned it.
[3] To the Coventry Letter.

sence. I confesse tis happiest when there is more care
for the matter than the manner, tho this last is much
easyer sought for. As to the other it is *Donum Dei*,
and you know to whom it was sayd at Merton Colledge " Young man you were borne with 3 quarters
of what you know ".[1]

Having named this colledge, I must not omitt to
tell you that Neddy does well according to the disci-
pline of the place. He is already turned disputant in
the Hall.

As you thrive by the order of the 2nd (that seemes
to shew a certainty made in the present Rent, and in
the Arrears) pray lett me know it, as of all other things
wheather to profitt or losse — for when I cannot
rejoyce with you I will mourne.

Yrs

163. *Petty to Southwell.*

[The answer to the Coventry Letter, which formed part
of the " Novum organum " here referred to by Petty, is a
voluminous document of some thirty pages of foolscap. I
have not printed this in the *Papers*, but have given the answer
to the *Sale and Settlement of Ireland* (*Papers*, No. 18). Petty
had at length formulated this reply, though two years before
he had insisted that it should be left to others (*supra*, p. 149).

By the " Journal of the General Assembly " it seems that
Petty meant the Journal of the ' Supreme Council ', which
had assumed control of Ireland during the Rebellion. I
cannot discover that this Journal is anywhere extant.]

Piccadilly, 16 Junii 1687
Dr Cozn

I have put the paper you desird into Phill
Madox hands. It contaynes :

1. A defence of the present Settlement.
2. An answer to the ' Coventry Letter '.
3. An answer to the *Sale and Settlement of Ireland*.

[1] *Supra*, p. 179.

4. Part of the Journall of the Generall Assembly. The latter (or 4th point) by mischance I have not, but soon may.

I expect more dismall Newes about the Tecrohan concerne.

_____

The Present Evills of Ireland are :

That the value of all the Lands this yeare 1687 is but little more than half what the same was Anno 1683.

The value of the Cattle and stock about $\frac{3}{4}$, Of the housing about $\frac{3}{6}$, The mony and plate but $\frac{2}{3}$.

The diminution of the whole is about 9 millions 200^m pounds, the interest whereof is 920^m pounds. But 920^m is about the $\frac{1}{7}$ part of expense of the people in Ireland. And this decay of $\frac{1}{7}$ part will also cause a decay in the King's revenue of $\frac{1}{7}$ part of what rises from Importations, Excise on drink, Ale and wine licences (Quitrents, harths and Exportations being another business). Adieu.

W. P.

This paper is a ' Novum Organum ' and therefore keep it.

164. *Southwell to Petty.*

[Kingsweston] 2 July 1687

Deare Cousin

Yours of the 16th past should not have had soe late an acknowledgement, but that I have beene ill, and twice bloodded, &c.

I doe this day expect, by the lawyer, what was copyed in three of the Irish points that you mention ; and I hope you will ere long give me alsoe the satisfaction of the 4th.

I am in sympathy with you for what may happen on the Tecrohan Account ; but who needes wonder at any event on that Syde, when the prints which now come out make Church of England Loyalty a sort of ridiculous fable ? This I confesse lyes heavy as a

milstone on my heart, and I would faine beleive that
such papers have noe 'Allowance', tho soe Inscrib'd.[1]

As to the *Novum Organum* you were pleasd to
send me, in stating the points as to Irish Revenue ;
you may be sure I will keepe it as my directory, and
as I doe all manner of Papers that come from your
hands.

Wheather Cousin Charles be at home or abroad,
my service to him and to the whole family.

Ever yrs

165. Southwell to Petty.

[Kingsweston] 8 July 1687

Deare Cousin
Since my acknowledgement of yours of the
16th past I have received and Read the papers, and
doe think I never was better entertayned in my life.
I could say many things of soe excellent a discourse,
but will Comprize all in the words of Seneca, speaking
of the Law : *Non Irascitur sed Castigat.* The 4th
point which you thought wanting (being part of the
Journall of the Supreame Councill) is there as well
as the rest, and serves as voucher in some particulars
of the preceding discourse.

I am told from an Intelligent hand, as if there
were hopes the Settlement would not be shaken,[2]
what ever is done with the Charters. And surely
if those who have power, and noe passion, did but
read and consider your discourse (as perhaps they
have done), they must be convinced that the Settlement
cannot be broaken without strange confusion in all his
Majesty's affaires in the Kingdome.

But I heare of 11 Lords whose Outlawryes are
discharged, and surely this lookes not onely as the

---

[1] Southwell, though speaking in guarded language, means, of course, that
he hopes that the Declaration of Indulgence and the attacks on Irish Protestants
were not directly inspired by King James II.

[2] The Act of Settlement was not repealed till 1689.

forerunner of a Parlyment,[1] but as some assurance to them of having estates to support the dignity of Peerage.

You say nothing as yett of what has hapned about Tecrohan, and your silence is a very good signe.

The late dissolution makes my hopes of seeing you very remote, and this not onely in love (?) to the Country, but as being on ground ; for of ten letters from the other syde, there is not one Bill.

My most humble service to my lady and the little ones. I have beene reading this day "the Hind and Panther Transverst"[2] and doe fancy none could make more of it than my Cousin Charles, for he would reach all the good humours that are in it.

I am allwayes Yrs

166. *Petty to Southwell.*

[Sir Isaac Newton's *Principia*, after being ' exhibited ' at the Royal Society in 1686, had just been published. As we shall see later, the book excited the highest encomiums from Petty.

Petty was quite right in thinking that his *Essays in Political Arithmetic* were likely to bring trouble to M. Auzout (*supra*, p. 247). Auzout was indeed so much afraid of this that he caused a letter to be written to the Royal Society begging them, if they printed his answer to Petty, not to say whence he had obtained his figures (H. Justel to Edmond Halley, *Royal Society Letter Book*, and Hull, p. 522 *n.*).]

Dre Cous.   Piccadilly, 9° July 1687

To prevent any discontinuance I answer your last, about Ridiculing (' with allowance ') of Church

---

[1] There were fifteen Catholic Peers whose outlawrys had been reversed in the Irish Parliament which eventually met on May 7, 1689 (Lecky, ii. 182).

[2] Dryden's poem *The Hind and the Panther*—written in the interest of the Roman Catholic faith which the author had recently embraced — had been published in April of this year. It was answered by *The Hind and the Panther Transversed, or the Citty Mouse and the Country Mouse*, the work of Charles Montagu (afterwards Lord Halifax) and Matthew Prior. Dryden is said to have been deeply wounded by the "cruel usage" he thus experienced "from two young fellows to whom he had always been very civil ".

of England's Loyalty, by saying That I take Loyalty
to bee an habituall disposition to obey the Law, and
that for God's sake.   I now ask you—1°. What are
the Lawes ?   2°. What the Church of England ?

My cake is againe dough in Kerry.   Mr Newton's
excellent book is come out.   They are like to knock
Monsr Auzout on the head both at Rome and Paris,
for what They say hee gave mee occasion to write
about London.   I have heard nothing from the
foe in Holland.   Have a care of your health—by your
own observation and not other Medicination

I am Y^rs

W. P.

I hope you have received all my papers from Phill.
Madox.

167. Southwell to Petty.

[Kingsweston] 12 July 1687

Deare Cousin

Yours of the 9th gives Answer to my last
about Ridiculing (with allowance) the Church of
England Loyalty ;   by saying first, that you take
loyalty to be an habituall disposition to obey the law
and that for God's Sake.   And then you aske :

1°. What are the Lawes ?

2°. What the church of England ?

I answer (1) That the Lawes are Rules of Duty, with
Rewards annext to the obedyent and punishment
to the Stubborne.   (2) Tis a church which makes
Loyalty to the Prince a Religious Law, or in your
owne words ' an habituall disposition to obey such
law, and that for God's Sake '.

But if Ridiculing with Allowance then be the
Reward of this Law, I desire to know of you, what
shall be the punishment ?

If an Englishman should rise up in this generation,
and shew cause to magnify London above Rome and
Paris—If he should advise the Prince of the Citty

how to prevent seditions and privations, and the Cittizens how to Stifle a Plague. Would it not be hard if the Apprentices should teare this man, as Dr Lamb,[1] for a Conjurer? and harder yett if they should doe it 'with Allowance'? But if, to mitigate the matter, a Reason should be given for this Severity (as namely that the Fame and Service herein did affict some great men of Paris and of Rome, and that Mons[r] Azout was in danger uppon it), I then say alsoe that it may be lawfull to deny to him the Rocks and Mountaynes of Kerry, who measured out to others the meadowes and Fatt of the Land.

Pray lett me know why is your Cake dough againe in Kerry, and how fares it with Tecrohan?

I thanke you for your advertisement about my Health. I have acknowledged your Papers, and admired them as Seneca did the Law—*Lex non Irascitur sed Castigat.*

I am ever Yrs

Pray are you satisfyed, in Mr Newton's New Booke, with the Reasons he gives for the ebbing and flowing of the Sea?

168. *Petty to Southwell.*

[Petty is here contemplating yet another expedition to Windsor, which apparently took place before August 16. The 'Extra Discourse', which he had prepared for this occasion, was a paper entitled *The Weight of the Crown of England*, which in its shorter form (consisting of ten points) I have printed in the *Petty Papers* (No. 79). Its author set great store on its powers of persuasion and hoped it would prove 'The Bible for Ireland' (*infra*, p. 280). Perhaps, as Southwell anticipated, the paper proved to be beyond His Majesty's powers of comprehension (p. 282). But in any case Petty was eventually compelled to admit that it got him

---

[1] ? John Lambe, the astrologer. Having been imprisoned for fifteen years for the practice of 'execrable arts', he lived for a time under the protection of the Duke of Buckingham, but was attacked by a mob of apprentices in 1628 and died as a result of his injuries.

' no butter to his parsnips nor hobnails for his shoes '
(p. 283).]

Piccadilly, 23ᵈ July 1687

Dr Coz

Yesterday Charles,Monsʳ Mesnel,and Crofton
went away for Holland by the way of Harwich.

Fitzgerald of Tecroghan nonsuited himself last
terme, but will come on agayne the next. Wee are
strong in all parts but the Maine—which is Juries.
I am going to Windsore to remove the rub in my
Kerry buisines ; Tis a pittifull one, If something
deeper bee not the true Cause. I have an Extra
discourse to shew the King if things fit right.

As for Mr Newton's book, I would give 500£ to
have been the author of it, and 200£ That Charles
understood it. My bad eyes disable mee to make the
most of it, for diagrams cannot bee read by others.

Mr Pen, a mighty man, is or will bee shortly at
Bristoll. I receive nothing in Ireland and nothing
from it, but am yrs

W. P.

169. *Southwell to Petty.*

[Kingsweston] 27 July 1687

Deare Cousin

I see by yours of the 23ʳᵈ that Cousin Charles
is departed and well attended. He has the best of
my good wishes, and pray lett me heare of his safe
landing and well doing—for we ought to be concernd
for the good of the next Age.

I see how Fitzgerald fences against your Sharp
Weapons, as knowing he cannot wound you but by
the black legion of 12.¹

I hope your Windsor Journey will vacatt (?) The
Rubb about Kerry, and that you alsoe had a fitt
season for the discourse you carryed. I am afire to

¹ *I.e.* an Irish jury, which would be certain to give a verdict for Catholic
against Protestant.

know it, and P. Madox will write it and carry it by a safe hand to me. And whereas you would give 500£ to have beene Author of Mr Newton's booke, I would give a 1000 to be the Author of the least of yours; Tho from Ireland, of 1600£ due to, me I can squeze but one. I am therefore Retrenching all I can, and from 3rd Rate [have] to Sayle in a 5th.

W. P.[1] had on Sunday 3000 at his congregation where he preached vehemently twice that day and magnifyd the King's Indulgence. I expected to see him here, but am told as if he departs to morrow, and is sent for by the King. Time will tell us his errand.

All duty to my lady and respects to the little ones.

170. *Petty to Southwell.*

D^{re} Coz^{n} Piccadilly, 4° Aug 1687

Charles was well at Rotterdam the 29th, but was 4 times 24 hours at sea.

I send you the Contents of the discourse I mentioned. I intend it to bee The Bible for Ireland. I have shewne it in parts to some great Men, but not yet to the King; but will shortly.

The Customs of Dublin have, in this last quarter, fallen from 4 to 3, and the Excise from 7 to 6. Now altho it hath been sayd with a lowd voice That the people of Dublin are half run away[2] (and by good observers that 1100 houses are voyd) Yet your Cousin assures you that in the last quarters hee finds more burialls and Christnings than in any of the 10 quarters before. And therefore sayes that The people do retrench their expence in strong drink by $\frac{1}{6}$ part and also in their housing, by crowding 7 familyes into 6 houses;

---

[1] William Penn, who had lately returned from a missionary journey in Europe, was now engaged on a preaching tour of England. The Declaration of Indulgence had been published in April.

[2] A large number of Protestants had left the country when Clarendon was superseded by Tyrconnel.

for 1100 is the $\frac{1}{6}$ part of the houses in Dublin. The
fall of lands appeares to mee by the fall of the Price
of butter, Cheese, Milk, eggs, flesh, &c.

Adieu

171. *Southwell to Petty.*

Kingsweston, 13 Augt 1687

Deare Cousin

I have yours of the 4th and have read the
papers inclosed, which are either for transplanting or
Propagation. The things are mighty, and call unto
my mind that when Paul reasoned of Righteousnesse,
Temperance, and Judgement to come, Felix trembled.
You know Columbus made the first offer to us of his
Goulden World, and was rejected; That the Sybill's
Bookes, tho never so true, were undervalued; and
Mr Newton's demonstrations will hardly be understood. The market rule goes fair in everything else,
Tantum valet quantum vendi potest. Soe as tho I doe
not suspect you can be mistaken in what you assert,
since you enumerate soe many solid as well as bitter
objections thereunto; yett the dullnesse of the world
is such, the opposers soe many, your fellow labourers
soe few, and your Age soe advanc'd, that I reckon the
worke Insuperable. However I am glad that your
thoughts are all written downe, for Posterity, as
favour'd by great Accidents, may cultivate what the
present Age neglects. And in the meane time since
you propose to entertayne the King on these subjects,
lett me advertize you what his good Brother once sayd
at The Councill Board—That he thought you one of
the best Commissioners of the Navy that ever was;
That you had vast knowledge in many things—" But "
sayd he " the man will not be contented to be excellent,
but is still Ayming at Impossible Things ".

You know I am [in] possession [position] of saying
any thing to you that comes in my head; but this I
say for your service, that being already advanced in

his Majesty's opinion for things that he Compre-
hends, you doe not growe lesse by going beyound his
Reach.

I rejoyce to heare that Cousin Charles gott safe,
tho after good tossing, to the other syde. Your letters
will not be lesse welcome if you sprinkle them with a
little good tydings of him and of his Improvements.
I say the same for the rest, and am ever

Yrs

Pray Cousin, did you ever use any Art to Improve
your memory? Tully *De oratore* uses many words
to shewe how it may be Improved by Images, but
I desire your saying.

172. *Petty to Southwell.*

Pickadilly, the 16 Augt 1687

Dr Cosin

I have had noe Letter from Charles since the
7th Instant from Amsterdam. I am not solicitous
about his studys and the Course of his Life, for he is
too Solicitous himselfe. I onely say God send him
good luck, and then a little Learning will serve his
turn. For of the hundred prosperous men which wee
have seen since the year 1660, neither the Learning
nor parts of five have been admirable, and the forty
[? ninety] five contemptable ; nor have one quarter
of that hundred thriven by following the Course which
their parents put them into.

I doe perfectly approve of your advise concerning
my Mountybanck papers. But we must eate Toades,
and wash our hands in Molten Lead, to sell of our
oynments for the Itch !

I gave the King a paper at Windsor Intitled *The
Weight of the Crown of England* in 20 short Articles,
more stupendious than what I sent you. I desired the
King to pick out of the whole one Article which he
wished to be true and another which he thinketh to

be false, and Comand me within 24 houres, and within
one Sheet of paper, to show him my further thoughts
Concerning them.   All was very well taken, but
without getting better Buter to my parsnips or hob-
nayles for my Shoes ; and poor Isaac Newton will
certainly meet with the same fate in the world, for I
have not met with one Man that puts an extraordinary
value upon his Book.

Now Because you cannot believe that my Project
can gaine the nation 140 millions, I send you now
another paper to show how 1619 millions may be
gotten in 25 yeares ; [1] and have the 5 points whereon
the same is Bottomed, as well demonstrated as in the
Pulpett and at the Barr is usual.   You will ask me
why I persist in these fruitless Labours.   I say they
are Labours of pleasure, of which ratiocination is the
greatest and most Angelicall.   And being by my age
near heaven, I think it high time to build myself a
Tomb on earth out of these materialls, to which I hope
you will furnish mortar in due time.

You will say the Double bottome hath poysoned
all my proposalls ; to which I say that the Closett I
showed you, containes the solution of all Questions
in Shipping and Sayling.   A vehement Combina-
tion against me made the fourth attempt worse than
the first.   I courted the King's Mysteryes, and like
Actaeon would have seen Diana nacked, and was
therefore sett upon by many Cruell dogs.

The Paper I sent you concerning the fall of the
people's Expence and the King's Revenue, proves
admirably and woefully true as the enclosed Scrap
demonstrates ; for the people must grow fewer when
the Births and Burialls doe both decrease, and the
Customs and Excise doe the Contrary.

Concerning an Artificial Memory ; [2] I believe the

---

[1] This was "On Doubling the People" (*Papers*, No. 95), where Petty attempts
to show that if the population of England, Ireland and Scotland were doubled
the capital valuation of the three countries would rise from 1095 to 2714 millions
of pounds.

[2] Cf. *Philosophical Transactions*, No. 178, "On the Strength of Memory",
by Dr. Wallis (1685).

ancient orators had itt better than any body now, as
to matters, paragrafes, sentences and words. I myselfe had somewhat of the Latter, and could att the
first hearing remember any 50 Nonsensicall Incoherent
words ; and not onely repeat them readily forwards
and backwards, but alsoe readily which was the 3rd,
19th, 37th &c. It was a thing of noe use but to gett
the admiration of ffoolish people.

I have tyred you enough—Adieu

W. P.

173. *Petty to Southwell.*

Piccadilly, 6° Septemb. 1687

D^{re} Co^{z}

I long since answerd your excellent letter
of the 13th past by sending you the most extravagant
paper I ever wrote, viz, of gayning 1600 millions
and of eating Toades &c. I doubt whether you ever
receyvd it, or have been sick, Tho such Whynsyes
require neither answer or other regard. However I
say *All is true.*

Charles is come back, a little sooner than we
thought, for not having his health ; but hath made an
Emprovement which I think wonderfull, and answerd
all the ends I apprehend in travell, giving as good
an Accompt of Holland, Flanders, Brabant, &c as
I desire.

I believe I shall shortly passe from hence by
Bath and Wells to Canington, 3 miles westwards of
Bridgwater, to see some lands neere Minehead. Wee
all present you and your family our services &c.

174. *Southwell to Petty.*

Badminton, 10 Septr 1687

Deare Cousin

I have beene for 3 weekes from home, either
in attending his Majesty, as he past and repast the

whole length of our County,[1] or assisting my Lord of
Ormond, as he is here deteyned and therefore afflicted
with the gout.   He has stood on his leggs but one
day since he came heither, and talkes of being lifted
into his Coach on Tuesday next, in order to passe
to his House at Kingston Hall [2] in Dorsett Shire.
I will then hasten home and pay duty for your long
and obleiging and amazing letter of the 16th past, which
was not to be done in progresse.

But I am just now reproached againe by yours
of the 6th Instant and by one from my lady, full of
kindnesse to my daughters, whom I but just saw at
Bathe as they past by.   I wish you all prosperity in
the purchase you have in hand ; And surely if you
come to Bathe, you must come to Kingsweston, or
never expect to prosper in your designe.

I am glad my cousin Charles is returned with
health and soe full fraighted in soe short a time.
Neddy is here now with me and plays well at Billiards.
I know not yett if he learnt Logick as fast when at
Oxford, for as yett I have not had time to enquire.
He is however a pretty sober young fellow.

When you heare what the great and gracious
Interview at Chester [3] has produced and what we are
likely to trust too, I pray send me a word ; and with
most humble duty to my lady, I am ever Yrs

R. S.

175. *Southwell to Petty.*

Deare Cousin   Kingsweston, 28 Sept. 1687
Uppon a fresh Review of your letter of the
16th past, the particulars are of that Bulke and
importance and my digestion soe incompetent, that

---

[1] The Queen having been ordered to Bath, King James had made a sort of
progress through the Western Counties, promising everywhere that he would
settle liberty as firmly as Magna Carta (Burnet, *James II.*, p. 216).

[2] Kingston Lacey had recently been bought by Ormond.

[3] Tyrconnel had been summoned to meet King James at Chester in consequence of the complaints against his administration in Ireland.

I must sweare, as the honest Recusant did of Queen Elizabeth, That ' if she was not the Head of the Church, he wisht she were soe '.

But first as to my Cousin Charles. I see you resigne him to the impression of his Starrs. And as one Tree will not become another, or oakes and Cedars much alter their Shape, soe you will allow that withyes are to be twisted towards what one would have them to be, and dead wood must by Carving be brought into Figure. And, it standing thus betweene your son and myne, perhaps we are both in the right !

I perceive you have tryd the Artificiall Memory and undervalue It. If the Ancient Oratours had it with advantage and for use, It seemes their method is Lost. The Chiefe Rule we now have left is onely exercise and conning of things overnight. But if you know better, I will aske questions herein at your coming downe. You must then alsoe expect I shall be very importunate to see the 20 Articles which conteyne the *Weight of the Crowne*, which you presented his Majesty—and certainly with the most peculiar Test I ever heard, viz : to pick out any one He wished to be true, and any other He suspected to be false, and that in 24 houres He should have demonstration. But tho you complaine [that] after all that you gott neither Butter or Hobb-nayles hereby, yett you fare much better than He who found out the Malliable Glasse.[1]

You doubtlesse touch a very sore place when you suspect the surviving malice of the Double shipp. Your fate compard herein to that of Acteon's goes very farr, as having courted the K[ing]'s Misteryes. Yett I may say that if this last word should be mistaken for ' Mistresses ', then to have had a fresh one and of your procurement, as well as of any others, sounds

[1] It is recorded in Richard Grafton's *Chronicle or History of England*, under date 1568, that " a certeyn craftsman had found out the art of melting glasse, in such sort as he made the same malliable ". It seems from Southwell's reference that some misfortune must afterwards have overtaken this inventor.

not as a matter that should have turnd to your disadvantage !

Your observation of the Poverty that is already growne, and must ensue while mouthes encrease and yett eating growes lesse, is so much more a valuable stroake in your Art of Calculation as it is seene felt and understood by all. And doubtelesse the other great things you mention may be as Rationally founded, though unequally comprehended. And I confesse unto you that, tho the world should never be wise enough to wedd what you propose in the Multiplication of Men and the benefitts flowing from it, yett if you have as strong motives for the Truth of these matters as usually convince men from the Pulpit or at the Barr, I cannot wonder that you are Ravished with the harmony and charmes of Ratiocination. You very well call it a ' Labour of Pleasure ', but not so properly ' Angelicall ', since tis perhaps the onely pleasure the angells want. For Intuition of truth may not Relish soe much as Truth that is hunted downe.

But if you intend Pyramids out of these materialls to beare testimony of your good will to mankind, when you passe to a better life, you should take care while you are among us to explaine all and leave as few Hyrogliphicks as is possible. And I, if I live, will not fayle to assist my Godson to hand them to the Presse. Tho doubtlesse it were better done while you are yett on this syde the pitt.

You see how little I can say to those mighty things you honour me withall ; But I keepe them Charily together, and my son may find Charmes where I now Languish. He is now with me and to stay all the winter ; since Oxford is already, and is growing more, an unquiet place.

                    I am ever Yrs
                              R. S.

176. *Southwell to Petty.*

Kingsweston, 5 Oct. 1687

Deare Cousin

Tho already I have answered in my Slight way, or rather acknowledged, your excellent letter of the 16th of August, yett as I often revolve on what you write and cannot think it halfe soe gratefull to admire you as to be your friend, lett me speake of your inimitable guifts, as I am led by our Relation, or by that confidence you have in my sincerity, or by the clause of your sayd letter which followes :

"You will aske me why I persist in these fruitlesse Labours ? I say they are Labours of pleasure, of which Ratiocination is the greatest and most Angelicall. And being by my Age neare Heaven, I think it high time to build myselfe a Tomb on earth out of these materialls, to which I hope you will furnish morter in due time."

I say hereunto that doubtlesse your Heir or Executors will not be wanting to tell the world in good marble what you were. But they will have more joy to Record what you have done for your Family, than what you have over-done for a deaf and ungratefull world. I think you excell most of mankind in reputation already. Why then would you give 500£ to have beene the Author of Mr Newton's Booke ? I am afraid this Thirst for Glory will hurt your Children, create you more envy then benefitt. It were high time to knock off. There are better contrivances which may gaine friends either to prevent or to mitigate the Evills at hand ; such as personall services to those in power or to their dependants, or a sprinkling of money where eloquence will not passe.

My next concerne referrs to the Papers you are likely to leave behind you ; and to this I will only say what I had once from our friend M^r Ab Hill,[1] on occasion of his being left a Trustee to the learned Dr Barrow.[2] He noted first that Dr Gunning,[3] a Seraphick man, late Bishop of Ely, had left nothing behind him but a heap of Misticall Scraps, Whereas Dr Barrow scarce left one handfull of loose papers ; soe carefull had he beene to finish all he ever tooke in hand, either printing what he wrote, or leaving his thoughts and collections all ready for the Presse.[4]

Lastly, to add a word in Reference to my Godson, your Heire. Lett his parts bee never soe good, there is noe safety in trusting any young man with the Temptation of a large Cash. If it be true, as the world reportes, that you are a great moneyd man, why have you lost all this time to vest it in good land ? Lett not too much caution or curiosity leave it at last undone.

I am now almost asshamed of this long lecture, and am considering if you will take it in good part. But I hope the best, because my passion and respect for you and yours is the burthen of this song. And seeing it is soe indeed, I will even preach on, and againe tell you, and even my good Lady alsoe, That the Ant is made the Emblem of Self-wisdome :

Ore trahit quodcunque potest, atque addit acervo.[5]

and the Scripture has other emblems, as in that of making the Living Dogg better then a dead Lyon.[6]

Deare Cousin, excell noe more then you have done. Putt a stopp to the Miriads of Men and the Millions of Money which you have discoursed of. For tho you bestow on these matters as much embroydery of Demonstration as the Witt of Man can present, yett

---

[1] Abraham Hill (1635–1721) was for many years Treasurer of the Royal Society. He published a *Life of Dr. Barrow* in 1683.

[2] Isaac Barrow (1630–1677), divine, mathematical and classical scholar. Newton was his pupil.

[3] Peter Gunning (1614–1684), ancestor of the famous ' beauties '. He was Bishop of Ely from 1675 till his death.

[4] Petty, unfortunately for his editor, did not take the hint which is here offered by Southwell.

[5] Horace, *Satires*, i. 1. 34.   [6] Ecclesiastes ix. 4.

if your fellow creatures are left still in the Darke, you are but in St Paules Case, who sayes that if he spoke in an unknowne tongue, he should passe but for a Barbarian. And in things which are very stunning, men will not hearken to the voyce of the Charmer, charme he never soe wisely. *Ergo Anima, siste gradum* and remember what followes, in your owne words :

> " Sublimis Abissus Abissos
> Invocat; et quales humana non Bolis ulla mensuret
> mentis "[1]

Let me end with good wishes that noe Cousin of myne have anything to doe with Dr Heylen's[2] Case, who wandred a whole night in Bagly Woods, just neere his house, after he had written the Geography of the whole Earth.

I am ever Yours

R. S.

177. *Southwell to Petty.*

Kingsweston, 10 Oct 1687

Deare Cousin

Yours of the 4th[3] came to me the next day after I had sent you some lincks of very Sawcy but friendly thoughts. As to your Purchase,[4] I here send you what the Surveyour answers. He is a plaine frugall man. And as to instructing Mr Plumbly, I

---

[1] This is a quotation from Petty's *Colloquium Davidis cum anima sua*, a translation of his own paraphrase of the 104th Psalm, which was published in 1679. The English lines run :

> " One deep abysse
> Calls for a thousand more, each whereof is
> Unfathomable by all the sounding lines
> Of Kings, Philosophers, and of best divines."

[2] Peter Heylyn (1600–1662), Fellow of Magdalen College, Oxford. He published in 1657 *Cosmographie, in Four Books, containing the chorographie and Historie of the whole world and all the Principal Kingdoms, Provinces, Seas and Isles thereof.*

[3] This letter is missing.

[4] Of a property near Canington, to which allusion has been made. *Supra,* p. 284.

think what you said goes through the whole Alphabett, nor doe I think that ever such a Scheme was made before. I cannot yett find where to wedge in a word, but I will try when tis faire weather, for now I am very dull.

If you lay out but 2500£, it must be in Revertions for your Grandson and when the Tenements are full Stated. Our Neddy read these Instructions with marvellous relish, which is some signe he may gett them into his head ; but he is just now as hott as mustard uppon Logick and proposed to me to write his thoughts to Cousin Charles on that dry Subject.[1] I told him Charles might shew it his father, and soe he might burne his fingers. At last being earnest I lett him take his cource, for the exercise may doe him good though Charles has better things to mind. I wish however that Charles would urge him to write 20 letters more on the severall parts of this doctrine, for perhaps the being made accountable may doe him some good.

The ill weather putts me out of humour to write more at present, than that I am Y^rs

R. S.

178. *Petty to Southwell.*

[The last two letters from his friend (and especially that of October 5) had caused Petty some searchings of heart, and he now proceeds to answer them by two of his own. It may be noted that in the first he pleads guilty to no less than five lawsuits on hand. In two of these (with Lord Dunsany and Fitzgerald of Tecroghan) he states that he is the defendant, in the other three he was presumably the plaintiff, the Farmers, Lord Kingston and McGillycuddy being those against whom he sought to obtain justice.

It may be guessed that the papers relating to Ireland ' of five hours' reading ' and ' ready for use ' were those subsequently published under the title of the *Political Anatomy of Ireland*, while the others ' concerning particular designs ', were no doubt some of the miscellaneous items printed among

---

[1] He did so, and Charles—or rather Sir William—answered him in the letter of October 18, printed below (p. 299).

the *Papers*. Petty's somewhat cynical references to ' great men ' in this letter may be compared with those in his *Ars Aulica et Ecclesiastica* (*Papers*, No. 134).

In his allusions to the payment he received for the Down Survey, Petty is perhaps hardly fair to the surveyor, Mr. Jacobs, whom he was thinking of employing—for though it may be true that Petty did not receive in cash more than three farthings per acre for the land which he had surveyed, it is clear that he derived numerous incidental advantages from that survey, especially in the way of obtaining large tracts of forfeited land for his own use on very easy terms. It was always a sore point with him that the Government would not pay him for his Copper Plates, *i.e.* the engraved maps of Ireland published under the title, *Hiberniae Dilineatio* (Hull, *Bibliography*, No. 31, p. 651).

In the second reply (*infra*, p. 294) Petty, after condensing Southwell's criticisms into twenty points, returns to the charge, and deals with him in characteristic fashion.]

Pickadily, ye 13th Octobr 1687

Dr Coosin

To yours of the 3d[1] and 10th Instant This day received, I answer thus hastily that of the 10th, That you may not think yours of the 3d displeased me. I acknowledge that Letter to have been full of friendly freedom, and that therewith you dressed my many sores with a tender and gentle hand. I could write ten sheetes in answer to itt—every line there deserving soe much consideration.

1°. I hope that mine of the 4th has satisfyed you That I doe not altogether run mad upon gaining 1619 millions, But would be glad to get five per Centum for my money.

2°. I am not so bent upon the *Weight of Crowns*, as to contemn the valueing of Lands.

3°. I am solicitous to plant my son upon *Terra firma* whilst I live.

4°. If you do not like Ratiocination, why have you engaged Dear Neddy soe deeply in it ?

5°. I study my own private and particular Affaires, though sometimes I take a Vagary and fit of De-

---

[1] *Sic*, but 5th (*supra*) is evidently intended.

bauchery into the publick. *Si pulchrum sit pro Patria mori*, why not to bestow a few hours upon it ?

6°. I have but few Law suites considering my circumstances. I sud my Lord Kingston and must sue the old Ffarmers for great sums, for what by grosse Justice is due unto me. I wish the suite against M'Guily-Cudy &c might be prevented, in which are many scurvy Circumstances. I have in my late writings Concerning Ireland cleared the Duke of Ormond against the Narrator of *the Sale and Settlement of Ireland*,[1] who accuseth his grace for having more Acres of Land than would have satisfied all the Adventurers ; Whereas I shew the occasion of that Calumney to have been his grace's having 200^m acres (by the Extreame Columne) of our Lands in Kerry, which in Truth were 30^m acres by the Legall measure of the Reduced Columne, nor scarce were worth 3 thousand pound per annum before the Warrs. I further show that though his Grace had them when the Pamphlet was written, yet he quitted them the next yeare upon Judgement of the Court of Claimes, having held them but five yeares in all. As to the Suites wherein I am Defendant, it is that of Dunsany, for which I referr you to the voyce of the people ; and the other against Tecroghane, wherein I hope next Hilary Terme to prove 4 or 5 Priests to have been forsworne last Trinity Terme. These five Suites are of 40 thousand pound Importance, and must not be tamely abandoned, as others have been.

7°. As for Kerry ; my order of Settlement is ready, but some will have me pay 2000 pound to those that owe me 7082 pounds.

8°. As to my papers ; Those relating to Ireland (and which are neare five hours reading) are correctly ready for any use, and soe are a bundle of others concerning particular designs. The rest I will finish as I can, and as I deserve.

9°. As to my applicacõns to great men ; they have done me more good than harme. If you know of

---

[1] *Supra*, p. 273.

anything that may recoyle upon me, pray warn me of itt.

10°. I concur with you that a man may best doe his business by personall service to great men, and by sprinkling gratuities amongst the leser sort. And I doe accordingly serve men of Indiferent goodness in Indiferent matters, but cannot stoop to be a Pimp or a Pander, to be a Parasite or Sycophant, or to be a Toole to any base design.

11°. Lett me add a word to Mr Jacob's Letter, who demands three pence per acre, besides his own and his son's charges. When I Imploy him I will doe as other men have done, But let me tell you That your Coosin had scarce three farthings per acre, without anything for Charges, or for his Coper plates and archives. Nor had he much above one thousand pound profitt for measuring round about the world—For he measured the equivalent to eight times about the world for 9 thousand pound.

12°. Charles doth not think it decent to answer his Cozen Neddy's Letter the same day that he received itt.

179. *Petty to Southwell.*

[London ? October 14 1687]

Dr Cozen

To show you how much I esteem your Letter of the 5th Instant, I have here divided it into 20 dry short Paragraphs,[1] and have stript it of all the witt and silken sayings wherewith the solid sense was adorned; and have withall reduced your 20 points to a fewer number of my own, vizt :

(1) That Ratiocination is not Angellicall. That we ought to be moderate in the use of itt and such delights of the mind. You call demonstration Imbrodery. You say that Marble Inscriptions will make a better monument Then Ilustrous writing.

---

[1] See Enclosure, *infra.*

(2) You press the obligation of providing for a family ; of making oneselfe capable of great Aliances. You show the danger of Leaving much money to Children. You preferr purchaceing of Land. You press the practice of the ant.

(3) You warn me against Thirst of glory, against buying a great name too dear, against emulating Mr Nuton (sic), against talking of Myriods and Millions, against the applications about publick, vast, and sublime matters to great men. You advise me to gratify particular persons, to treate onely of vulgar matters, least we be counted Barbarians. Not to study Maliable glass ; not to shute at great Services for the World, (which may recoyle at ones selfe) ; not to be a great Geographer, and be bewildered in one's owne Land.

(4) You advise the preventing and ending of Law suites ; the sorting and methodising of such papers as may bee fitt for publick view ; to put a period to Kerry Controversy at any rate, (which is never the better for all the graces, accesses and Receptions we have had), and that as suplicants we must undeceave ourselves.

If I did not sincearly thank you, I would at one dash approve all you have said ; But standing upon my integrity I will (1) except against severall of your Doctrines. (2) I will plead not guilty to some of the faults you suspect me of. (3) others I can excuse and extenuate. (4) I will show how my practice doth and hath complyed with many of your documents. (5) I will heartily cry *pecavi* upon most of the other points.

I say that Ratiocination is nothing but Adition and Substraction of *Sensata*, and that Angels, seeing and hearing at Immense Distances and being of great Celerity in their Motions, doe perform greater exercises of Reason than men can doe. I also say that Ratiocination and the pleasure thereof encreases by practice, Soe as the more a man doth the more he may. Contrary to the nature of Sentiall pleasures, It

continueth to extream old age and shall goe with us
to heaven ; and I had rather represent heaven by the
facultyes and exercises of sublime Ratiocination Than
(as some doe) by Musick, or than (as others doe) by
beauties.   Nor doe I conceave there is any sin in
Ratiocination, for it is the seeking of truth ; and God
is the Truth and a Rewarder of them that seek him,
even allthough they should miss of finding him.   Nor
doe I know why God may not be as well pleased
with our Considering the systeme of the World, The
motions of bodyes, The Censation and Generation
of Animalls, as with the manner how grace is infused,
and faith inspired into the Souls of men.

I am sorry you called Demonstration 'Imbrodery'.
When we would demonstrate the goodness of Cloath,
we singe of the Nap thereof, soe as to see the spinning
and weaving of the yarn and the pile of the wooll ;
Rekoning noe Imbrodery, flowering, or Diapering of
Stuff to be the Essential goodness of the Garment.

Lastly, as to Marble monuments.   Can you shew
me any Marble Inscriptions soe Antient as the
writtings of Homer and Esoph, or of Archimedes ?
Much less of the holy men who described the Creation
of the World and the Destruction of the same by
Noah's flood.   Moreover Inscriptions upon Tombs
mention but a few things, speaking onely the afection
of the writer towards the Defunct.   But Homer and
Esoph may continue by repeated Transcriptions to
the world's end.

As to the burden of providing for Familyes.   Do
you mean that a young man of 20 yeares old should
provide for all That may depend from him before
four score ? and that, not onely for his ordinary food
and Rayment, but against all the extraordinary
Disasters and Calamityes incident to man, without
any care or labour of their own ?   For my part I
have made my 3 children to Learn and Labour
proportionably to their ages and the common rate
of others ; and a man may as well exceed in his aimes
and solisitudes concerning this matter, as in talking

of Myriads and Millions. I have laboured for them
64 years. I do not make my house a Bridwell unto
them, nor myself a Bedel. I will take to myselfe as
much as I can use, and divide the rest according to
their meritts ; and it will become them to be thankfull
for soe much, without grumbling that *per fas aut nefas*
I had not gotten more. To conclude, I do not think
that I have managed this matter soe as to be worser
than an Infidell. I have been an Ant, but not an
Ant which *ore trahit quodqunque potuit*, but onely
quod jure potuit, quod posset honore.

Concerning Alliances, That is to say Marriages.
I sett done (?) with the Greek posey of my Romsey
Schoolmaster's Ring, which is in English : ' He that
is married according to himselfe is well married '—
that is to say in parity or proportion of parts, person,
parentage, and Fortune. The comon opinion of the
world shall be My Rule. I will not sweat to make
my daughter a fortune, nor to be hony for Drones,
and I desire to enable my son to live within the
Compass of that wive's fortune which himself best
loveth.

Concerning Leaving money or Land to a son. I
incline to your opinion. It is better to leave a son
50^{m} £ worth of Land well setled, than 50^{m} £ in
money. But if he be an Ingenious active Lad, it
is better to bestow 5 thousand pound upon him in
an office worth one thousand pound per annum, than
to sett him to plow upon a Farm of 250 pound per
annum. Five thousand pound will buy but 250 pound
per annum in Land, about 400 pound a yeare in
houses. A thousand pound a yeare in offices will
buy as many ships as should bring in 2 thousand
pound per annum, and as many low priced horses as
may be hyred for above 4^{m}.

Soe that it dependeth upon a good Judgement to
determine with what species of effects to stock one's
children. You may see by my last Letter what
Inclinations I have to Land, and how I have instructed
myselfe to purchace it ; and yet a good Bargain

dependeth upon time and Chance, and it is a good Bargaine to gett five per cent for one's money.

(Enclosure.)

You advise me
  (1) To follow my owne private affaires, not the publiq.
  (2) To seek assistance by personall services and guiftes.
  (3) Not to hope for favor from making poll[itical] proposalls.
  (4) But rather envy and hatred with derision and devision.
  (5) To get lands in England and not [money ?].
  (6) Not to write things beyond ordinary Capacityes.
  (7) Not to aspire to great undertakings of any kind which all men will obstruct.
  (8) To make an end of Kery at any rate.
  (9) To prevent and compound law suites.
 (10) To have my papers ready for the presse.

  (1) I do so for the most part.
  (2) I have done so and that very often without effect, yet I shall try again.
  (3) (4) I agree, but think my late applications have done mee rather good than harme.
  (5) I have endeavored it and do still, but find much discouragement.
  (6) I write indeed many extraordinary Things, but all in the intelligible and demonstrable termes of Number, Weight, and Measure.
  (7) I have many schemes and designes for small as well as great undertakings. Nor do the latter but take them as they seem good and pleasant.
  (8) (9) I have few suites in proportion to my sevrell Interests, and I wish I could finish that wherein the Duke of Ormond and

McGillycuddy are concerned.   I hope to
finish with Lord Kingston.

(10) I have many Important papers redy for the
presse, and many more Intelligible and usefull perhaps not fit to bee printed.   Others
I perfect daily.

180. *Petty to Southwell.*

Piccadilly 18 Octb. 1687

Dr Coz^n

Your Godson sends the enclosd to his Cosen
Neddy, which besides the acompt of his voyage contaynes what I teach him of the right use of Words,
reason, good Judgment, Stocking himself with *Sensata*
—all with due respect to the Universityes, who seek
Truth as the Courts do Justice.

I am recovering my Kerry labours, being
                                Y^{rs} & c.

(*Enclosure.*)

181. *Charles Petty to Edward Southwell.*

[Though the enclosure which follows was ostensibly
written by Charles Petty (now aged 15) in reply to a letter
which he had received from Edward Southwell, it is easy
to see that, apart from Charles's record of his travels, most
of it must have been inspired, if not dictated, by his father.
The hand of Sir Robert may similarly be detected in Edward
Southwell's long reply to Charles Petty (*infra*, p. 307).

The two elder correspondents perhaps hoped by this
means to impress one another with the attainments of their
respective offspring, but on November 24 (*infra*, p. 323)
Petty throws off the mask and once more takes up the cudgels
in his own name and hand.]

London, Octob^r ye 18. 1687.

Dear Cosen

In your kind letter of the 10th you say :
1°. That Reason is an excellent guift of God.   2°. That

Mann's Innate Reason is Strengthened and formed by the Art called Logick. 3°. That this Art, altho it Containe many odd words, ought not to be laught at. 4°. That Logick is learned in the University better than else where. Let me add a 5th point : that you have learned it better than most others, as appears by your two Instances, One of a good argument and the Other of a fallacy.

I agree with all your Propositions, Reserving this little, vizt : That the forming of arguments may bee best learned where those who Practice it are most numerous, but the Invention of *Media* succeeds best where there is the greatest Stock and Plenty of things and Actions usefull to Man's Life, and where men are most often forced to argue and persuade in earnest. So as you have done well in learning the former Part at Oxford in one Summer's time, and you doe as well in trying your Tooles upon *Meum* and *Tuum* at Kings-Weston. But my Father telleth mee that the 6 principall words which you have put so hansomely together in your instances, are none of them words of sence nor of a Single Signification ; for each of them hath many meanings, which must bee cleared before you can make a good sylogisme of them, vizt : Kingdom, Election, lasting, Faction, Vegetable and Plant. And my Father sayes hee gave Sir Robert a Specimen there of many years since.[1]

But Cousin our goeing to the University is Necessary. Those who are there, and who have been there, are a Great Body of Men, and are or will be in great offices and authority ; and Consequently will bee able to Crush and Run Downe any single Man that stands at Defiance with them, and will make a Lowder laugh against words of a single signification than any Single Man can make against their Insignificant Gibrish. God forbid wee should say that Universities were Instituted by Crafty Potentates, not to Improve their Reason but to deprive them of it.

[1] *Papers*, ch. v. ' Dictionary '.

You have told me, Cousen, how you have spent
your time and Require mee to tell you how I have
spent [mine] (less that in Travell), which was as followeth, vizt : From the Saracens Head at Algate to
Harwich, I spent my time with an Ingenious Gent
of great Quality who had been many years a Domes-
tick servant to the Pope, well conversant in the
Spanish Policy of the Netherlands, and had been many
years in Sea Service. Upon him I kept Pumping
from morning till night, who had the Patience and
Kindnesse to answer mee.

That Road was very Obnoxious to Robbing, so
it concerned us all to hold our Pistols and Blunder-
busses in the best Posture for our Defence. Wee
put many Cases concerning the various manners of
being Attacked and which Part each man was to
act in It, and passed our Conjectures upon every
man that came neere us what designe hee might have
upon us.

Our Passage from Harwich to the Briel[1] might
have been in 12 houres, but wee were 5 times 24
upon it. In all which time, to take away the Tedium
of our bad Passage, I applyed myself to talk with
the Sea Men of all the accidents that had beefallen
them in their Severall Passages, and what Remedyes
they used in them ; and in 5 dayes learned to speak
the Language of the Sea and to understand the ship
wee were in.

At Length wee landed within 4 miles of the Briel,
where at first sight wee seemed to come into a new
world—for such is all Holland. The Briel Standeth
upon the mouth of the Meuse which Runns through
its Canalls and is a Place (because of its ill Port)
more fortified by nature than by Art. It hath but
a small Garrison now, because the Dutch will keep
nothing at a Great Expence that is not of Present
use. The most Remarqable thing in it is the Steeple
of the great Church. To get to it you must goe up
320 steps, from whence you have a View of all the

[1] Brielle, the port of Rotterdam.

Province of Holland. It is very thick peopled, as most of the Townes in Holland are. The Island in which it standeth, and that is called by its name, is the most fertile Part of all Holland and Corne grows noe where else.

It will be very tedious to tell you what I did or observed in every Towne; wherefore I will reduce them to the following Heads:

1. Wanting no Language, I attempted no more Dutch than to speak with the Vrowe Friester and Voorman and to goe with [them] into the markett about a few necessary things; and was pleased to observe what Parity and Equality the Voorman or Waggoners tooke to be between themselves and the Sparkes they carryed—aprehending as I think that men who live Plainly and honestly by their owne Laboures, were as Good men as those who make a Flourish by the fruits of their fathers (?) flateryes, Frauds and Oppressions.

2. I tooke notice of the Meats, Drinks, Cloathes, Houses, Expence, and Labour of the Severall people through whom I passed, taking notice of their pretence to Piety Compared with their Morall Probity.

3. I went every where into the marketts to see with what Pro[vision] each Place was furnished, and compared the Prices of the [town] with those of our Ordinary.

4. I Enquired what Policy was used about the Cleaning and Paving of the Streets, Night Watches, and what Remedys they used against Beggars and Thieves.

5. I Enquired the names, and endeavoured to see the persons, of those who were eminent for their Authority, Wealth, Learning, Arts &c; and what Ladys were eminent for their witt or beauty— especially of the persons mentioned in Our Gazetts.

6. The Gardens and Plantations in Holland and Flanders are very considerable.

7. By Sight of the fortifications I enabled myself

to understand what I had seen in Bookes and heard in Discourse Concerning them, and always asked 2 questions : one was, 'what number of soldiers each fortified Place would containe ? ' and the other was, 'against what greater number of Besiegers that Garrison would Defend itself for 3 months ? '

8. I observed with what affection the People in Severall Places spoke of the Prince and Princesse of Orrange, as also of the French and English, and of the French Protestants Refugies.

9. I observed the outward appearance of Piety and order in many Religious Congregations, and more especially of the Catholiques in Flanders.

10. I made a Grosse Conjecture wether the Townes were thin or thick peopled in Comparison of London, and went to see every Remarquable thing in each Towne.

11. I computed the difference of my expence in severall Places, and compared the Coynes and Exchanges in Each ; and when I came home made up my account all Reduced into English money to a farthing, and spent no more than my kind father approved of.

12. I carefully considered wether in any Place I had seen I might learn any exercises of Riding, Fencing, Dancing, as also Mathematicks and Philosophy, with the Grosse notions of Trade, better than at London, or Informe myself better than there of every Crick and Corner of the Habitable World. And particularly wether the Scenes or Theaters and Balls are more considerable anywhere else than at London, and wether I could be anywhere better fed or Taught than in Picadilly.

Such Observations as these I made through all Holland, North Holland, Brabant and Flanders. The Prince of Orrange talked with me above half a quarter of an houre about my owne Travells and my father's writtings. I dined with some of the States Generell ; I was specially admitted to see their ma[gazines] and

was on board their best men of Warr. I was at
Narden [1] where the manner of Drownding Amsterdam
by the Sluces of Narden was expounded to mee.
I saw at Utrecht the great mischiefs which the French
at their being there did to that Place. I saw in
Huesden [2] Garrison great numbers of English Soldiers
who had lately been disbanded in Ireland. At Antwerp,
the Rector of the Jesuits, being a noble man of mind (?)
showed mee Extraordinary Respects—I say ' Extraordinary ', for if hee did the same to every body hee
led a very troublesome Life. The Governour of
Brussels son did the same, upon account of my
Father's late Bookes.

At Nieuport I parted from Mr Mesnel [3] because
hee durst not goe into the french Territorys. I went
alone through Du[nkirk] and Gravelines to Calais,
where staying some dayes for a wind, I att last mett
with a bad one, which kept us 18 houres at sea, Split
our Top Saile, and made the sea break often over our
Stern, and when it should have brought us into Dover,
turned Calme. Soe as the sea both goeing and coming
proved to mee a Schooll of Navigation wherein I was
well whipt ! But there and in former Passages I
think I have learned to comand a ship as well as a
famous sea Capt of the King's Ship (whom my father
well knew), who did not know the Pump from the
Capstan, and signed a warrant for a bale of Canvas
to Coat the Pump with.

From Dover I rid Post to London in one Day
and Danced afterwards. This is the Story of your
affectionate kinsman & most humble serv^t

CHARLES PETTY.

I must Dear Cousin take some further notice of
your famous university maxime, vizt : *Quae Conveniunt in aliquo tertio conveniunt Inter Se.* For the
3 principall words thereof, *Conveniunt, Aliquo Tertio,*

---

[1] On the Zuider Zee, a few miles from Amsterdam.
[2] I cannot identify this place ; perhaps Houten is intended.
[3] His French tutor (*supra*, p. 279), probably a Huguenot.

and *Inter se*, are all of them ambigous and not of single signification. For *conveniunt* signifies locall meeting and Covenanting, with severall other things. Your *Aliquo Tertio* are 2 adjective words without a substantive to either, and may have as many sorts of substantives as there are predicaments. As for *conveniunt inter se*, I say That if you would have sugar and cinament *Convenire inter se*, you must pound them both into powder and mingle both powders ; for then you will have one particle of Cinament between 2 particles of sugar, and one particle of sugar between 2 of Cinament throughout the whole mixture. And other ' inter - se's ' are but metaphoricall and Catachresticall. By this maxim you may say that an applle is a body, and that an oyster is a body, therefore an applle is an oyster. That God is a Spirit and the Devill is a Spirit ; Ergo &c. Wherefore take heed of this maxim : *quae eidem sunt equalia, sunt Inter se equalia*, which is abused by the Schools who hereby make the words *in aliquo Tertio* to signify the same as *Inter se*. Nevertheless the arguments about an applle and an oyster might be framed thus : Every apple is a body, Every body is an oyster ; ergo, every apple is an oyster. For here every Proposition is universall and affirmative, but some of them false.

Wherefore, Dear Cousin, I say of these Sylogisms with Mr Hobs : *Hos tarde disco, disco tamen abjicioque*.[1] After this Rate my father and I talk of Logick when wee are in the Park. Wherefore, Dear cousin, stock your self mightily with *Sensata*, and exercise yourself in adding and substracting of them, for that only in Logick. And to discern the small differences between your *Sensata* is what is Commonly Called good Judgement. Every Country fellow will find out the fallacy of Schoole arguments, altho they cannot tell the Schoole names of their faults. Vintners

---

[1] The phrase occurs in *Vita Tho Hobbes*, the philosopher's autobiography in Latin verse, line 43 : " Quos tarde disco, disco tamen abjicioque, admittorque meo quaeque probare modo ".

will Impose bad wine upon their Customers, presuming they cannot tell the names of their faults in vintners Phrases. My father saith hee hath known a Country Butcher to bee an excellent anatomist, saving that hee would call a Tendon by the name of a Buckle, a membrane a Vilme, an Artery a Pipe &c. Now the first of these fellows understood wine, and the latter the fabrick of Animals ; altho they did not know the names taught by them who teach nothing else.

To conclude, the Universityes are almost necessary, but not for Substantiall learning ; and I will goe to them (as you have done) to learn the Language which is spoken there.

182. *Southwell to Petty.*

Kingsweston, 26 Oct 1687

Deare Cousin

Tis too great a fault to have had yours of the 13th soe long by me without acknowledgement, since in 12 short articles [1] there is such an Audit of your selfe and your Affaires, that I know not if ever I received a more important memoir in my life. There is one thing especially which Shines therein, and that is your Kind and Candid acceptation of what I had presumptously writt. I will henceforth place your Selfedenyall and Consideration in the sphere of other great things, and am glad my other accusations have but served to enlarge the panygerick.

I will here speake onely to a very few of the 12 Articles, since I am soe contentedly putt to silence on the Rest. You say in the 4th, Why doe I strive to engage Neddy soe deepe in Ratiocination, if I do not like It ? I answer that I doe like it and admire it, even where the envy of it has done hurt. But Neddy's Byas is soe little dangerous on that hand and the powers Elastick are so strong on the other, that we are sure we cannot transgresse. Besydes we take The

---

[1] *Supra,* pp. 292-294.

Law (which hee must conquer), to be as obstinate as Carthage, and that nothing but these Bombs will tame It ; And hence it is that we both implore your ayd as any thing unto this end falls in your way. And Neddy does allready pronounce That with all the Law he shall gett by your enablements, he will pursue M\^cGilly Cuddy, his Heires, Executors, and Assignes, over all the Reekes of Kerry.

As for the 9th Article, That you desire to be warned if there be any thing which may Recoyle. To this I answer, that it was spoken in friendly feare, least you might dropp any thing from Papers, to the exaltation[1] of Thunder and Lightning.

I will end with a few hints, and but very poore ones, in the paper Inclosed, which have reference to those Two you sent me in yours of the 4th Instant, about purchasing of Land and the Science of securing thereby 5 per cent ; for want of which Science your poore Cousin has suffered. And from Ireland tis worse againe as to his particular, Long letters and noe money being all the Rent he getts. Wherefore you cannot but pardon our being soe Sollicitous about Reprisalls uppon the Law, and for getting if possible into the Cittadell of Reason which comands It.

I am ever Y^{rs}

R. S.

Our Neddy is tumbling over *Witts Com̃on Wealth*,[2] and wine-drawing the neighbouring Parsons,[3] in order to send Cousin Charles some Luggage by the next Carryer.

183. *Edward Southwell to Charles Petty.*

Dr Cousin   [Nov 1687]

I did on the 24th answer one branch of yours of the 18th, but having taken more breath, and

---

[1] *Sic*, but *excitation* seems to be intended.
[2] *Wit's Commonwealth* originally published in 1597 and reputed to be by John Bodenham.   [3] See next letter.

scratched very often where I did not Itch, I found all too little for what I ought to say. But as I must say something to keepe up the [ball ?], soe tis noe great matter wheather it be right or wrong ; since we may both be at last the better for our jangling :

Amantium irae amoris redintegratio est.[1]

But, because you compare Logick to Computation, it may be best to extract what particulars occurr in your owne letter, or in other [ways] referr me too Sir William's ; and then adding all, I may endeavour to substract somewhat for my advantage.

Sir William says in the cover of yours that yours conteyned what he taught you " of the Right use of Words, Reason, good Judgement, stocking yourself with *Sensata*, all with due respect to the Universityes who seeke Truth as the Courts do Justice ".

[As to] his *Discourse of Duplicate Proportion* which I have heard my father say he had the honour to read to the Royall Society in 1674.[2] I take notice of a Dictionary that Sir William makes to explaine 16 hard words [which] often occur in that discourse ; as of Place, Body, Right. And I fancy that those explanations or definitions are some [of] those choice *Sensata* wherewith he advises the mind should be stockt. And in his dedication of the Discourse to the Duke of Newcastle, he sayes that the mind of a young man should not only be instituted in the mathematicks, but stored with variety of Matter, Data, and Phaenomina, uppon which the said Mathematics might exercise and be applyed unto. Lines and numbers without matter &c are but like lute strings without a lute or an Hand.

I have had the advantage to looke into a rich magazine of Sir William's Correspondence with my Father for long before I was borne, and I believe

---

[1] The quotation (with the substitution of *integratio* for *redintegratio*) is from Terence, *Andria*, iii. 3. 23.
[2] *The Discourse made before the Royal Society the 26 of November 1674. Concerning the Use of Duplicate Proportion, etc.* Printed for John Martyn, 1674.

I shall hereafter digg deepe [in this] mine, and especially if you will beare with my troublesome queryes when I make them. But there among other papers I find a Specimen of the Art of Ridiculing,[1] which ought rather to be calld the Art of Reasoning, since the proofs are strong and demonstrative, onely the materialls ridiculous to which they are applyd. Here I would tell you there is a further example (if you heard it not before) of the King of France's statue in the large quadrangle at Paris with Illuminations sett up at each corner :

" La Feuillade pourquoy tu nous berne
A mettre le soleil entre quatre lanterne."[2]

But my pretention is to bring in here a letter from Sir William to my Father of the 16th September 1682, and to which I suppose you doe in yours refer where you say That the Single signification of words ought to be cleared up, as Sir William a long [time] since intimated to my Father. Now the clause runs thus : " I have perused the Logick paper, but cannot more explaine it. For the scope of it is : 1°. to pick out 50 Principle words of the Questions, and then to sett downe and number all the meanings you can fancy of every [one], and then to new State your Question according to the precise signification of each word as you pretend it. Secondly when that is done to find out your *Data* or *Media Probationis*, and to ratiocinate (in that ridiculous manner you know of) and that will bring you to a solid conclusion."

I have asked my Father what was his Logick Paper sent to Sir William and he says he cannot remember [but thinks] it was a scheme framed by Sir William to find out if England were better or worse for the much Building in London, and that (his offering it was Logick) my Father desired him to

---

[1] *Papers*, No. 136.
[2] The Duc de La Feuillade, who earned great distinction in the wars of Louis XIV., had just constructed the Place des Victoires in Paris and set in the middle thereof a gilt statue of the monarch bearing the inscription " Viro immortali ". It was destroyed in 1793.

make it out, but thereof he gave no more than the 2 rules which here are mentioned.

And now I come to the fresh instructions that I find in your own letter of the 18th instant, which I thus extract. You say :

(1) That the forming of arguments may be best learned where those who practise it are most numerous —as in the University.

(2) But the Invention of *Media* succeedes best where there is the greatest stock and Plenty of things and actions usefull to man's Life, and where men are most often forced to argue and perform in earnest— as in the wide world.

(3) That words which have many meanings and are not of a single sence and signification, inust first be cleared up before we can make a good Syllogisme.

(4) That Universitys may deprive some men of Reason, instead of Improveing it.

(5) That the famous University maxime *Quae conveniunt in aliquo tertio conveniunt inter se*, and that of the Schooles, *Quae eidem sunt equalia sunt inter se equalia*, are miserably abused for (*a*) they are compounded of words of very [uncertain] sense. (*b*) that the first of these will lead a man to say that every apple is a body, that every oyster is a body— *ergo* every apple is an oyster ; That God is a spirit and the Devill is a spiritt *ergo*——. (*c*) You further say that the words of those 2 Latine sentences, viz, *In Aliquo tertio* and *inter se*, are hereby confounded and made the same thing, and so produce the absurd-ityes above said.

(6) From hence you deter (?) me from such maximes and such sylogisms, and say in the Phrase of Mr Hobbes :

Hos tarde disco, disco tamen abjicioque

(7) You preach (?) your father's first doctrine—to stock myselfe mightily with *sensata*.

(8) And to exercise myselfe in adding and sub-stracting of them ; which onely is Logick.

(9) And lastly that the small differences between these *sensata* is what is commonly called good Judgement.

But you conclude with 2 Instances of the vintner and the Butcher, as if they were to the same purpose, and to shew plaine men may know things when the learned know only the names. Yett these same seeme quite different, for if the vintner brewes and sofisticates and getts wealth by knowing Druggs which his customers are Ignorant of, soe he is as knavish as any Logician whatsoever!

Cousin I have trimmed up the materialls which you putt into my view, and I shall goe neere to make you laugh before I go any further. For having been desirous to make you such answer as might keepe life in our future correspondence, I called in to my Ayd several of the neighbouring Parsons, who passe for shrewd men at a syllogism, and they are generally smoakers who tell you that the Narcotic quality in Tobacco gives a Fixation to thought. They read your Travells with great attention, often crying, "Pray Sir that article again!", and "What is the gentleman's age and what his Parentage?", and "On my life he will come a shrewd man!" They were all in good humour till they took notice of a back stroake or two, which is given to Universitys, and chiefly when Hobbs was quoted. As for example: "How", sayd one, "I would sooner renounce smoaking, then I would follow that Hobbs." "Nay" said another, "I would smoake for ever rather than imitate what such a varlet has done—He Logician! Why did not our Dr Wallis kick his Algebra about his eares, and outdoe him too even at Plaine Rayling?" But a third was more sedate, for he distinguished the matter saying: "Gentlemen, we are present not uppon Mr Hobbs' Divinity but his Logick. The man had parts, tho proud and perhaps ungratefull; for he ownes he had learnt sylogisme the old way, and that afterwards he kicked it down, as many others do the scaffolding by which their building gott up." "Now Sir", sayd he to me, "I take it you pretend the Study of the Law, and if you must read for it Books of those who studdyed old Logick and framed all their Arguments and Reasonings by those Rules, I think you had better keepe the High Roade and tread the same path be it for better or for worse." Sayd he "Every fencing master has a different way of killing, and there may be as much difference in the methods as there is in Pace, Trot and Gallop, or as sayling a shipp that rowles and tosses one more then another. But if all come to the same ports and in the same time, why should one forsake company for a little hour of ease? Besydes", sayd he, "there are good Pilots in the new way, and it requires happy parts to hitt it aright, and to mantayne it against opposition. Soe that on the whole matter you had as good goe about by the Bridge as to venture over a new sound. Did not Suarez, Mr Chillingworth[1] and Sanderson,[2] and does not Sherlock[3] now goe by this old way? Therefore I advise you *stare in vias antiquas.*"[4]

There was in the company a neighbouring vertuoso who did not smoak. Soe he began with *Ars Longa vita brevis*. He sayd with all submission that there was great difference between the bare eye and a prospective glasse; that there were things not known of old, and even a great difference between these very glasses as they are in length and goodness. That as there is a vast disproportion in the methods of curing the body, why not the same also for the minde? And that, if a man could find out the shape and moulding which could carry him aright, it were an inestimable jewell—It would save time and make every demonstration the stronger. He made a com-

---

[1] William Chillingworth (1602–1644), the theologian, who after embracing the Catholic faith reverted to Protestantism.

[2] Robert Sanderson (1587–1663), Bishop of Lincoln, and publisher of several religious and philosophical works.

[3] Richard Sherlock (1612–1689), Divine; or William Sherlock (? 1641–1707), Dean of St. Paul's. Both were authors of controversial treatises on religious matters.

[4] Jeremiah vi. 16.

parison of one of the stamps in the Tower for the King's Coyne, how much it required to be a good one, but then how all the mettle that fell from it bore an elegant impression.   He concluded that in your letter he saw great beames of light and right.   If he had an entire Systeme from the same fountaine he could go through the whole worke.

The Parson that spoke last replied again That altho the arts were very good, yett he had long since learnt many the same, he thought in the old Common way, " For " sayd he " the very first page Saunderson tells you that knowledge is the end of Logick, and if this knowledge be obstructed by any thing in the matters before you, tis either because it is obscure or too general and doubtfull; and there are proper cures for each as it happens.   Definition is the first, division for the second, and Reasoning or Argumentation is the third. And here " sayd he " I will frame a short familiar example to each " :

" (1) If we know not who sett our house on fire in the darke, we cease not till we find his name and Christian name,—which are the *Genus* and *Differentia* of the man,—or for more certainty wee may add his place of abode; for those men are *outlawed* and distinguished from all others.   And that which is thus done by a man may be done by a word, to strip it from all double signification and to bring it to a single sense, which is the thing so much inculcated.

" (2) If on the said firing of the House, wee had been told that one of such a family had burnt it, the first care would be by distinguishing to separate all those of the family who neither would or could be guilty, and so to come at last to the man that was.

" (3) And if there should be no possible preference of this Burning but the doubt remayne, then Reason would bidd us conjecture to whose account amongst all our Enemyes it could most turne to doe us such mischiefe.   And if we guesse the most likely man, then to search into his lying down and up rising about the time in order to find out proofe ; and if none does appear to fasten it on him by Repoach and Comon Talk untill he bring proofe to clear himselfe."

" This " sayd the Parson, " is what I think answers your comparing of Logick to adding and substracting. And what you call good Judgement in discerning the small differences which may arise betweene the *Sensata*, that is the proofes *pro* and *con*, which may be had as to the guilt or Innocense of the party above said. Soe that altho we may differ in the names, we seeme to agree in things, and not onely in the ends but in the methods ; like how doctours that prescribe alike, tho in different Languages.

He further added that often it falls out that men dispute warmly when both mean the same matter, onely they feel the same object through different mediums. One sees the Stick in the water as magnified and made crooked, the other in the cleare ayr. Soe this has yellow spectacles on his nose and the other has none. And therefore tis commonly the labour of the counsel for the opponent to shew the Respondent that they are of the same opinion, saving the false appearances that are between them ; and that if those could possibly be true as the other takes them, he would be of the same opinion. Alsoe here the Parson, returning to his Pipe, desired me to speak [of those] axioms which were in dispute and which are common to Euclide as well as to [logick]. And as to them I say as followeth :

That tis pitty other languages are not as copious as that of China, that so everything might have a proper name and every name a thing.

That altho you show how these 2 axiomes may be perverted, yett I find it requires a mighty stock of perversness to do it, as is manifest in the examples produced, which doe neither quadrate with the Rules of Logick, nor obey the natural Byas of those 2 axiomes. For they only tell you that where 2 things agree in a 3rd, they doe as to such agreement resemble each other. But not surely in other points, when they are not compared with a 3rd, or when the comparison is perversed, as in this :

> Tom Thinn lovd the Lady Ogle,
> Count Coningsmarke lovd the Lady Ogle,
> Therefore the Count killd Tom Thinn.[1]

This is true in fact, but the true conclusion had been to say " therefore they both did love her ". But the other conclusions are as harsh and untoward ; as if one should say that because two lines which are drawne from the circumference may make an angle in the center, therefore the same 2 lines should make an angle in the Circumference. Soe that if according to the Comon Phrase we speake *ad idem*, I doe not see how those two honest Axioms can doe any hurt.

As to your advise of collecting a world of *sensata*, I do admire It, and doe begg of you, dear cousin, to send me 20 good ones, such as may not onely be fitt to store up and serve many purposes, but such as may Instruct me how to choose and doe the like. These are the same I suppose which Sir William calls varyety of matter, *data*, *Phenomina*, and his *Media Probationis*. But whereas he had then in his thoughts such of these as might most properly beare the application of lines and numbers and mathematicks, you know my worke is to be Law and Right Reasoning ; and therefore lett me have from your store such of these Jewells as you can spare me, and which have chiefly their aspect that way.

But for the present I begg alsoe every advertisement and every good help which may bring me to a happy end of this thing calld Logick. For I love it noe otherwise then [all] children their nurses for the Teat's sake, and for what I may hope to suck forth from it. But if there were one way to the wood better than an other and within my reach, I would give a finger to find it out. Wherefore [help] me herein and you will perpetually oblige

S^r

---

[1] See p. 323 *n.*, *infra.*

If this letter were not already unmercifull [I] would give you a little of the [rules] I go by in the framing of Syllogismes, but I will reserve a Scantling thereof to the next.

184. *Petty to Southwell.*

[Petty was still unrepentant concerning his lawsuits, and here launches forth into a fresh (and apparently most un-deserved) attack upon the Duke of Ormond—not on account of any fresh wrongs which he had suffered at the Duke's hands, but because Ormond had occupied some of his lands in Kerry more than twenty years before (*supra*, p. 4). In using the parallel of David and Bathsheba, Petty probably had in mind Dryden's poem *Absalom and Achitophel*, rather than the Biblical version of that story.

The Duke and his sons, with ' his servant Sir G. L. ' (George Lane, created Viscount Lanesborough), had no doubt ' got much ' out of the Rebellion, but it must be admitted that Petty himself was by no means impeccable in this connection.

The ' Specimen of Algebra or Logick ', addressed in the form of a letter to Edward Southwell (*infra*), has already been printed in the *Petty Papers* (No. 86).]

Dre Cozn   [London 3 Novembr 1687]

You did in your late friendly letter blame me for not getting some *Terra firma* in England. I an-swered you by an Essay shewing I had thought of the Matter in earnest, and you sent me a paper where-with (as with okum) I calked up the leakes of my said Essay. You advisd me in the same letter to com-pound my present Lawsuites and prevent new ones. I answered you by telling what lawsuites I have, and wished I could prevent one for about 15,000£, and the root of all my sufferings—McGillicuddy &c. You in your last promise that Deare Neddy shall (I suppose when hee is a Maynard[1] or Hales) feret McGillicuddy, but say nothing of *&c.*

In the meane time, Cousen, hoping what I am now saying shall not recoyle and kill mee, I tell you The

---

[1] Sir John Maynard (1602–1690), the famous judge, whose will was so obscure that a private Act of Parliament was required to settle the disputes to which it gave rise.

Duke of Ormond is David, that I am Uriah, my estate in Kerry is Bathsheba. You should be Nathan, and then my said Estate would bee the poore man's Lamb &c. Nathan told David That hee had Wives and Concubines enough, without taking Bathsheba from Uriah, without murdering Uriah—a worthy Man who had served him bravely in his Wars and difficulties, as I had done the Duke and his Interest before the King's restoration, and now lately to my great hazard.

The Duke, his 3 sons, and his servant Sir G. L., gott more by the Rebellion of Ireland and the K[ing]'s restoration than all the Lands of Ireland were worth as they left it, as in Anno 1653; besides advantages which cannot well bee expressed by sums of mony. You may now say 'What is that to you?' I answer, 'Hee needed not my Bathsheba, nor the poore Man's Lamb'. I might adde, That the Ship *Settlement* (wherein I am a passenger) was thereby made Top-heavy and Lap-sided, so as shee could not beare Saile, nor work in foule weather.

Wherefore, dear Cousen Nathan, go downe to Gilgal and tell old David (the finest gentleman of Europe and whom I ever sought to serve) before hee dyes, That hee should not have medled with Bathsheba, nor have caused Uriah to bee killed, who by his Meanes hath been set in the forefront of all battells.

I have sent Neddy the best present I am able to make him, viz, a specimen of my Algebra or Logick, which—with what I have formerly sayd of settling the signification of words—is as much as I think necessary. Doing as wee would be done unto, is a very short Rule, but requires much practise; and so doth the Logick I recomend.[1] Adieu.   W. P.

Postscript in Lady Petty's hand.

You see, Sir, that we are Like a Catt in the Cubbard and must Leap forth. We are now in a fight with the Farmers—send us your prayers. . . .

[1] This letter has been wrongly quoted under date March 1667, in Fitzmaurice's *Life*.

185. *Petty to Edward Southwell.*

[3 November 1687]

(OF ALGEBRA)

Sir,

You have asked me once or twice what Algebra was. I answered that it was a kind of Logick, and a more refined way of reason upon common and easy principles, by adding and substracting not onely numbers but the several species of things. Also I might have added that the art of adding, substracting, multiplying and dividing of species, with their rootes, powers and proportions, is called the Algorithme of Algebra ; and is done by noting the severall species of things by letters or other characters, and by signifying the severall operations of your Algorithme by characters; all which characters or marks are called Symbolls.   The principalls whereof are contained in the small table underwritten :

1.	$A = 4$	A equalls 4
2.	$A + B$	A added to B
3.	$A - B$	A less by B
4.	$A B$ or $A \times B$	A multiplyed by B
5.	$\dfrac{A}{B}$	A divided by B
6.	$\sqrt{q}A$	The square root of A
7.	Aq	The square of A
8.	$A : B :: C : D$	As A is to B, so C to D

I next propound an easy question to bee answered by Algebra, or a Chayne of argument drawne out of these two common notions onely, vizt :

(1) Things that are equall to a third thing are equall to one an other.

(2) If equalls be added to equalls the totall will bee equall, and if substracted the remainders will be equall.

Soe have you enough for answering the question following, which is thus stated, vizt :

A thresher thrashed out 40 quarters of wheat and barley. He was to have a shilling for each quarter of wheat, and sixpence for each quarter of barley. At the end of his worke he received 28 shillings for wages.

The question is how many quarters of wheat and how many quarters of barley he had thrashed out ?

The first thing to be done is to state the case in symbols, which is done thus, vizt : let W be the marke of the unknowne number of quarters of wheate, and B of the unknowne number of quarters of barley ; and because 1 shilling is equall to 2 sixpences, let the number 2 signifye a shilling, and consequently lett 28 shillings be expressed by the number 56, and then the case will be stated in symbolls thus :—

The case & question	$\begin{cases}(1)\\(2)\end{cases}$	$2W + B = 56$ $W + B = 40$
	$(2) - W$	(3)	$40 - W = B$
The chayne and series of argument	$(1) - 2W$	(4)	$56 - 2W = B$
	$(3) = (4)$	(5)	$40 - W = 56 - 2W$
	$(5) + W$	(6)	$40 - 56 = W$
	$(6) + W$	(7)	$40 + W = 56$
	$(7) - 40$	(8)	$56 - 40 = W = 16$
	$(2) - (8)$	(9)	$40 - 16 - B = 24$

Thus have you 9 equations whereof the 2 first are the state of the question, and the 2 last are the answers to the same, and are to be read in words at length, thus :—

(1) Twice the quarters of wheat and the quarters of barley are equall to 56.

(2) The quarters of wheat and quarters of barley are equall to 40. (Qy. How many quarters of wheat and how many quarters of barley ?)

(3) 40, less by the quarters of wheat, are equall to the quarters of barley—substracting the quarters of wheat from both sides of the equation.

(4) 56, less by twice the quarters of wheat, are equall to the quarters of barley—substracting twice the quarters of wheat out of each side of the said equation.

(5) Is the 3rd and 4th equation repeated.

(6) 40 equall to 56, less by the quarters of wheat—adding the quarters of wheat to each side of the 5th equation.

(7) 40 and the quarters of wheat, equall to 56—Adding the quarters of wheat to each side of the 6th equation.

(8) 56 less 40, vizt : 16, equall to the quarters of wheat substracting 40 out of 56.

(9) 40 less 16, vizt : 24, equall to the quarters of barley by the 2nd and 8th equations.

Now it may bee here asked how one should know when and what to adde or substract as hath been done?

Answer : That the number of W or B being sought (and because if either bee known, the other is known by easy consequence), the Ingenium of the operation is to pitch upon one of them, as upon B, and then to expresse B by 2 or more equations. Lastly by severall additions or substractions to disentangle the mixtures of numbers with letters, so as numbers only may stand as one side of the equation, and a single letter or the other, as that $56 - 40 = W$ or 16, and that $40 - 16$ (or 24) $= B$.

By which chayne of argument it appears that of
the 40 Quarters of corne, 16 were wheat and 24 barley ;
and that the Thrasher haveing had 28 shillings of the
whole, had 16 shillings for the 16 quarters of wheat
and ten shillings of the 24 quarters of barley ; in all
28 shillings as was supposed.

Memorandum : That in the foregoing question the
Algorithme was simple and the acciomes very few
and plain, but yet many intricate questions may be
solved even by so much. But where the algorithme
is more operose, and where the stock is all the truth
in nature that can be expressed in number, weight, and
measure, it is not to be imagined what a number
and variety of light truths may bee deduced by
Algebra.

Memorandum : That as much Algorithme and
acciom may be learned and mastered in three months,
as will produce the solution of a vast number of im-
portante questions ; but the dextrous use and application of the same, soe as to bee free from oversight and
Paralegisme, may well require three years study and
practice.

This I have written that you may see whether you
will ingage your son upon this faculty and way of
Logic, as also at what yeare you will begin to put him
upon it.

The contents of this Paper are : (1) To tell what
Algebra is. (2) What Algorithme is. (3) What
symbolls are. (4) To state a question in symbolls.
(5) The stock of axiomes and truths. (6) To forme
the chayne and series of Argument. (7) To keep an
account of each equation in the Margent.

So as in Algebra : (1) The Algorithme is the
Tooles. (2) The stock of axiomes as the Materialls.
(3) The practice and a good head as the workeman-
ship. (4) The finding out abstruse truths is the work,
and out of a few truths to draw out infinite true con-
c[lusions] and to preserve the method of numbering
unconfounded is the exc[ell]ency.

Archimedes had Algebra 1900 yeares ago but

concealed it. Diophantus had it in great perfection 1400 yeares since. Vieta, DesCartes, Roberval, Harriot, Pell, Outread, van Schoten and Dr. Wallis, have done much in this last age.[1]

It came out of Arabia by the Moores into Spaine and from thence hither, and W[illiam] P[etty] hath applyed it to other then purely mathematicall matters, viz : to policy by the name of *Politicall Arithmitick*, by reducing many termes of matter to termes of number, weight, and measure, in order to be handled Mathematically. The second, 5th, and 10th Bookes of Euclid, doe make a great parte of the stock above mentioned.

186. *Southwell to Petty.*

[As he hints in this letter, Southwell had intended to deal more fully than he does here with the Paper on Algebra which Petty had sent ' Neddy ' a fortnight before. His papers contain a reply in draft which—owing no doubt to his unfortunate facial affliction—was never completed. After giving the matter another fortnight's consideration, on November 26 (*infra*, p. 325) he returns again to the charge. An interesting point in his draft reply is a reference to the fact that Thomas Hobbes had once " lamented (to Petty) that he had not taken the art of algebra more into his studdys ".]

Kingsweston, 15 Nov. 1687

Deare Cousin

I must noe longer forbeare telling you how the late ill weather has brought a defluxion on my face ; and tho the paine of it has been sufficient, yett I have not thought it the lesse for retarding my acknowledgement of your excellent favour of the 3ʳᵈ and the specimen of Algebra it conteyned. I must herein begg your Patience for a time, only that your Cousin

---

[1] Diophantus of Alexandria, *fl.* A.D. 350; Franciscus Vieta (1540–1603); Descartes (1596–1650) ; Gilles de Roberval, French Mathematician (1602–1675) ; Thomas Harriot published *Artes analyticae praxis* in 1631 ; John Pell (1610–1685) ; William Oughtred, author of *Clavis Mathematica* ; Franz von Schooten republished Vieta's works in 1646 ; John Wallis (1616–1703).

Neddy has entred it fairely in his booke, next after the Specimen of Ridicule;[1] and hopes to gett it in his head, as perfectly as he has gotten this, which he is much delighted withall.

As soon as I am able, I am to be at Badminton, as well as others, in order to be cathechized. But this being onely to tell you I am not current, I will say noe more, but am Yrs

R. S.

187. *Petty to Southwell.*

London Novem^{br} ye 24 1687

Deare Cosen

Altho the letter written in my wife's hand was enough to trouble you with, yett since Cosen Neddy has sumoned a Sinod of Smoakers and Lusty Logicians against my poor Boy Charles, give me leave to help him a little against them, viz. :

1. Wee never found any fault at all with the axiome *Quae eidem sunt Equalia, sunt inter se Equalia,* but said that the same had bien abused by the School men making another Axiome of it, viz, *Quae conveniunt in aliquo tertio, Conveniunt inter se*—which I do not like, notwithstanding your two Instances or Crutches which you have offered to support it. You say " T. Thin Loved Lady Ogle and that Coninsmark loved Lady Ogle.[2] Did therefore Thom Thin and Coninsmark agree or *convenire inter se ?* " To help you out I say they did, for Conin and his friends agreed to kill Thin, and Thin and his friends to hang Coninsmark. My Lady Ogle had an *aliquid* (but whether a *secundum, tertium* or *quartum* I know not) wherein they both would faine have been, but if both of them

---

[1] *Papers*, No. 136, and *supra*, p. 191 *ff.*

[2] Thomas Thynne of Longleat (1648–1682). He married in 1681 Elizabeth Percy, the Northumberland heiress, widow of Lord Ogle. He was murdered in the year following by, or at the instance of, Count John Philip Königsmark, a Swedish nobleman, and one of her unsuccessful suitors. Lady Ogle was afterwards better known as the Duchess of Somerset.

had mett in that *aliquo*, I doubt they would not have Agreed *inter se*.

2. Againe lett the Radius of a Circle namely *A*, meet with another Radius *B* in the center of the same Circle, which you may call if you Please *aliquid tertium* ; and yett you said two Radii agree in their Extremes only in one point (which point is nothing), but do differ and are distant every where else and do not at all *Convenire inter se*.

3. Your Smoakers sayd That Sanderson and other great Logicians have said, as wee say, (To which wee say the wiser They) to witt : That Logick is only addition and substraction. Truly, since Reason has been from the beginning of the World, I cannot be so arrogant to think that I had the first Notion of it !

That Dictionary I have often mentioned was Intended to translate all words used in Argument and Important matters, into words that are *Signa Rerum* and *Motuum*.[1] But the Treasury of *Sensata* are the many Miscelany papers of my Scripture which I add and substract, Compose and distribute, as Printers do their Letters.

As for the method of the Law, you shall have it when you come back from Gilgal ; and As for the many small Rules of Logick mentioned in your letter, they seem to mee of little more use than Rules how to distinguish one man from another, whereof ten thousand Are not so good as 2 minutes view of the Persons you would distinguish.

To Conclude, you have done well in sending Neddy to Oxford, and Charles must do the same when things are more quiet there. In the Mean time wee do from day to day the best wee can to quench the anxietie which Ireland by Every Post afflicts us with.

I am y^ors &c.

---

[1] Cf. " The Dictionary of Sensible Words ", 1685 (*Papers*, No. 46).

Postscript by Charles Petty.

Dear Cosen Neddy

You having given Occasion to talk of my Lady Ogle's *aliquid*, my Father did exempt me from answering you which I hope you will excuse in your affectionate kinsman & most humble serv^t

CHARLES PETTY.

188. *Southwell to Petty.*

Kingsweston, 26 No^br 1687

Deare Cousin

I sent you a little messenger to tell you I was ill, and nothing lesse could attone for being thus long in acknowledging yours of the 3rd. It had two sheates of the Institution of Algebra, and how little soever I am yett master of this first Essay, yett knowing with what will you sent it, and what mountaines you have beene able to remove by It, I value it uppon every account as a most inestimable Jewell.

You say for Incouragement that much of this Art may be learned in 3 monthes ; but add as candidly that it will require 3 yeares to perfect It, and refer to consideration wheather to embarque our Neddy in It and when ?

My first answer hereunto is this : that you are the first man that ever brought Algebra into Humane affaires,[1] and what is more, you have given it the utmost improvement. And perhaps you were borne for it, since to this day noe man is risen up to make any thing of it, tho tis now twenty yeares you have Instructed the World therein.

As for my son, he is young, and not borne I feare to stand under Saule's weighty armour, nor can we add a cubit to his stature. Soe that we must Jogg on in some trodden paths and take up a load proportion-

---

[1] Southwell means, of course, that Petty was the first to apply the statistical method to economic affairs.

able to his understanding; and the law being the marke we ayme at, It must suffice to take in those enablements which lead thereunto, and then stopp.

As for your letter which Inclosed these sheets, I read it with greife and sorrow. For you are displeased with the old drooping Duke, and soe concernd for your *Lamb*, as if he were fitt for the wolves. What he gott is as publick as Acts of Parlyament could make it, but I never heard that his 3 Sons gott one Acre; and I have heard that all Sir G. Lane's acquisitions makes not 3000£ per annum, tho he had many offices. Time was that all the marriners thought the shipp happy to have the Duke a passenger; and she had foundred in 71, if others (who were even Builders) had not beene opposed by him. I lament on the other syde that there should not be gratefull remembrance for what you did in the dayes of distresse, and especially when he is soe often and soe deeply wounded for gratitude to H. C.[1] You have alsoe as you say adventurd lately to your hazard in an vindication, of which I would bee glad to have the particulars from you that I may imploy them aright. For tho I cannot be your Cousin Nathan, yett I would strive to imitate Moses, who sayd in a time of danger and comon captivity, " Bretheren why strive you ".

I pay most humble duty to thankes to my lady for her last Postscript, and Neddy is impatient to heare from his Cousin Charles, but often sayes *non vacat exiguis.*

Yrs ever

R. S.

189. *Petty to Southwell.*

[The two letters which follow are without date or signature. They are both apparently by way of reply to Southwell's last communication.

---

[1] Henry Cromwell, whom Ormond had helped after the Restoration in the matter of his Irish property.

Petty was nearing his end, and though he never refers to his health he must have been for some time past a very sick man. His bodily infirmities seem to have provoked a restlessness of mind which found a vent in writing. I have remarked elsewhere (*Petty Papers*, Introduction) on the progressive increase both in letters and writings which characterises his later years. It is possible that the two letters were merely drafts, subsequently set aside in favour of the short note of December 13, with which Petty enclosed a full statement of his case against the Duke of Ormond. They seem at all events to have provoked no reply from Southwell.]

[London, end of Novembr 1687 ?]

Dʳ Cousin

Having done with Logick and Algebra, let us trim over and renew what was said of the Duke of Ormond, viz :

1. I sayd That Hee was as David and Mee Uriah ; that the Kerry land witheld from mee by him 5 yeares was as Bathsheba, and in Nathan's sense ' The Poore Man's Lamb ' ; that I was this Poore Man and his grace The great Sheepmaster.

2. That his grace and his 3 sons, with his Eminent Instrument Sir Geo[rge], got as many advantages by the King's Restoration, as were the equivalent to all the Lands of Ireland as they were worth between Dec 1650 and Sept 1653.

3. That thereby The Ship ' Settlement ' became Top heavy (so as lesse able to beare saile), and Lop sided (that is heavyer of one Side and part than of the other), which hinderd her working. I have also intimated That, by reason of many defective timbers even about her keele, shee could not lye on ground without danger of damage.

4. I conclude with a wish That some Samaritan would help mee to my lamb, would cleere the quitrent for the time they witheld [it] and the yeares value, as 5 yeares enjoyment beare to the whole ;—without taking anything for the Wrongs, damages, suppressions, Importunityes, Indignityes, which I have suffered in 20 yeares last past on this accompt.

To these things you answer and say :

1. That for what has been done to my Lamb I would make his grace fit to bee throwne to the Wolves.

2. That what his grace hath had, was most publicq and by acts of parlament, (that is) most just.

3. That his 3 sons never had one foot of Land, nor Sir Geo[rge] above 3000£ per annum—besides offices.

4. That a time was when all the Marriners thought the ship happy who had the duke for passenger.

5. That this ship had foundered Anno 1670 without his help.

6. You say something of my being gratefull to one who did much for me in Evill times.

7. That hee hath suffered for his gratitude to H. C.

8. You speake of a Vindication I lately made, which was against the Author of the *Sale and Settlement* his assertion That his grace had more lands than would satisfy all the Adventurers.

9. That you cannot bee My Nathan, viz, to get mee even the Skin of the Lamb I lost.

10. You record Moses his advice not to strive.

I follow your last point and advice of not striving, by not answering unto [you] without Symbolls or Algorithme and descanting upon every one of all your 10 points, but remayne quietly

Yrs &c for ever

. . . oro, miserere laborum
Tantorum misere animi non digna ferentis.[1]

190. *Petty to Southwell.*

[London, beginning of Dec 1687 ?]

Dʳ Cᵒ

When Barbers have shaved all over with the razer, They clip of the stragling hayres with their

---

[1] Virgil, *Æneid*, ii. 143.

Cisers. Wee have shaved away our Logick and Algebra, as also as concernd Uriah. Wee now clip the hayres following, which are as big as Cables, vizt :

1. I did not say The Dukes Acquisitions were secret, or things to bee made out by Algebra, but fully agree with you that they appeare in Acts of Parlment and are Notorious.

2. I did not say That either of his 3 sons had lands by the Settlement. They need it not ; but had Offices and honors to the value of ——.[1]

3. I never Murmurd at the Number of Sir George Lane's Emoluments, but rather say That hee had not so much as hee deserved.

4. In my late letters I told you how I vindicated his grace from the Author of the *Sale and Settlement*, who sayd that Anno 1667 His Grace had as much lands as would have satisfyd the Adventurers, who have about 390 thousand acres. Whereto I answered That 200^m were only waste Lands in Kerry, calld 200^m acres by the extreme Collume, but were reduced to 30^m by the Legall measure of the reduced Collume ; nor worth 3000£ per annum before the wars ; nor what would make $\frac{1}{40}$ part of the adventurers satisfaction. I further shewd how fairely Hee quittd them Anno 1668 ; but sayd nothing how he came into them 1663.

5. You have heard his Grace complaynd of for what Hee did for H. C., and I have heard H. C. reviled for what hee had done for Ld O ; [2] and W. P. was twice almost under water for what he had done on the same accompt.[3]

6. You say you cannot bee Nathan. I sayd it in jest, nor do I wonder at what you say in earnest. ' Let Nature work '—' Wee shall live till wee dye '—*Hulche pulche* &c

7. As for our boyes. Let them go their severall

---

[1] Blank in MS.   [2] Lord Ossory, eldest son of the Duke of Ormond.
[3] Petty had been early connected with Henry Cromwell as his physician, and later on he was instrumental in preserving for Cromwell's family the lands which they had obtained in Ireland. There is amongst the MSS. a power of attorney given by Cromwell to Petty in 1661.

wayes. They will *tandem aliquod convenire* in some good *Aliquo tertio* and by Oxford Logick *inter &c.*

To conclude, by letters from J. Waller of the 3rd instant hee tells of a new double-bottom built in Kerry of 2 decks, which performeth in all points to admiration. The devill cannot long stiffle what I had so amply demonstrated, whereof The monuments are in the Closet I shewd you.

I run to ruine apace at Dublin. Mr Houblon's correspondents of Seville wrote 11 July and 13 October last, That father Nicholas Fitzgerald, son of Sir Luke of Ticroghan and the Lord Netterville's [1] daughter, was living then and there; But a Nun this terme sware shee saw him dead, put into his coffin, and buryd 1683; and a fryer sware hee sold his clothes and have a ryte good masse said for him. What remedy doth The top-heavy lopsided settlement provide for good debts satisfyd with stolen goods, or onely sworn as aforesaid to bee stolen?

191. *Petty to Southwell.*

[This was Petty's last letter—dictated to his wife and signed with her initials. He was still fulminating against the Duke of Ormond, and characteristically accompanied his note by a Paper containing a fresh account of this time-honoured grievance. The document in question is however no longer extant.

He died three days later. The news was conveyed to Southwell by M. Mesnil, the French tutor who has been mentioned in the preceding pages. In this letter M. Mesnil tells how the ministrations of Dr. Lower and a surgeon named 'Hobs' failed to assist the dying man, and how, "A fin de mourir pas seulement en vray philosophe mais aussi en bon chrétien', he summoned Dr. Birch (the Duke of Ormond's chaplain) to his bedside—" Enfin à minuit sonnant, il rendit l'âme avec aussi peu d'agitation qu'il en avait eu les derniers jours de sa maladie; mourrant ainsi de la manière qu'il avait souhaité toute sa vie de le faire ".]

---

[1] John, second Lord Netterville of Dowth, prominent in the Irish Rebellion, *d.* 1659.

London, ye 13 Decemb^r 87

Dear Cousen
    Your last offerd me occasions to have tossed
poses against the Old Gentleman[1] who has been gotten
to hurle Flints against your Cousen.
    On Saturday senight I was taken with a great
Lameness, I have nevertheless shewn how both
Farmers are over paid all their demands of 8183£,
and am hastning to make even with all the rest of
my opressors. The enclosd Paper (Markt Number 2)
is what concerns his Grace. I think I shall never
willingly abate of it. I'm sure it is not halfe the
wrong I have sufferd, nor is your Lambe above the
100th part of the grand Flocke. Doe what you pleas
with it—some Course or other must be taken—Adieu.
    I have only to add that we are all here your
affectionate humble servants
                                                    E. P.

192. *Southwell to Petty.*

Kingsweston, 16th December 1687

Dear Cousin
    I was yesterday in some fright upon reading
from Phillip Madox the report of your sickness, but
the favour of yours of the 13th dispelld the cloud,
as making slight of the matter. However it will be
very welcome to mee to hear that you walk again as
you did before.
    I see and congratulate that you have been able
to lay so great a Tanto (?) at the Farmours doors, and
that you are hastning to make even with all others.
    As for the demand of 7774£ 10s-, which yett (as
you say) is not half the wrong you have suffered,
and of which you shall never willingly abate—the
figure I hold between my Friend and Patrone, as
well as ignorance in the particular meritts of the case,

---

[1] The Duke of Ormond.

makes it fitt for mee above all other to be silent;
and I can assure you that if the old Gentleman had
half such a demand from you, I would not be his
Herauld tho he should desire it. Things of anger
and the prospect of warr (in a warm attaque and as
warm a defence) drives the Common friend into a
corner; and he stepps not out till he finds both
convinced in their Hearts that it were their Common
Interest to be quiet. From these Motives, and
because you also leave mee to do what I will with
the paper, I will keep it to myself; and the rather
because I rarely hear from him since the gout has
disabled him, and as seldom write.

Even you who are the Claymer, seeme tenderly
to wish that you had nothing but poses to toss against
him, and I am sure I do as cordially wish that at
this time of day, and while both are in the storm,
there were nothing but sweet odours, as the tossing
of Incense, between you.

With all true service to my Lady and little ones,

I am ever yʳˢ

R. S.

193. *Southwell to Lady Petty.*[1]

[Kingsweston, Dec 23. 1687 ?]

Honᵈ Madam

It was but yesterday that I received the
terrible newes which has soe afflicted me, that I know
not wheather I should comfort your Ladyship or your
Ladyship me.

I ever thought for almost 26 yeares past that Sir
William Petty was in severall respects the greatest
among mortalls that I ever saw, and the world can
never sufficiently deplore his losse. Your Ladyship
has formerly known sorrowes and must overcome

---

[1] Cf. Southwell's letter of December 23 to Samuel Pepys on the same occasion
(*Hist. MSS. Com.* 15th Report, p. 181).

these alsoe. Tis happy your children are soe well growne up as to be companyons and comforts to you.

He is gone to a better life, and where his great soule has fulnesse of knowledge, and room to admire what there he finds, as we did him whilst he was among us. To dye with a composed mind, and all the circumstances of a good Christian, is what either he or we could wish, or can desire to imitate him in. I will pay to his memory all the service I am able, and begg your Ladyship and all my deare Cousins to believe that I am,

Madam

194

EPIGRAPH

Sir William Petty Kt who, for his Tallents in Philosophy, Physick, Navigation, Poetry, Surveying, Calculations and Politicall Arithmetick, was in his Generation most eminent.

He dyed 13 December[1] 1687. An. Ætat 64.

[Endorsed by Southwell " Epigraphe for Sir William Petty ".]

Petty was buried in the Abbey at Romsey, where he had first seen the light. He had once (*supra*, p. 283) talked of making for himself by his writings ' a tomb upon earth ', but in his will he left a sum of £150 for the purpose of a memorial in more concrete form. None such, however, was erected at the time. Even the site of his grave, though said to have been once marked (Fitzmaurice, p. 315), had by the middle of last century been lost. It was about this time that an obelisk, designed by Charles Barry, was erected on the Wiltshire Downs, a few miles from Bowood, by the third Marquis of Lansdowne. Curiously enough the purpose of this monument was not left on record. Succeeding generations have thus been free to speculate whether it was erected

---

[1] *Recte* 16th December.

in commemoration of the accession or marriage of Queen Victoria, the birth of Edward Prince of Wales, as a boundary mark of the Bowood estate, or merely as one of those ' follies ' which were dear to early Victorian landowners.   It was only recently that there was discovered among the Bowood Papers a draft inscription for this obelisk (evidently made at the time of its erection), which clearly showed it had been originally intended to commemorate Sir William.

There would seem, however, to have been a change of plan, for while the monument in question remained innocent of any inscription, another memorial was erected by Lord Lansdowne a few years later in Romsey Church.   This was executed by Westmacott, and represents Petty in recumbent effigy.   It bears the following inscription :

" In memory of Sir William Petty, a true patriot and a sound philosopher, who, by his powerful intellect, his scientific works and indefatigable industry, became a benefactor to his family and an ornament to his country.

" Erected by Henry Marquis of Lansdowne, 1858."

Southwell's assurance (*supra*, p. 288) was thus at length made good.   " Your heirs will not be wanting to tell the world in good marble what you were.   But they will have more joy to record what you have done for your family, than what you have overdone for a deaf and ungrateful world."

SIR ROBERT SOUTHWELL

FROM AN ENGRAVING BY JOHN SMITH AFTER KNELLER'S PORTRAIT AT THE ROYAL SOCIETY

INDEX

THE END